WEALTH PROTECTION

Build and Preserve Your Financial Fortress

Christopher R. Jarvis, M.B.A.

&

David B. Mandell, J.D., M.B.A.

John Wiley & Sons, Inc.

*We dedicate this book to our families for their
endless love and support.*

Published by John Wiley & Sons, Inc., Hoboken, New Jersey
Published simultaneously in Canada

For general information on our other products and services, or technical
support, please contact our Customer Care Department within the United States
at 800-762-2974, outside the United States at 317-572-3993 or fax 317-572-4002.

Wiley also publishes its books in a variety of electronic formats. Some content
that appears in print may not be available in electronic books.

Library of Congress Cataloging-in-Publication Data:
Jarvis, Christopher, 1970–
    Wealth Protection, Inc. : how to protect your assets from taxes, lawsuits
and other risks / by Christopher Jarvis, David B. Mandell.
      p. cm.
    Includes bibliographical references and index.
    ISBN 0-471-22142-2 (cloth : alk. paper)
    1. Executions (Law)—United States.   2. Debtor and creditor—United
States.   3. Estate planning—United States.   4. Tax planning—United
States.   I. Mandell, David B., 1968–   II. Title.
KF9025 .J37 2002
332.024'01—dc21   2002005429

Printed in the United States of America

10 9 8 7 6 5 4 3

ABOUT THE AUTHORS

Christopher R. Jarvis, M.B.A., has experience as an actuary, invest-
ment advisory representative, entrepreneur, and financial consultant.
He is currently the managing partner in the firm Jarvis & Mandell,
LLC (www.jarvisandmandell.com).

Mr. Jarvis has been quoted in the *Wall Street Journal* and the *Los
Angeles Business Journal* and has co-authored financial and legal texts
for doctors, business owners, and financial planners. Chris has been
booked to speak to the International College of Surgeons, the Beverly
Hill Bar Association, the Association of Chamber of Commerce Executives, The Summit (CE seminar for attorneys and accountants),
the UCLA Law School, the Learning Annex and The Anderson
School (MBA Program at UCLA). Chris's articles have been featured
in over 25 national publications and he is the featured financial expert in Medscape's *Money & Medicine* section.

He holds an honor's degree in applied mathematics from the
University of Rhode Island. He earned a Master's of Business Administration from UCLA where he majored in finance and entrepreneur-
ial studies and was awarded the Ken Kennedy Fellowship. Mr. Jarvis
also holds a seat on the board of governors for the *Sigma Phi Epsilon
Education Foundation.* He can also be found in Lexington's *Who's Who
in Finance.* Mr. Jarvis lives in Los Angeles, California.

David B. Mandell, J.D., M.B.A., is an attorney, author, and renowned
authority in the fields of risk management, asset protection, tax, and
financial planning. He is the sole shareholder of the Law Offices of
David B. Mandell, PC (www.mandellpc.com) and is a principal in the
financial firm Jarvis & Mandell, LLC.

As a writer, Mr. Mandell has co-authored *The Doctor's Wealth Protection Guide"* and *Risk Management for the Practicing Physician*©, which
is certified for Medical Continuing Education credits. His articles
have appeared in over thirty leading national publications, including
*The American Medical News, Physician's Money Digest, InFlight Magazine,
Yachts International,* and *JCK Circular,* the nation's largest jewelry business publication. In addition, Mr. Mandell lectures to professional
and consumer groups across the country.

Mr. Mandell holds a bachelor's degree from Harvard University
from which he graduated with honors. His law degree is from the
University of California Los Angeles' School of Law, where he was
awarded the American Jurisprudence Award for achievement in legal ethics. While at UCLA, Mr. Mandell also earned a M.B.A. from
the Anderson Graduate School of Management.

Acknowledgments

The authors would like to thank the following advisors, each of whom is an accountant, attorney, or other financial or insurance professional. These generous people have contributed valuable insight and experience which benefited not only this book, but our practices as well. We work closely, in fact, with many of these advisors on a daily basis in the planning for our clients. Thanks to: Peter Breitstone, Steve Block, Alan Brown, Celia R. Clark, Roccy DeFrancesco, Jim Duggan, Tom Dyer, Dale Edwards, Stephanie Enright, Neil Finestone, Dr. Arnold S. Goldstein, Howard Hafetz, Thomas Handler, Debra Hoag, Mike Jones, Larry Keller, Adam Kirwan, Arnie Klein, Gordon Klein, Larry Lebowsky, Kim Michel, Bill Nosal, Walt Parsons, Paul Pichie, Mike Salmon, Mark Sims, and Glenn Terrones.

We would also like to thank those people whose help was integral in the creation of this text. Our agent, Larry Chilnick, and our editor, Deb Englander, were invaluable. Renee Cardriche and Monica DeAngelis provided us with great research, saving us so much time so that we could continue working with clients while writing the book. We would like to thank Gordon Klein, George Peng, and Ron Rimkus for reviewing the technical elements. We also want to thank our parents Jane and Charlie, and Dot and Ray for reviewing dozens of editions of the book and for their endless support in this and every other endeavor we have undertaken.

Contents

PART IV
INVESTING

PART V
ASSET PROTECTION

PART VII

RETIREMENT PLANNING

PART IX
BUSINESS PLANNING

Introduction:
Why We Wrote This Book

Like our own families, your family needs Wealth Protection planning.

Between the two of us, Chris and David, we give nearly 100 seminars per year. Invariably, we begin each talk with a lawyer joke and a brief case study. The joke usually lightens the mood, and the case study illustrates the dangers of inadequate Wealth Protection planning. As we start this book, we want to skip the joke and get right to sharing our own families' experiences. We're not going to pull any punches or exaggerate. We don't need to.

In fact, what happened to our families motivated both of us to pursue Wealth Protection planning. We entered this field—and wrote this book—to help other families avoid the financial pain and emotional suffering that our own families endured.

As you're reading this book, remember that we're not only authors and advisors, but also members of families who illustrate both the positive and the negative experiences that can be part of Wealth Protection planning. From our stories, you will see why Wealth Protection planning is fundamental to the long-term security of every family. (If, after you read the book, you are still left with a yearning for good lawyer jokes, visit our web site www.mywealthprotection.com, and you'll be sure to get your fill.)

CHRIS'S STORY

I must preface this story with the fact that my mother, Dorothy, is a very proud woman. She doesn't like people to know about her problems and rarely asks for assistance. Dorothy is the kind of woman who cares deeply about everyone around her, has many friends, and will always sacrifice herself for the happiness of others. Fortunately, her sense of caring is stronger than her sense of pride, and she asked me to use her experience in an effort to help others help themselves. For this, I am grateful.

My stepfather, Tom, was a successful attorney. He came from a wonderful family and had a great sense of family values. More important, he loved my mother and treated her with the most respect and admiration I have ever witnessed in any relationship. He also treated his children and stepchildren very well and was extremely generous in sharing his success with all of us. He was a wonderful man, worthy of a relationship with my mother.

My mother's relationship with Tom was particularly rewarding for me because I had watched my mother struggle financially to take care of me and my two siblings for years. She worked multiple jobs to try to pay the bills, but she never let us know how bad things were financially or how much her divorce from our father had hurt her emotionally. It wasn't until after I saw how happy Tom made her that I realized how stressed, frustrated, and unhappy she had been before she met him.

Like most children, especially teens who still idolize fathers, I didn't know how to react to a new stepfather. But, when Tom swept my mom off her feet and made her truly happy for the first time in over a decade, I couldn't do anything but embrace him. I was thankful that someone was able to make my mother as happy as she made everyone around her.

It seemed as if life was repaying my mother for all the sacrifices that she had made. Not only was Tom the most loving and caring person she had ever met, he also made a very good living. Instead of scraping to pay the mortgage on a small home, she and Tom bought their dream home in the suburbs—a beautiful English Tudor with a bedroom for each child and stepchild. They also bought a summer home and some rental real estate. They even had the ability to vacation twice per year and take the children on some of their trips. I bet Mom felt like she was Cinderella and her life was forever changed for the better.

Unfortunately, midnight approached and the ball was ending. One night, only two years into the marriage, Tom was rushed to the hospital with internal bleeding. I was away at college, and my mother called me to say that Tom would be in the hospital for a week or two for some tests. Like any obedient child, I disregarded my mother's wishes and rushed home. When I arrived, I was relieved to find Tom in good spirits and alert. He told me to go back to school and take my exams. He said he'd see me at Christmas.

I returned to school, focused to finish my first semester at the University of Rhode Island. On the night before my first exam, I received a phone call. It was my mother. There had been some complications, and Tom had just passed away—at age 41. Mom said that she would be fine and that I should just stay at school. I left school and drove home immediately. This would be the worst Christmas of our lives.

As you would expect, the emotional healing process took a very long time. Unfortunately, that would not be the only pain. Because Tom had property in numerous states, the probating of his will took almost two years. During that time, my mother was unable to sell the properties to interested buyers and had to use the modest insurance proceeds to pay bills along with the 11 percent interest rate mortgage on their dream house.

To make a long story short, because of their failure to plan for the worst, within five years of Tom's death, the high mortgage payments on all the property and the subsequent real estate downturn destroyed Mom. She couldn't make the payments, but she couldn't find a buyer either. The impact of the recession on New England in the late 1980s was severe. Even though interest rates were then approximately 30 percent less than what she was paying, the banks denied her refinancing because she did not "qualify" for that size loan based on her income.

In the end, Mom lost her house and all of her property and was forced to file for bankruptcy. She had to leave her dream home, move to an apartment, and ask her boss to cosign a rental agreement. Now, her pride, as well as her heart and pocketbook, had been damaged by the tragic loss of her husband.

Even though Tom was a successful attorney who had an estate planning division in his own law firm, he hadn't done the necessary planning. Why? He probably hadn't thought about the financial repercussions of the worst-case scenario. Though there is nothing we could have done to prevent Tom's passing, a few basic planning strategies could have saved Mom's pocketbook and her pride.

DAVID'S STORY

My Uncle Steve is very close to my immediate family. Uncle Steve made it a point to participate in the lives of all his children and nephews. In fact, I can't remember any of my basketball games or water polo matches when he wasn't in the stands cheering.

Steve is a real estate developer who owns primarily residential properties. Back in the late 1980s, he was involved with a residential condominium project outside Hartford, Connecticut. As part of the deal with the primary bank, Steve had to personally guarantee a $2.5 million loan to his company—$2.5 million was more than twice Steve's entire net worth, and he had never signed that large a guarantee before. Nevertheless, Steve, like many entrepreneurs, had supreme confidence that his project would sell out quickly and that the loan would be paid on time without a problem.

Despite his confidence, my Aunt Karen had reservations from the outset. While Steve slept soundly, Karen always fretted about the debt.

Unfortunately for Karen, her worst fears came to reality. It seemed that just when the construction crew broke ground on Steve's project, the economy began to turn sour in the New England area. By the time the construction was complete and the condos ready to be sold, the local real estate market was dead. Buyers were few and far between. Even though Steve and his team had brought the project in on time and within budget, the turn in the economy was too powerful to overcome. Sales were much too slow to cover the loan payments to the bank, so with every additional week, the debt continued to build. By the time the last condo was sold, the loan had been called. Steve personally owed over $1 million to the bank.

By this time, the stress on Karen was taking its toll. She had trouble thinking of anything but their financial problems. She grew depressed and developed a nervous tic. Our family tried to be positive and comforting, but there was little we could really do. Even Steve, the eternal optimist, couldn't imagine a positive solution. As close family members, we saw the fighting and the increasing marital stress. We also knew their ultimate fear: that they might lose everything in bankruptcy.

Fortunately, my family's story ended more positively than that of Chris's family. Before moving forward with any negotiation with the bank or with the bankruptcy process, Karen and Steve went to see an asset protection attorney. Incidentally, this is the same attorney with whom Chris and I have worked on many cases.

The attorney advised them to follow a detailed plan, which included (1) paying the loan sporadically with small payments in an effort to buy time, (2) establishing and funding a pension for Steve and the two other employees of his company, and (3) moving to Florida, where they would eventually file for bankruptcy protection (the move, by the way, wasn't very dramatic in their case because they were spending much of the winter in Florida anyway).

Karen and Steve followed the advisor's plan. Although enduring the bank's pressure to pay was certainly stressful and moving to Florida was a sacrifice, their plan proved to be successful. When their bankruptcy hearing took place two years later, the bank in Connecticut did not even participate. The bank had written off the loan and taken it off their books. In fact, Steve's particular loan officer was no longer with the bank.

Following their Wealth Protection advisor's plan, Karen and Steve were able to shield the lion's share of their savings, paying out only $30,000 to creditors and protecting nearly $1 million. Most important, Karen and Steve were able to put this one major wealth threat behind them and preserve what they had worked so hard to build. I'm happy to report that their family finances and their marriage are now more secure than ever, although the lingering effects of their ordeal are still evident to those who know and love them.

From our two experiences, you can see how Wealth Protection solutions can turn a potentially devastating bankruptcy into a minor loss and how lack of advanced planning can cause unnecessary financial and emotional stress. Why did Dorothy lose so much more than Karen and Steve? The tragedy of Tom's death was an event that could neither be reversed nor delayed while strategies were put into place for Dorothy. Karen and Steve were luckier—their debt problems could be prolonged while their planning took hold. The ability to do some Wealth Protection planning was truly the difference.

Even though Karen and Steve kept their wealth, their situation took its toll on them emotionally. If they had implemented Wealth Protection planning in advance, however, they would have been reassured that their wealth would be safe, despite the bank loan. This would have significantly reduced the stress on Karen and her marriage.

IS YOUR FAMILY LIKE OURS?

Do our stories seem familiar to you? Can you see the lack of prior planning hurting your family as it did Dorothy? Would you know to whom to turn if you were in a situation like Karen and Steve's? In our law and financial planning practices, we have helped thousands of clients avoid many different "wealth threats." If you can't identify with Dorothy or with Karen and Steve, maybe you can identify better with one of these people:

- Dr. Bill lost what he thought was a frivolous lawsuit and had to come up with $2,000,000 in damages.
- Larry and Wendy pay over $100,000 *per year* in income taxes.
- Dave fell off a ladder painting his house, hurt his back, and couldn't work for over nine months.
- Julie seems to get modest returns while paying significant taxes on her investments.
- Jim runs a successful business but lives frugally while he sees owners of similar businesses enjoying much better lifestyles.
- Mike and Shelley recently had their first child and have no idea what legal documents or insurance products are right for them.
- Daniel and Andrea's son just got accepted to an Ivy League school, but they can't afford to send him.

If you can imagine yourself in any of these situations, then Wealth Protection planning will help you considerably. In this book, we will provide solutions to all of these scenarios. You'll learn how Dr. Bill could have shielded his $2 million from that lawsuit. You'll see how Larry and Wendy can reduce their income tax bill by over $100,000 (or more) per year. From Dave's disability situation to Daniel and Andrea's educational funding challenge, comprehensive Wealth Protection planning addresses them all.

PART I

THE SYSTEM/ THE BOOK

CHAPTER ONE

WHY THIS BOOK SHOULD COST $5,000

This book allows you access to top advisors' secrets and strategies—and have them tailored to your Wealth Protection situation

I magine for a moment that instead of reading this book you are opening the door of a ritzy professional office in a New York City corporate center. When you open the door, you are greeted by a receptionist, who asks you to sit in the waiting area while she offers you a cup of coffee and explains what will happen today.

First, you will meet with an asset protection, tax, and estate planning attorney from one of the top-rated law firms in the country. He graduated from the nation's best schools, has written two books on areas of his practice, and has lectured to fellow attorneys and accountants in professional seminars.

In your meeting with the attorney, he will take over an hour to ask you questions about your goals in the areas of asset protection, tax, and estate planning, analyzing what types of planning you have already done with prior attorneys or accountants. Once his questions are answered, he will give you an overview of the types of strategies and tools that might make sense in your legal plan. He will even give you articles and executive summaries on these solutions, so you can review them later at your leisure.

Next, you will break for 15 minutes and go to another office where, for another two hours, a leading financial planner will evaluate your investments, insurance, retirement plan, educational funding, and other financial issues. This financial planner, who has an M.B.A. from a leading university and is the author of over a hundred articles in his field, has just flown in from Beverly Hills, California, to meet with you.

In your two-hour meeting with the financial planner, he will ask you questions about your present financial situation. Your answers will help him provide you with recommendations for such issues as saving for retirement, reducing income taxes, protecting your family finances in the case of a premature death or disability of the breadwinner(s), saving for college education costs, saving for long-term-care costs for you and for your parents, using charitable gifts to benefit your family, and maximizing the estate you leave your heirs. Like the attorney with whom you met, the financial planner will give you materials to read so you can review them later and discuss them with your family members or advisors.

After this meeting, you will break for lunch. Meanwhile, the attorney and the financial planner will be discussing your case, coordinating their evaluations and recommendations into one cohesive Wealth Protection plan.

When you return from lunch, you will meet with both advisors, who will not only explain their coordinated Wealth Protection plan for you, but also provide you with this plan in the form of a clear, comprehensive write-up, which you can then evaluate at your leisure.

What would you expect to pay for this kind of tailored Wealth Protection advice from leading professionals? It's a good bet that the figure you choose would be closer to $5,000 than to the price of this book. Yet the detailed, tailored analysis of your plan from a coordinated legal-financial perspective is precisely what this book will provide for you, if you complete the risk factor analysis (RFA) and follow its results. (We'll discuss this more in Chapter 4.)

THIS BOOK WILL TRANSPORT YOU TO OUR OFFICES

Through this book, we have attempted to deliver to you the entire process just described, without the morning coffee or lunch break.

In fact, our goal is to make you feel that you are sitting right in our offices, where we ask you the same questions and give you the same detailed advice that we will in these chapters.

As we explained in our introduction, we feel strongly that families and individuals need to protect their wealth in order to avoid the problems our own families experienced. Every day, in our professional practices, we meet with clients, analyze their risks, and present a coordinated Wealth Protection plan to be executed.

When we set out to write this book, we wanted to recreate, to as great a degree as possible, the advisory experience we have with our clients in our own offices. This has been a challenging, but successful, task. The result of our hard work is a book that you can use not only to learn general principles, but also to create *your* Wealth Protection plan.

Of course, we welcome new clients in our practices and would like to meet with you to help you achieve your Wealth Protection goals. However, this is not always possible. This book can serve as a substitute for meeting with us personally, at least initially. Also, you can use the book to help you evaluate the type of "Wealth Protection specialist" you might need to help you achieve your goals—attorneys, accountants, financial planners, asset protection specialists, and others. This will prevent you from paying advisors who really don't have the expertise for your particular situation. In using the book in these ways, you may save yourself hundreds, if not thousands, of dollars in professional fees.

YOU NEED WEALTH PROTECTION PLANNING

You may think that you don't need this type of planning or won't benefit from meeting with the attorney and the financial planner. In our practices, we have assisted clients as varied as the entire population—from extremely wealthy families to individuals just starting their careers; from physicians and business owners to employees of Fortune 1000 companies, from high-profile celebrities to anonymous farmers. Moreover, our practices address goals from estate planning (like Dorothy and Tom, discussed in the Introduction) and asset protection (Karen and Steve also from the Introduction) to tax reduction, from retirement planning to benefits packaging, and more. From this vast experience, we can make this bold statement:

No matter your age, particular circumstances, or level of wealth, you need Wealth Protection planning.

How can we be so certain that you need Wealth Protection planning when we haven't had the opportunity to meet with you in our offices? We can be so certain because of the one principle we have each learned in our practices:

Every client wants to either build greater wealth or preserve existing wealth, or perhaps both.

Think hard. Does this axiom apply to you? Don't you want to build more wealth than you have today so you can enjoy it in retirement, leave it to your family, or give it to a worthy cause? If not, don't you at least want to preserve what you have already built so it isn't eroded by taxes, investment downturns, or lawsuits? If either of these goals seems worthy, then Wealth Protection planning should appeal to you.

Although you may think that your advisors have already put you in the right position in terms of Wealth Protection, we think that is unlikely.

YOUR ADVISORS HAVE NOT DONE ENOUGH

1. *Most advisors do a poor job, and their clients don't even know it.* You may feel that your present advisors are excellent, or perhaps competent. How can you tell? By their education? The size of their firm? Their reputation? Certainly, these are good criteria for screening an advisor, but they really don't tell you whether she's doing a good job once she is hired. How can you tell whether or not that trust you have will achieve the tax benefits it is supposed to? How can you evaluate whether this insurance product was really the best one for your situation? How can you tell if you paid too much in taxes this year be-

cause you neglected possible tax-saving strategies for your business? Often, there is no way for clients to truly evaluate any of these issues effectively. A new client of David's law firm recently discovered this costly lesson, although the ending was a happy one.

CASE STUDY: DAVID'S CLIENT— REAL ESTATE DEVELOPER

A few years ago, David's law firm was retained to perform a self-imposed tax audit on a client. The client, an extremely successful businessman and real estate developer, was concerned when one of his business colleagues was found liable for back taxes and penalties because of mistakes by his accounting firm. Nervous that he might become an Internal Revenue Service (IRS) target soon, the businessman hired David's law firm to do an audit of his income taxes for the past five years, both for himself and for his various businesses. What David and his tax partners found was shocking—a $5 million mistake! To find out what this mistake was, turn to Chapter 16.

2. *Even our society's wealthiest, most prominent families get poor advice every day.* Anyone can be caught in the trap of poor planning. Let's examine some examples.

- Elvis's family lost over $8 million because of poor legal advice. Elvis Presley, one of the most famous celebrities of the twentieth century, was someone who should have had top legal talent advising his family on estate planning. In fact, the Presleys lost over two-thirds of their net worth to estate taxes and probate fees when Elvis died. In this way, poor planning cost Elvis's family over 65 percent of their net worth. If this doesn't have Elvis singing the blues from his grave, then we don't know what would.

- The Wrigley family is one of the best-known family names in the United States. They built a huge fortune in the twentieth century on the strength of their chewing gum empire. Nonetheless, William Wrigley (the third generation of the family) was forced to sell one of the family's most precious assets, the

Chicago Cubs baseball team, just to pay the estate taxes due when both of his parents died in 1977. Estate taxes are quite easy to plan for, as you'll see in future chapters. But this leading U.S. family did not engage in such planning, and their financial fortune was vulnerable.

- Willie Nelson, Francis Ford Coppola, Kim Basinger, Burt Reynolds, Larry King, Stan Lee, and numerous other high-profile people have filed for bankruptcy over the past 30 years. Obviously someone was not giving them the proper Wealth Protection advice.

3. *Even with top professionals, advice is rarely coordinated into one plan.* In the next chapter, you'll learn why proper Wealth Protection planning must be implemented by professionals from different disciplines, including law, tax, finance, insurance, and so on. You'll learn about a key diagnostic question that always shows how well individuals or families have their planning coordinated. The question is: Do your accountant, lawyer, insurance advisor, broker, and financial planner all meet together at least once annually to review your particular situation? If you answer "no," then our first two points are moot. In other words, even if your existing advisors are competent, or even excellent, in their own fields, if they are not coordinated, then your plan is lacking. If this is true, you need Wealth Protection planning, if for nothing else than to coordinate your existing planning and to fill in the gaps where the lack of coordination has left holes.

Throughout the Introduction and this chapter, we have used the term *Wealth Protection planning.* From our own family stories in the Introduction and the various references here, you may have a sense of what we mean by this term. However, if you are going to get the maximum benefit from this book, it is important that you have a specific knowledge of what Wealth Protection really means. We'll examine this in the next chapter.

CHAPTER TWO

WHAT IS WEALTH PROTECTION?

5 key concepts are essential to understanding your plan

Before we begin addressing your Wealth Protection planning needs, it is crucial that you understand exactly what Wealth Protection planning is. Without a complete understanding of the field of Wealth Protection planning, it is nearly impossible to oversee your own wealth in an effective way for the long term. We have put together a working definition that will serve you throughout the book and in your personal planning:

> **Wealth Protection planning (WPP) is a multidisciplinary process of shielding your wealth from all internal and external threats.**

This is a fairly short definition, but there are five distinct concepts that you should grasp before continuing the book or beginning your individual Wealth Protection planning. After you truly understand what WPP is, you will have a greater appreciation for the value of this book to your overall financial situation.

CONCEPT #1: MULTIDISCIPLINARY

Protecting and growing your "wealth health" is like maintaining your physical health—you need to draw on the knowledge of many specialists with the oversight of a generalist. During your lifetime, you will undoubtedly spend more time with your primary physician than with any other doctor. However, the average person interacts directly with at least five other specialists and possibly indirectly with dozens more.

As a child, you may have developed allergies and visited an allergist or you may have broken a bone and seen an orthopedic specialist. As a teenager, you may have become concerned with your acne and consulted a dermatologist. At some point, you may have had your tonsils or appendix removed and had experience with a general surgeon and an anesthesiologist. Women will eventually consult a gynecologist and, perhaps, an obstetrician. As most people age, they will unfortunately have reason to consult a urologist, a cardiologist, an oncologist, or other specialist.

Throughout your life, you will probably consult with at least 5 to 10 doctors from different specialties and subspecialties. Different challenges require distinct expertise—and you will likely do the best you can to get the advice you need. In this way, your physical health demands a multidisciplinary approach. This doesn't make us hypochondriacs—it makes us smart!

The same principal of using a multidisciplinary approach should also apply to your financial "wealth health." Unfortunately, most of us are not as adamant about using this approach in our financial planning as we are for our health care. Believe us when we tell you that very few clients have addressed their "wealth health" with a combined legal-financial approach. Most prospective clients show the symptoms of a Wealth Protection plan that lacks a multidisciplinary interaction. Does yours?

How would you answer these questions?

- Do you write a check for any of your life insurance policies?
- Do you have separate firms handling different portions of your investments (pensions, IRAs, brokerage accounts, etc.)?

- Did you have a lawyer friend (not a specialist) draft your will or any of your more complex estate or tax documents?
- Have you put off funding any of your trusts or other legal entities?
- Is there a chance that your accountant, lawyer, insurance advisor, broker, and financial planner don't meet together at least once annually to review your particular situation?

If the answer to any of these questions is "yes," then you are a prime candidate for WPP, and you will benefit greatly from this book.

One of the reasons we have been so successful in our practices is that we coordinate the legal planning (David and his firm), the financial/insurance planning (Chris and his firm), and the accounting functions (typically, our contacts or the client's existing advisor) so that the client's plan works seamlessly. As an example, let's start with the first question.

If a client needs life insurance, Chris will search among thousands of products from hundreds of companies to find the right policy for the client. Meanwhile, David will draft the irrevocable life insurance trust (ILIT—the reason why is described in Chapter 20) to make sure that it complies with the client's goals and maximizes tax and asset protection. Then, Chris will make sure *the trust* purchases the policy to keep the proceeds out of the client's taxable estate and to avoid the IRS's three-year "look-back" restriction (discussed in Chapter 55). Finally, we will both make sure the client's accountant is up to speed on what the tax-filing responsibilities are. The benefit to the client from this simple transaction could be as much as $250,000 on a $500,000 insurance policy. Multidisciplinary, experienced, and coordinated—that is the way superior Wealth Protection planning should be delivered.

CONCEPT #2: PROCESS

Wealth Protection planning is not a one-time event. Rather, it is a process that continues from the beginning of one's earning years until at least one year after death. Just as life brings a constant flow of change, so is the challenge of Wealth Protection planning a continuous one.

One important reason that WPP is a continuous process is that your priorities will change over the course of your life. In the early stages of your career, before you have a family, wealth building may be the only focus of your plan. When you're only supporting yourself, you probably have little regard for an estate plan or for insurance planning (life, long-term-care, etc.). In the middle stages of your career, as a family enters the picture, a greater focus is shifted to providing for your family. At that time, creating a basic estate and insurance plan becomes important.

> While nearly every homeowner has insurance on his or her house, very few have adequate disability coverage. Yet there is less than a 4 percent chance of a fire in the home, but over a 70 percent chance of the homeowner's disability some time during his or her working years.

As you earn more income and accumulate greater wealth, you begin to focus more on asset protection planning and tax reduction. In the later stages of your financial life, retirement distribution planning will be primary. During retirement, most clients begin to focus on their estate planning—though you'll start earlier after reading this book.

Wealth Protection planning must continuously change in response to the dramatic events that always seem to invite themselves into our lives. The birth of a child, a divorce, a windfall investment, the premature death of a spouse, a large inheritance, a failing business, a disabling disease or injury—these are just a few of a thousand events that will require a significant modification to a family's Wealth Protection plan. In many cases, like the case in the Introduction of Tom's death, events cannot be anticipated. However, advanced planning can reduce the potential loss, and subsequent modifications to the plan can help put us back on track to reaching our goals. The case studies throughout the book will help illustrate this fact.

CONCEPT #3: SHIELDING

The basic concept of *shielding* is simple—protecting what's yours. In this book, we will discuss how to protect your wealth from various risks. Chapters 25 through 34 cover shielding assets from lawsuits, Chapters 35 through 37 and 39 through 40 show how to protect your income from disability and death, and Chapter 38 shows how to protect savings against the devastating costs of nursing home care. In these examples, shielding means "protecting."

You may also think of shielding as "minimizing" or "reducing." When we discuss shielding investments from market risks (Chapters 17 through 24) or shielding income and wealth from taxes (Chapters 7 through 16), shielding means "reduction."

From our experiences, we have found that clients neglect the areas of tax reduction and investment downturns more than any other. Often, otherwise bright and capable advisors have no idea what strategies to employ to reduce income taxes. While over 99 percent of the people we poll at our seminars would like to reduce their income tax burden, fewer than 1 percent have heard of opportunities such as 412(i) plans, welfare benefit plans, or captive insurance companies. This book will fill those gaps and will introduce you to a whole new set of options to shield your wealth from unnecessary taxes.

CONCEPT #4: YOUR WEALTH

Do you have the best handle on your wealth? Not necessarily. We have had many clients walk into our offices with significant misconceptions about their wealth. Fortunately, in most cases, they vastly undervalue what they are really worth. When completing our asset questionnaire (Appendix 5), clients often leave out certain bank accounts, fail to include a time-share condo ("because it isn't worth anything yet"), or simply forget about various life insurance policies that were put in place years ago.

If we were to discuss your wealth in our offices, we would need to know about *all* of your assets. We would go down an exhaustive checklist to make sure we did not overlook anything. We would also ask you to give us the present and the projected values of your assets and liabilities. Because your wealth may be increased or diminished by foreseeable events, we will need to consider this in our planning. For example, your wealth may increase by a future inheritance from an elderly relative, or it may decrease by a future debt that will come due. If so, such events must be weighed in the plan. Further, you may have contingent assets, which may or may not come to fruition (like an option to purchase land if the value increases). Again, these must be considered.

When you complete the risk factor analysis (the RFA) in Chapter 5, you will see how exhaustive our list of questions is. We do not want you to leave out, forget, or ignore any asset, regardless of how small or elusive it may seem. If a Wealth Protection plan is to be comprehensive, it must deal with *all* of your wealth.

Another important point we must make here regards the concept of wealth. We know many of you, like thousands of people we speak to in seminars every year, may be turned off by the word *wealth*. In fact, the same is true for many new clients we meet in our offices. Whether they be young or old, single or married, a certain percentage of people will say the same thing to us when we bring up the concept of WP: "Wealth?" they say, "Who's wealthy? We've got some assets, but we're not *wealthy*."

> This is the number-one Wealth Protection planning mistake people make: *They wrongly assume that they are not "wealthy enough" for Wealth Protection planning.*

Wealth Protection planning is not just for the admittedly wealthy. Not even close. From the 24-year-old just beginning her career to the multigenerational family with hundreds of millions in assets, the variation among our clients is astounding. Nonetheless, each, in his or her own way, needs some degree of WP. Whether it means developing a better risk/reward ratio in an investment portfolio, saving for college costs, reducing income taxes, protecting assets from liability, or simply creating an efficient estate plan, WPP impacts us all. Whether you are truly wealthy or just starting out, in a high income tax bracket or a low one, an individual or the head of a family, WPP in general—and this book in particular—has much to offer you. Do not get stuck in the "I am not wealthy enough" trap. It is the first financial land mine you must avoid.

Concept #5: All internal and external threats

The final concept in our definition of WP may be the most important. That is because you will only value the importance of planning if you truly understand what we are planning against—those internal and external wealth threats. Before you began reading this book, you probably had in mind certain concerns about your wealth (you may not have verbalized them as threats). Most of our clients consider income taxes or investment downturns as threats. Perhaps you had others, like estate planning or college funding, as well.

> The average four-year college tuition in 2020 will be $273,000 (over $500,000 for Ivy League schools).

Regardless of what your specific "top of mind" threats were, it is imperative that you go beyond this initial gut feeling and realize *all* of the threats that could seriously jeopardize your wealth. It may turn out, in fact, that the threat that eventually does the most damage to your wealth is one that now seems insignificant. All the more reason why this factor is so crucial—*systematically recognizing all of the threats to your wealth is actually the first step in protecting it.* In the arena of Wealth Protection planning, ignorance is not bliss. It is foolish.

> This is Wealth Protection planning mistake number two: *Falling into the trap of ignoring wealth threats.*

Although it will take time and money to learn about and to protect against the threats that make your wealth vulnerable, this investment will reap great rewards. You've taken an important first step by buying this book. Now take the time to read it, to complete the RFA, and to implement the planning where you need it most. You and your family will truly benefit.

You may already be convinced that you need to dig deeper and to investigate where your current plan is vulnerable. How do you know which wealth threats are lurking in your present plan? The answer to this question will depend on your job, your family situation, your level of wealth, and a host of other factors. When you take the RFA and read your score, you will get a thorough sketch of the key threats that make your particular situation vulnerable. That is still a few short chapters away, though. Let's make sure you thoroughly understand the types of threats that exist before you move on.

In our analysis of a client's situation, we differentiate between "internal" and "external" wealth threats. The difference, essentially, is the source of the threat. Internal threats come from your own situation or that of your family, whereas external threats are created by outside forces. Here are some common internal and external threats. The RFA will elicit specific threats particular to your situation.

Internal Threats
- Premature death or disability.
- Need for nursing home care.
- Divorce.
- Mismanagement of investment funds (poor allocation, speculation, etc.).
- Lack of professional guidance.
- Poor choice of advisors.

External Threats
- Downturns in the investment markets.
- All types of taxes.
- All types of lawsuits and claims.
- College and other educational expenses.
- Estate costs and administration fees.
- Divorce, disability, or death of a business partner/key financial source.

CHAPTER THREE

FINDING YOUR PERSONAL ECONOMY

To build and preserve wealth, you must focus on your Personal Economy.

IT'S *YOUR* ECONOMY THAT COUNTS

As a result of the bull market of the 1990s, Americans have become obsessed with the stock market and the nation's economic performance. CNBC, market updates, and "fed-watchers" have become a ubiquitous presence in our lives. Tracking the health of the economy is a daily soap opera, and the supposed experts on talk radio and television are household names. According to recent studies, the ups and downs of the market create a "wealth effect" on how positively or negatively we feel about our own economic status. If the market is up, we feel wealthy (as in 1999). If the market is down (as in 2000), we feel poor. Are you susceptible to this phenomenon?

Here's a quick test. Assume a financial news program is reporting these stories:

- Experts fear the economy is sliding into a recession.
- The Dow Jones Industrial Average (the DOW) dropped by 20 percent.
- The Nasdaq closed down 300 points.

- Alan Greenspan appeared on Capitol Hill and announced another change in the prime rate.

At the same time:

- A little-known change in the tax law eliminates a large deduction your business had been taking.
- Your mother was just diagnosed with Alzheimer's, and you have little savings and no long-term-care coverage to pay future medical bills.
- Your accountant informs you that you failed to heed his advice about the tax liabilities associated with retirement plan distributions.
- You need back surgery that may prevent you from traveling for work.

WHICH EVENTS ARE *REALLY* MORE IMPORTANT TO YOUR PERSONAL FINANCIAL SITUATION?

Of course, the second set of events is significantly more important to the security of your Financial Fortress than the first set is. While this may seem obvious, most people disregard this simple realization. Millions of us, in fact, behave as if the overall market news is a more significant factor in our personal finances than details of our own lives! Many of us succumb to the uneasiness surrounding the volatility of the market, which, in turn, makes us feel powerless to change our own Wealth Protection situation. This can become a vicious cycle where all planning is avoided.

We have now come to Wealth Protection planning mistake number three: *People focus on the macroeconomy of the nation, rather than paying proper attention to their own personal economy.*

THE CONCEPT OF THE PERSONAL ECONOMY

When we talk about stimulating your *personal economy,* we aren't talking about making decisions on the type of career to follow, ways to move up the corporate ladder faster, whether to get married or to have children. These are some of the life decisions you will have to make on your own. What we are talking about is, regardless of what choices you make, how you can make the best of your personal situation by building and preserving your wealth.

PART II

CUSTOMIZING THIS BOOK FOR YOU

CHAPTER FOUR

INTRODUCING THE RISK FACTOR ANALYSIS

I n Chapter 3, we explained the concept of *your personal economy.* The next two chapters will help you protect and stimulate your personal economy.

We have created a relatively brief questionnaire (85 questions) for you to complete. Once you write down your answers to these questions, you can proceed to the next chapter. We recommend writing your answers on a separate piece of paper, not in the book, for three reasons:

1. You will want to use that piece of paper to write down the chapters that we recommend you read as part of your *customized* program.

2. You will probably want to revise your customized Wealth Protection plan in the future, and your answers may change.

3. You may let a friend borrow the book, and you probably want to keep your answers private.

Every person who completes the risk factor analysis (RFA) will receive a different set of recommendations and will be directed to read different chapters. Also, each time you complete the RFA (assuming your life has changed at least a little), you will be directed to different chapters and will hopefully learn something new. This is how this book differs from other personal finance books. Though we cover over 60 topics in seven distinct sections (taxes, investments, asset pro-

tection, insurance, retirement, estate planning, and business planning), each person will get a different "book" to read.

Of course, if the RFA recommends that you read more than the
average of 10–20 chapters, it means that you either have more assets
to protect or have more facets of your complete Wealth Protection
plan to address. It may mean that you have been more successful and
therefore need to understand more subjects if you intend to keep
what you have acquired.

Please take a few minutes to complete the RFA, and feel free to
read the other chapters at your leisure. Also, feel free to go to
www.mywealthprotection.com for updated and more comprehensive
information that we couldn't fit into one book.

CHAPTER FIVE

THE QUESTIONS

Please find a sheet of paper and a pen or a pencil. Then, read each question and write your answer on the sheet of paper. After you complete the analysis, we will help you self-grade it and determine which chapters of the book will be the most helpful to you in protecting your own personal wealth and stimulating your personal economy.

SECTION A—TAX PLANNING

You have heard that there are only two certainties in life: death and taxes. We will cover death extensively in sections D and F of the RFA. The questions in section A are designed to help you reduce your taxes. We have yet to meet a client who thinks he or she is paying too little or "just the right amount" of taxes. Pay careful attention to these questions and the recommendations we give. If you don't want to reduce your taxes, please give us a call. We'd love to meet you.

1. Is your household income greater than $50,000?
2. Is your household income greater than $200,000?
3. Is your household income greater than $400,000?
4. Is your household income greater than $600,000?
5. Are you or your spouse over 45 years of age?
6. Do you receive rental income from any real estate you own?
7. Do you have either a Uniform Gift to Minors Account (UGMA),

an education IRA (individual retirement account), or a broker-age or savings account that you intend to use for college costs for your children or grandchildren?

8. Do you know that there is an 80 percent tax on your retirement plan?

9. Do you presently have a CPA (certified public accountant), a tax attorney, or a financial advisor?

10. Have you ever had your financial and tax plans reviewed by an-other professional (a second opinion)?

11. Do you own a business or a professional practice?

12. Do you have a charitable inclination? Would you give to a char-ity to help reduce your taxes now, to help a worthy cause, and potentially to help your heirs as well?

SECTION B—INVESTING

Most investors get into trouble because they get greedy, take too much risk, or just don't understand what options they have. Your answers to these questions will help us customize a reading list that will help you achieve your investing goals.

13. Did the financial events in the past few years cause you to take some of your money out of the stock market?

14. If you answered YES to question 13, are you unsure when you should invest in the stock market again?

15. Are you satisfied with all of your investments?

16. Are you sure your investments are not subject to large swings in the market?

17. Are you comfortable paying 32 percent to 50 percent in taxes on your investment gains?

18. Are you comfortable paying taxes on mutual funds even when their values go down?

19. Do you need income from your investments but want upside potential that is greater than bonds, certificates of deposit, or money market accounts?

SECTION C—ASSET PROTECTION

There are millions of lawsuits filed every year in this country. Only in twenty-first-century America can a burglar successfully sue the owner of a home he burgled for an injury he received on the premises or can a customer sue a restaurant for coffee that is too hot. Combine these cases with insurance companies who seemingly always look to deny coverage based on the "fine print," and you see how easily you can have a liability nightmare on your hands. Whether cases like these seem foolish or even ridiculous, those of us who don't protect ourselves may prove to be the fools. Remember, it was David's uncle's asset protection plan that saved him from losing everything!

20. Are you afraid of being sued and losing your assets?

21. Are you or will you ever be married?

22. Do you own valuable assets in your own name, in the name of a spouse, or in the name of your living trust?

23. Do you own any valuable assets jointly with a spouse or with another person?

24. Do you believe insurance will take care of any potential losses you might have?

25. Do you own rental real estate?

26. Do you own a business?

27. Are you a physician, an attorney, a real estate developer, or a contractor?

28. Do you have more than $100,000 of equity in your home, or is it worth $300,000 or more?

29. Do you have more than $100,000 in liquid assets and non–real estate investments (stocks, bonds, mutual funds, certificates of deposit [CDs], money markets)?

30. Do you own anything you would like to leave to your children?

31. Are you concerned that your children or grandchildren may lose the inheritance you leave them to a lawsuit or a divorce?

32. Are you a partner in a partnership of any kind?

33. Are you interested in offshore planning?

34. Do you have relatives in other countries?

SECTION D—INSURANCE

No matter how affluent you are, you undoubtedly value your life (and your ability to make more money) more than your possessions. If you have to support loved ones (spouse, children, or even parents), your life is even more important—your heirs can't recreate or replace you when you pass on. Remember what happened when Tom died? Chris's mother was left in a terrible situation.

These questions are designed to determine if you have (1) enough life insurance to cover the costs of living and educational costs for your children or a spouse you support, (2) enough disability coverage to replace your income if you are to become disabled, and (3) enough coverage to provide for the exorbitant medical costs if you, your parents, or your in-laws need long-term care.

This section requires few questions, as almost everyone needs to read the majority of this section for three reasons:

1. You will die someday.

2. There is a 70 percent chance that you or your spouse will become disabled during your lifetime.

3. There is less than a 1 percent chance that you, your spouse, your parents, or your in-laws will *not* need long-term care at some time.

35. Do you own life insurance?

36. Are you paying for your insurance with after-tax dollars?

37. Would you buy more insurance if your health were better and the insurance were cheaper?

38. Would your family be able to get by if the breadwinner stopped making money?

39. Do you get a tax deduction for your disability insurance premiums?

40. Does your employer pay for your disability insurance, or do you have a group disability policy through an association?

41. Would your parents or in-laws have enough saved to pay for nursing home costs of $300 per day for the rest of their lives if they became sick?

42. If your answer to question 41 is YES, would it be acceptable if your parents or in-laws spent your inheritance on their medical bills if you could have saved that amount?

43. Would it be okay for your parents *and* in-laws to move in with you if they couldn't afford nursing home care?

44. Would you and your wife have enough saved to cover medical bills of $300 per day if you became sick (assuming no health insurance)?

45. Do you own a business or a practice, or do you have equity in your home and a desire to buy more insurance at a reduced cost?

SECTION E—RETIREMENT

Do you work to live or live to work? Most Americans work to live and have their eyes on the prize at the end of the rainbow—retirement! Despite this typically common goal, we see a great fluctuation in clients' abilities to retire. Even among clients with the same income, their ability to retire early or with as much money as they had hoped is usually a function of the quality of their retirement plan. If you want to retire early, or retire wealthy, or retire happy, take the time to read these questions and the recommended chapters.

46. Do you have brokerage or savings accounts that you intend to use for retirement?

47. Do you participate in a profit sharing plan, a pension, a 401(k), or an IRA?

48. Are you concerned you won't have enough saved for retirement?

49. Are you retired already or about to retire?

50. Would you like to have "guaranteed income" during retirement so you don't have to worry about stock market returns or interest rate fluctuations?

51. Is there one breadwinner in your family who is saving for both spouses?

52. If you are married, or soon to be married, do you have more than a 10-year age difference or a 10-year life expectancy differential?

53. Are you potentially responsible for the financial well-being of your parents or in-laws?

54. Do you want to retire before age 59½?

55. Do you think you might accumulate at least $500,000 in retirement plan assets at any time in your life?

SECTION F—ESTATE PLANNING

Every year billions, if not trillions, of dollars are paid unnecessarily in the form of estate taxes and probate fees. Eighty percent of businesses don't reach the second generation because of poor intergenerational planning. In Chris's mother's case, poor planning led to her bankruptcy. Don't let oversights, bad planning, or procrastination ruin your life or the lives of your heirs.

56. Do you believe that estate planning is a waste of time because of the estate tax repeal of 2001?

57. Are you or do you anticipate being worth more than $100,000 at any time during your life?

58. Are you or do you anticipate being worth more than $1,000,000 at any time during your life?

59. Do you own life insurance?

60. Do you pay for your life insurance with after-tax dollars?

61. Are you or do you anticipate being worth more than $3,000,000 at any time during your life?

62. Do you own anything jointly with your spouse or with another person?

63. Do you own rental real estate?

64. Do you own a business or a professional practice?

65. Do you intend to leave your business or professional practice to your heirs or to sell it and leave them the proceeds of the sale?

66. Do you have more than $500,000 in a retirement plan or an IRA?

67. Do you have a stretch IRA or hope to use a stretch IRA to avoid taxes at death?

68. Did you know that 80 percent of your pension, 401(k), or IRA could be taken by taxes when you die?

69. Do you own stocks worth over $2,000,000?

70. Would you do your estate planning for half the price if you could?

71. Are either your parents or your in-laws still alive?

72. Do your parents or in-laws have an adequate amount of long-term-care insurance?

73. Do your parents or in-laws have a current living trust, and, if so, is it funded?

74. Do your parents or in-laws have life insurance?

75. Do you or your relatives own a family business?

76. Do your parents or in-laws have a retirement plan or an IRA?

77. Are your parents or in-laws living on the interest of their bonds, certificates of deposit, money markets, stock dividends, or retirement distributions?

78. Are you afraid of leaving an inheritance to your family and having them lose it if they get divorced? Are you concerned about losing your inheritance if you get divorced?

79. Do you have a charitable inclination? Would you like to leave something to a charitable organization?

80. Would you consider leaving something to a charity if it helped reduce your taxes and helped your family?

SECTION G—BUSINESS PLANNING

Starting and running your own business is very difficult. Believe us, we know. We have two businesses ourselves. You need to address certain risks so you don't lose what you have worked so hard to achieve. Luckily, in return for all the craziness involved in running a business, there are benefits that only you can realize. This section helps explain some of those benefits.

81. Do you have partners in your business?

82. Are you a partnership, sole proprietorship, or just a person with a business and no legal entity?

83. Does your business have more than $250,000 in annual profits?
84. Does the business have more than $1,000,000 in profits annually?
85. Are you concerned about losing your business to lawsuits?
86. Would you like to avoid employment headaches and reduce your overhead in the process?

CHAPTER SIX

THE INTERPRETATION OF YOUR ANSWERS

Over the next few pages, we will go over each of the risk factor analysis (RFA) questions and, based on your answers, give you recommendations on which of the following sections and chapters may best help you reach your goals. Of course, you can go ahead and read the entire book, but your answers to the RFA will help customize this book for you!

You may have purchased this book because you wanted to learn about a few specific tools and strategies. After you read the recommended chapters, feel free to look in the index or the table of contents for your areas of interest and peruse those chapters as well.

Of course, the recommendations in this section are generic and can never replace meetings with qualified experts in the areas of financial planning; asset protection; and tax, retirement, investing, and estate planning. However, we feel the RFA is the most comprehensive financial planning tool you will find in any book on the market.

Enjoy!

SECTION A—TAX PLANNING

Pay careful attention to these questions and the tax planning recommendations we give. If you don't want to reduce your taxes, please give us a call. We'd love to meet you.

1. Is your household income greater than $50,000?

2. Is your household income greater than $200,000?

3. Is your household income greater than $400,000?

4. Is your household income greater than $600,000?

No matter what number your response is, read Chapters 7 and 8 to learn how you will be taxed on your income and investments.

If you answered YES to any of questions 1 through 4, read Chapters 42, 43, and 44 on retirement plans. Certain strategies can help you save up to $20,000 per year in income taxes. You may wish to peruse the rest of the income tax section for other tidbits that may save you $5,000 here and $10,000 there.

If you answered YES to any of questions 2, 3, or 4, read Chapter 12 on the deductibility of long-term-care insurance.

If you answered YES to question 3 or 4, read Chapters 10 and 63 on welfare benefit plans.

If you answered YES to question 3 or 4 and are part of a company with over $2,000,000 in revenues, read Chapter 64 on captive insurance companies.

5. Are you or your spouse over 45 years of age?

If you answered YES to question 5 and to question 2, 3, or 4, read Chapters 42 through 50 on retirement planning, especially Chapters 43 and 44 on defined-benefit and 412(i) plans, respectively.

6. Do you receive rental income from any real estate you own?

If YES, you may be paying too much in income taxes and not taking advantage of some "income sharing" possibilities. Read Chapter 11 on income sharing. You also should seriously consider reading all of Part V on asset protection, especially Chapters 26, 27, and 30.

7. Do you have either a Uniform Gift to Minors Account (UGMA), an education IRA (individual retirement account), or a brokerage or savings account that you intend to use for college costs for your children or grandchildren?

If you answered YES because you have an UGMA account or a separate brokerage or savings account for your children, you are paying unnecessary taxes on your investments. You can avoid these taxes by implementing a 529 plan—read Chapter 14.

You should also consider a 529 plan if you have an education IRA and you want to put more money away in annual gifts. If you only put away $2,000 per year for your children, you probably won't have enough to send them to college. The 529 allows $11,000 to $22,000 per year (or more).

You also want to read Chapter 14 if you don't want your children or grandchildren to be able to access the money you leave them for college to buy other things.

8. Do you know that there is an 80 percent tax on your retirement plan?

If you don't even know this problem exists, you need to read Chapters 7, 8, and 15. You also need to review Part VII on retirement planning (Chapters 41 through 49, with special attention given to Chapter 48) and Part VIII on estate planning (Chapters 50 through 61). If you are familiar with this terrible tax threat, go directly to Chapters 57 and 58.

9. Do you presently have a CPA (certified public accountant), a tax attorney, or a financial advisor?

If YES, then read Chapter 16, Is Your Tax Advisor Helping You or Hurting You? When it comes to tax advice, most people never pay for a second opinion. They just assume that the advisors are doing what is best. Unfortunately, this is not always the case. In some instances, it can cost you more than you can imagine.

10. Have you ever had your financial and tax plans reviewed by another professional (a second opinion)?

If NO, then read Chapter 16 as well. If YES, have you reviewed your plan recently? This exercise is well worth the time and the money because it can save you thousands, if not millions, of dollars.

11. Do you own a business or a professional practice?

If YES, read Chapters 7 through 12. You should also read Parts V, VII, and IX on asset protection, retirement, and business planning, respectively. There are many options available to you to improve your personal economy through proper Wealth Protection planning.

12. Do you have a charitable inclination? Would you give to a charity to help reduce your taxes now, to help a worthy cause, and potentially to help your heirs as well?

If YES, read Chapters 13 and 61 on charitable planning (after reading Chapters 7, 8, 50, and 51).

SECTION B—INVESTING

Most investors get into trouble because they get greedy, take too much risk, or just don't understand what options they have. Your answers to these questions will help us customize a reading list that will help you achieve your investing goals.

First of all, everyone should read Chapters 17, 18, and 19. This required reading will explain what investment options exist, identify some pitfalls, and explain how taxes and inflation are commonly overlooked by investors.

13. Did the events in the past few years cause you to take some of your money out of the stock market?

14. If you answered YES to question 13, are you unsure when you should invest in the stock market again?

If you answered YES to either question 13 or 14, then you should follow up your reading of Chapters 17, 18, and 19 with Chapters 20 through 24. Chapter 20 shows you how to get back into the market, and Chapters 21 through 24 offer investments that have some bells and whistles that can reduce your risk, without sacrificing all upside investment potential.

15. Are you satisfied with all of your investments?

16. Are you sure your investments are not subject to large swings in the market?

If you answered NO to either question 15 or 16, read Chapters 17, 18, 22, 23, and 24. The strategies covered in these chapters offer benefits you may not know exist.

17. Are you comfortable paying 32 percent to 50 percent in taxes on your investment gains?

18. Are you comfortable paying taxes on mutual funds even when their values go down?

If you answered NO to either question 17 or 18, then read Chapters 19, 21, 22, and 23. These chapters offer strategies for reducing taxes on investments. This can have a significant impact on the amount you accumulate for future use.

19. Do you need income from your investments but want upside potential that is greater than bonds, certificates of deposit, or money market accounts?

If YES, read Chapter 24 on convertible bonds.

SECTION C—ASSET PROTECTION

As we mentioned before, in twenty-first-century America a burglar can successfully sue the owner of a home he burgled for an injury he received on the premises and a customer can sue a restaurant for coffee that is too hot. Combine these cases with insurance companies who seemingly always look to deny coverage based on the "fine print," and you can see how easily you can have a liability nightmare on your hands.

Therefore, everyone must read Chapters 25 and 26.

20. Are you afraid of being sued and losing your assets?

If YES, definitely read Chapters 25, 26, and 27 to start, then read the remainder of Part V.

21. Are you or will you ever be married?

If YES or MAYBE, read Chapter 26 on problems with joint ownership and 34 on divorce.

22. Do you own valuable assets in your own name, in the name of a spouse, or in the name of your living trust?

23. Do you own any valuable assets jointly with a spouse or with another person?

If YES, read Chapter 26 on problems with joint ownership, Chapter 52 on wills and living trusts, Chapter 53 on A-B living trusts, and

Chapter 29 on family limited partnerships (FLPs) and limited liability companies (LLCs).

24. Do you believe insurance will take care of any potential losses you might have?

If YES, please think again. There are so many exclusions in insurance policies, and jury awards are climbing at an alarming rate. Read chapter 27 on insurance and read the other necessary chapters in Part 5.

25. Do you own rental real estate?

If you answered YES to any of questions 22, 23, 24, or 25, you must read Chapters 25, 26, and 27 and especially Chapter 29 on FLPs and LLCs.

26. Do you own a business?

If YES or if you intend to own a business in the near future, read Chapter 66 on corporations, Chapter 26 on ownership forms to avoid, Chapter 29 on FLPs and LLCs, Chapter 30 on trusts, and Chapter 68 on professional employer organizations.

27. Are you a physician, an attorney, a real estate developer, or a contractor?

If YES, you have extremely high liability exposure. We have written books exclusively on asset protection for you. Make it a point to read all of Part V on asset protection.

28. Do you have more than $100,000 of equity in your home, or is it worth $300,000 or more?

If YES, go to Chapter 33 on protecting your home.

29. Do you have more than $100,000 in liquid assets and non–real estate investments (stocks, bonds, mutual funds, certificates of deposit [CDs], money markets)?

If YES, you should read Chapters 28, 29, and 30.

30. Do you own anything you would like to leave to your children?

31. Are you concerned that your children or grandchildren may lose the inheritance you leave them to a lawsuit or a divorce?

If you answered YES to either question 30 or 31, you should read Chapters 28, 29, 30, and 34 and all of Part VIII on estate planning. There is much you can do to protect your heirs and the inheritance you may leave them.

32. Are you a partner in a partnership of any kind?

If YES, you must read Chapters 26, 29, and 34.

33. Are you interested in offshore planning?
34. Do you have relatives in other countries?

If YES to either question 33 or 34, read Chapters 31 and 32. These chapters will explain what you can and cannot do with offshore planning. It is not just for the rich and famous. Offshore is very helpful for people with over $100,000 of liquid assets.

SECTION D—INSURANCE

This section requires few questions, as almost everyone needs to read the majority of Part VI, Insurance Planning, for three reasons:

1. You will die someday.
2. There is a 70 percent chance that you or your spouse will become disabled during your lifetime.
3. There is less than a 1 percent chance that you, your spouse, your parents, or your in-laws will *not* need long-term care at some time.

For these reasons, everyone must read Chapters 35 through 38.

35. Do you own life insurance?

If YES, you may want to understand your options. There is probably a way for you to reduce your costs or increase your coverage for the same price. Read Chapters 35 and 36.

36. Are you paying for your insurance with after-tax dollars?

In over 99 percent of the cases, the answer is YES. If you are like most people and are paying for insurance with after-tax dollars and if you have a retirement plan or your own business or practice, you should read Chapters 10, 43, 44, 48, 57, and 58.

37. Would you buy more insurance if your health were better and the insurance were cheaper?

If YES, read Chapters 39 and 40. These chapters show unique ways to get insurance on people with poor health and ways to reduce the out-of-pocket cost of insurance.

38. Would your family be able to get by if the breadwinner stopped making money?

If NO, read Chapter 37 on disability insurance.

39. Do you get a tax deduction for your disability insurance premiums?

40. Does your employer pay for your disability insurance, or do you have a group disability policy through an association?

If YES is your answer to either question 39 or 40, you may have fallen into a tax trap or may have insufficient coverage. Read Chapter 37.

41. Would your parents or in-laws have enough saved to pay for nursing home costs of $300 per day for the rest of their lives if they became sick?

If NO, read Chapter 38 on long-term care.

42. If your answer to question 41 is YES, would it be acceptable if your parents or in-laws spent your inheritance on their medical bills if you could have saved that amount?

43. Would it be okay for your parents *and* in-laws to move in with you if they couldn't afford nursing home care?

44. Would you and your wife have enough saved to cover medical bills of $300 per day if you became sick (assuming no health insurance)?

If you answered NO to any of questions 42, 43, or 44, then read Chapter 38 on long-term care. Long-term-care insurance has become very popular as a way to protect against high medical bills, to reduce income taxes today, to protect an inheritance from being depleted, and to serve as an estate planning tool.

45. Do you own a business or a practice, or do you have equity in your home and a desire to buy more insurance at a reduced cost?

If YES, then you may have a means to obtain what we call "free" insurance. It isn't really free, but it may be something that you can purchase for $0 out of pocket and that can provide a significant benefit to your family. Read chapter 40.

SECTION E—RETIREMENT

Do you work to live or live to work? Most Americans work to live and have their eyes on the prize at the end of the rainbow—retirement! Despite this typically common goal, we see a great fluctuation in clients' abilities to retire. Even among clients with the same income, their ability to retire early or with as much money as they had hoped is usually a function of the quality of their retirement plan. If you want to retire early, or retire wealthy, or retire happy, take the time to read these questions and the recommended chapters.

Everyone must read Chapters 41, 42, and 49.

46. Do you have brokerage or savings accounts that you intend to use for retirement?

If YES, you are probably paying too much in taxes. Did you know that the average mutual fund investor pays 32 percent in taxes on all of his or her gains? If you don't want to give away a third of your appreciation, you should read Part VII (especially Chapter 41, Chapter 45 on variable annuities, and Chapter 46 on life insurance). You should also read Chapters 17, 18, and 19 and Chapters 21, 22, and 23 in Part IV on investments.

47. Do you participate in a profit sharing plan, a pension, a 401(k), or an IRA?

If YES, then you should know what you are able to do under the various rules. If NO, and you want to participate, you should know what you can do. In either case, read Chapter 42.

48. Are you concerned you won't have enough saved for retirement?

This is very common, so you probably answered YES. If you want to put more money away for retirement, you should read Chapters 42 through 46, which will show you many ways to put more money away each year and will help you achieve your retirement goal.

49. Are you retired already or about to retire?

50. Would you like to have "guaranteed income" during retirement so you don't have to worry about stock market returns or interest rate fluctuations?

If you answered YES to question 49 or 50, read Chapter 47. This chapter shows you how to use life annuities (which are different from variable annuities) to lock in income during retirement. You should also read Chapter 44 to learn how to achieve a guaranteed retirement income. This is a very important tool for retirees.

51. Is there one breadwinner in your family who is saving for both spouses?

If YES, then you have a serious risk. If the breadwinner dies or becomes disabled, the other spouse will be left with no retirement. To avoid this problem, read Chapters 44, 46, and 49.

52. If you are married, or soon to be married, do you have more than a 10-year age difference or a 10-year life expectancy differential?

If one spouse is much older than the other or one is sick and the other is not, then there is a serious risk that medical bills may decimate the retirement savings of the younger or healthier spouse. To avoid this problem, read Chapter 49 on long-term care and Chapter 46 on life insurance. Overlooking this problem can cause a financial disaster.

53. Are you potentially responsible for the financial well-being of your parents or in-laws?

If YES, read Chapters 49 and 60. By purchasing long-term-care insurance on your in-laws and parents, you can protect your retirement savings (and potentially your inheritance) from being spent on medical expenses.

54. Do you want to retire before age 59½?

If YES, read Chapter 46. There are ways to use life insurance as a retirement tool. This must be considered because it is often the only way to save for retirement on a tax-deferred basis and to take money out for retirement expenses before age 59½ without a 10 percent tax penalty. In fact, withdrawals can be 100 percent tax-free!

55. Do you think you might accumulate at least $500,000 in retirement plan assets at any time in your life?

If YES, you may be subjecting your heirs to an 80 percent tax trap without even knowing it. This is the most overlooked part of any financial plan. Read Chapters 48, 57, and 58 to learn how to avoid the trap.

SECTION F—ESTATE PLANNING

Every year billions, if not trillions, of dollars are paid unnecessarily in the form of estate taxes and probate fees. Don't let oversights, bad planning, or procrastination ruin your life or the lives of your heirs.
Everyone must read Chapters 50, 51, and 52.

56. Do you believe that estate planning is a waste of time because of the estate tax repeal of 2001?

If YES, read Chapter 51. This is integral to your planning success.

57. Are you or do you anticipate being worth more than $100,000 at any time during your life?

If YES, go to Chapter 52 on wills, and review Appendix 3 on intestacy laws.

58. Are you or do you anticipate being worth more than $1,000,000 at any time during your life

If YES, go to Chapter 53 on A-B trusts. Otherwise, you will probably cost your family hundreds of thousands of dollars in taxes and probate fees unnecessarily.

59. Do you own life insurance?

If YES, read Chapter 55. Without an irrevocable life insurance trust (ILIT), up to 50 percent of your insurance will never reach your heirs.

60. Do you pay for your life insurance with after-tax dollars?

Most likely, the answer is YES. If you want to have the government pay for up to 50 percent of your estate plan, read Chapters 47, 57, 58, and 59.

61. Are you or do you anticipate being worth more than $3,000,000 at any time during your life?

If YES, you should read all of Part VIII on estate planning. A few hours of your time could save over a million dollars in unnecessary taxes and fees. You need to read Chapters 57 and 58 if you don't want to lose 80 percent of your retirement plan to taxes at death.

62. Do you own anything jointly with your spouse or with another person?

If YES, this could be a disaster. This is how children and spouses are unintentionally disinherited every day. Read Chapters 26, 52, and 53 and, most important, Chapter 54 if you want to avoid this problem.

63. Do you own rental real estate?

If YES, go to Chapter 56. This could help you to save taxes every year and to avoid unnecessary estate taxes without losing any control of your assets.

64. Do you own a business or a professional practice?

65. Do you intend to leave your business or professional practice to your heirs or to sell it and leave them the proceeds of the sale?

If YES to question 64 or 65, read Chapter 65 on buy-sell agreements, Chapter 68 on PEOs, and all of Part VIII.

66. Do you have more than $500,000 in a retirement plan or an IRA?

67. Do you have a stretch IRA or hope to use a stretch IRA to avoid taxes at death?

68. Did you know that 80 percent of your pension, 401(k), or IRA could be taken by taxes when you die?

If YES to either question 66 or 67 or NO to 68, read Chapters 57 and 58. Otherwise, you may inadvertently leave 80 percent of the plan assets to taxes at death. The stretch IRA is a very big tax trap—we recommend against it in most cases. You need to know your alternatives.

69. Do you own stocks worth over $2,000,000?

If YES, then read Chapters 13, 58, and 61.

70. Would you do your estate planning for half the price if you could?

If YES, then you should consider the welfare benefit plans discussed in Chapters 10 and 63 or the advanced strategy discussed at the end of Chapter 58. If the government will give you a break, you should take it.

71. Are either your parents or your in-laws still alive?

If YES, read all of Part VIII on estate planning, and get them a copy of this book. It may add hundreds of thousands, if not millions, of dollars to your inheritance.

72. Do your parents or in-laws have an adequate amount of long-term-care insurance?

If NO or MAYBE, read Chapter 60.

73. Do your parents or in-laws have a current living trust, and, if so, is it funded?

If anything but YES to both parts of question 73, read Chapters 52 and 53.

74. Do your parents or in-laws have life insurance?

If NO or MAYBE, read Chapter 36 on life insurance, Chapter 55 on ILITs, Chapter 34 on divorce, and Chapter 60 on long-term care.

75. Do you or your relatives own a family business?

If YES, read Part IX, especially Chapters 63 and 65.

76. Do your parents or in-laws have a retirement plan or an IRA?

If YES, read Chapters 57 and 58, and also give copies of those chapters to your parents and/or in-laws. If they don't plan, you may lose 80 percent of your intended inheritance to taxes at their death.

77. Are your parents or in-laws living on the interest of their bonds, certificates of deposit, money markets, stock dividends, or retirement distributions?

    If YES or MAYBE, read Chapters 47, 56, 57, and 58.

78. Are you afraid of leaving an inheritance to your family and having them lose it if they get divorced? Are you concerned about losing your inheritance if you get divorced?

    If YES to either part of question 78, read Chapters 30, 34, and 55.

79. Do you have a charitable inclination? Would you like to leave something to a charitable organization?

80. Would you consider leaving something to a charity if it helped reduce your taxes and helped your family?

    If YES to either question 79 or 80, read Chapter 61.

SECTION G—BUSINESS PLANNING

Starting and running your own business is very difficult. Believe us, we know. We have two businesses ourselves. You need to address certain risks so you don't lose what you have worked so hard to achieve. Luckily, in return for all the craziness involved in running a business, there are benefits that only you can realize. This part helps explain some of those benefits.

We encourage you to read every chapter of Part 9, Business Planning. However, we provided a few questions to help direct those of you who are short on time and can't afford to read all six chapters.

Everyone should read Chapter 62.

81. Do you have partners in your business?

    If YES, you need to have a buy-sell agreement. Read Chapters 63 and 65.

82. Are you a partnership, sole proprietorship, or just a person with a business and no legal entity?

    If you have done nothing in the way of filing for legal status, read Chapter 66 on corporations. Operating as a sole proprietor or a partnership puts you at too much risk for lawsuits and doesn't give you any real tax advantages. Chapter 66 is an important one for you to read.

83. Does your business have more than $250,000 in annual profits?

If YES, read Chapter 63. This may help you "kill two birds with one stone" because you can get benefits for you and your employees while reducing taxes.

84. Does the business have more than $1,000,000 in profits annually?

If YES, read Chapters 63 and 64. These are very advanced strategies that offer very sizable benefits—to those who qualify.

85. Are you concerned about losing your business to lawsuits?

If YES, read Chapter 67 on advanced asset protection strategies.

86. Would you like to avoid employment headaches and reduce your overhead in the process?

If YES, read Chapter 68 on PEOs.

PART III

TAX PLANNING

CHAPTER SEVEN

MAKE SURE YOU DON'T
GIVE AWAY MORE THAN
NECESSARY

Most likely, you didn't have to complete the risk factor analysis (RFA) to accept that you would prefer to legally pay less in taxes. Who doesn't want to reduce his or her tax bill? Nonetheless, you answered at least one question in the RFA that directed you to this section . . . and that is important. You may be looking for ways to save for your retirement on a tax-deductible basis. You may wish to reduce the taxes on the capital gains from your investments. You may want strategies to provide benefits for you and your family on a pretax basis. Regardless of the reason, you are in the right part of the book. Part III will help you understand how the tax-planning portion of your Wealth Protection plan can be designed to improve what you add each year to your Financial Fortress.

The famous Judge Learned Hand once said: "No American is required to pay any more tax than the law would allow . . . there is not even a patriotic duty to do so." You will realize that each tax-reduction strategy is designed to offer some social benefit. When reading this part, you should look for a strategy that offers you and your family a benefit you need. The additional tax savings will be an extra benefit.

We are not recommending that you stop paying taxes. Instead, we're advising that you use these tried-and-true strategies that are based on Internal Revenue Code (IRC) sections and supported by revenue rulings, case law, or private letter rulings.

If you are not sure how much taxes eat into your income and family net worth, you should read the next chapter, Uncle Sam's Pieces of Your Pie. The subsequent chapters will discuss many tools that may help you reduce, defer, or even eliminate some of these taxes while providing you, your family, or your business some other much-needed benefits. In particular, we will also cover such tax-saving tools as retirement plans, individual retirement accounts (IRAs), insurance, annuities, closely held insurance companies, private placement insurance and private annuities, long-term-care planning, and health insurance planning. If tax reduction is a major goal of yours, be sure to read the other chapters of this part as well.

CHAPTER EIGHT

UNCLE SAM'S PIECES OF YOUR PIE

Before exploring all the ways you can legitimately reduce your taxes, you should first understand how much money is on the table. If you thought you could only save a few hundred dollars per year, you might find the cost of this book and the time spent to read the book and create your Wealth Protection plan to be worthwhile. If you thought you could save thousands if not hundreds of thousands of dollars from this book and its recommendations, you might take the exercises more seriously. Of course, if you thought you might save hundreds of thousands if not millions in taxes over your lifetime, you might even send us a thank you note or a holiday fruitcake. If you want to send us half the savings, we wouldn't want to insult you by refusing your generous gift. With that said, let us begin by explaining the problem at hand. Then, we'll move on to addressing it.

We all know that we pay income taxes on our salaries. Do you know exactly how income taxes are computed? Most people believe that they move from income tax bracket to income tax bracket—increasing the percentage they pay on each dollar earned as they move forward. The truth is that every single person pays the same tax rate on his or her first $8,556 of income, while every couple filing jointly pays the same rate on their first $18,456 of income. When someone makes money in a higher bracket, he or she pays the higher amount. Let's look at the 2002 "married filing jointly" bracket in Table 8.1.

TABLE 8.1   TAXES PAID BY A MARRIED COUPLE
               FILING JOINTLY (ACCORDING TO 2002
               TAX LAW)

INCOME ABOVE	BUT LESS THAN	YOU PAY
$0	$6,456	0.0%
$6,456	$18,456	10.0%
$18,456	$51,552	15.0%
$51,552	$109,704	27.0%
$109,704	$176,769	30.0%
$176,769	$311,904	35.0%
$311,904	Over	38.6%

Let's look at an example to see how this works.

CASE STUDY

Rob and Janelle are married and file jointly. Rob makes $50,000, and Janelle runs an in-home business that generates $10,000 per year. For simplicity, assume they have no deductions and live in a state with 0 percent state income tax. They have $60,000 of total adjusted gross income.

- On the first $6,456 of income, they pay 0 percent. $0
- On the next $12,000 of income, they pay 10 percent. $1,200
- On the next $33,096 of income, they pay 15 percent. $4,964
- On the remaining $8,448 of income, they pay 27 percent. $2,281

Total tax $8,445
Marginal tax bracket   27%
Effective tax rate ($8,445/$60,000)   14.1%

Assume that Rob and Janelle spend $3,700 per month on their expenses and save the rest.

Gross income	$60,000
Income tax	$8,445
After-tax income	$51,555
Expenses	$44,400
Retirement savings	$7,155

If Rob put away 10 percent of his salary into a tax-deductible vehicle (like a retirement plan), their finances would look like this:

Gross income	$60,000
Deduction	$6,000
Taxable income	$54,000
Income taxes	$6,825
Net income	$47,175
Expenses	$44,400
Savings	$2,775

Since Rob now has $6,000 in pretax retirement savings, so their total retirement savings is $8,775 instead of the $7,155 he had before!

After you pay your taxes on your salary, you're home free, right? Wrong!

You will either spend the money and pay sales tax, or you will save the money. If you save the money, you have to put it somewhere. Predepression generations often put the money under their mattresses or in a safe or buried it in their yards. Our generation is more comfortable with certificates of deposit (CDs), money market accounts, stocks, bonds, mutual funds, real estate, and other investment vehicles. What happens to this money?

The investments are generally designed for income or for growth. In some cases, an investment may offer both. Income investments give you regular income. Your bank accounts, CDs, and money markets give you an interest payment each year. If you own bonds, you receive a coupon every six months or every year (we will not discuss zero-coupon bonds here). You may own stocks that pay a quarterly dividend. If you own rental real estate, you collect rents. All of these forms of income—interest payments, dividends, coupons, and rent checks—are *added* to your salary. If you are in a 27 percent marginal income tax bracket, like Rob and Janelle, then you will have to pay tax of 27 percent on that investment income. If you are in a 38.6 percent marginal tax bracket, then you will pay 38.6 percent in taxes on that investment income. Of course, if you are not in an income-tax-free state, you could pay up to 10 percent in state income taxes as well.

Growth investments are designed to *grow* in value. These are typically stocks and some mutual funds. The money you invest with a company is used to grow the firm. The company reinvests its proceeds to potentially increase the net worth (value) of the company . . . and of course the value of your shares. You do not receive a regular check from the company. Rather, you have the right to sell your shares of the company. If you realize a profit on your investment, you are responsible for taxes on your "capital gains." There are two types of capital gains, long-term and short-term. A *short-term gain* is defined as "realized (sold) appreciation of an asset that you owned for less than one year." If you have a short-term gain, it is treated exactly the same way (for tax purposes) as the interest, coupons, and dividends previously discussed. In Rob and Janelle's case, their short-term capital gains would be taxed at 27 percent (plus any applicable state income taxes). Of course, if their combined incomes and investment income reach $109,704 (see Appendix 4 for tax tables), then each additional dollar will be taxed at 30 percent.

If you hold an asset for more than one year, the government gives you a benefit. You can pay long-term capital gains tax rates. These rates are 10 percent of the growth for individuals who are in the lowest tax bracket (because you cannot pay a higher rate for capital gains than your marginal tax rate) and 20 percent for all other taxpayers (plus applicable state taxes). This benefit is an incentive for investors to keep their funds in one place and not to be constantly shifting them, which could significantly disrupt business. It also acts as a deterrent to short-term, potentially unethical, trading.

Back to the example: Suppose Rob and Janelle invest their $7,155 of after-tax savings into a 5 percent money market account. This generates a $358 interest payment annually. They must add this $358 to their $60,000. Because they are in a 27 percent marginal tax bracket, the additional federal income tax liability will be $97. Thus, the $358 interest will only really be worth $261 to them (a 3.6 percent return instead of the 5 percent they thought they were getting).

So you pay your income taxes and your sales taxes and your income tax or capital gains tax on investments. That should suffice. Right? Wrong again.

When you pass away, Uncle Sam has an estate tax for those of you who might be worth more than $1,000,000. That $1,000,000 may include the value of your home, retirement plans, real estate, brokerage accounts, and insurance policies. At present, the tax rate is 50 percent. Half of what you leave your children could go to taxes. (For a complete description of this tax, how it works, why the supposed repeal is a fairy tale, and how to avoid the unnecessary costs associated with it, please read Part VIII on estate planning.)

Lastly, there is a combination of taxes that severely threatens those of you who hope to be worth over $1,000,000 and who might die with retirement plan or IRA money. There is something called IRD—income in respect of a decedent. We will discuss this in great detail later. We just wanted you to know that it is very possible and highly likely that a $1,000,000 retirement plan or IRA will be worth only $170,000 to $300,000 to one's heirs—after the IRS takes their (not-so) fair piece.

Now that you know what we are hoping you can save, you should be more motivated to dive right into the strategies and solutions that exist and to move one step closer to reducing the taxes that constantly eat away at your Financial Fortress.

The alternative minimum tax (AMT) is an extra tax some people have to pay on top of their regular income tax. The original idea behind this tax was to prevent people with very high incomes from using special tax benefits to pay little or no tax. But for various reasons, the AMT reaches more people each year, including some people who don't have very high income and some people who don't have lots of special tax benefits. The AMT targets business owners because they can treat themselves as salaried employees subject to individual income tax or as stockholders subject to corporate tax.

The AMT liability generally applies for those with a large number of personal exemptions, a large amount of state and local taxes paid, large amounts of miscellaneous itemized deductions, large deductible medical expenses, ISOs (incentive stock options), and large realized capital gains.

CHAPTER NINE

RETIREMENT PLANS

As you probably know, the IRS allows you to take deductions for contributing to your own retirement plan. The deduction is allowed because the government wants you to fund your own retirement and not rely solely on an underfunded Social Security program. Because a tax-qualified retirement plan is often a cornerstone of a Wealth Protection retirement plan, it is often the most important tax planning you can do.

There are many types of tax-deductible retirement vehicles. However, they all fall into one of two categories: defined-contribution plans or defined-benefit plans. *Defined-contribution plans* are plans that restrict the amount you can contribute to the plans on an annual basis. These are covered in great detail in Chapter 42. Conversely, *defined-benefit plans* restrict how much can be in the plan at any time. These are explained in further detail in Chapters 43 and 44.

In Part VII on retirement planning, you will learn that defined-contribution plans usually allow you to deduct between $10,500 and $40,000 per year (depending on your income level and the type of plan you use). Though defined-benefit plans generally work well for people near or over 50 years of age who also meet other criteria, they can create deductions as high as $60,000 to $200,000, or more.

The retirement plan is an integral part of every Financial Fortress. As you will learn in Part V on asset protection, qualified retirement plans are protected from lawsuits as well. But like all planning tools, they have their pitfalls. First of all, plan assets generally cannot be accessed before you reach age 59½ without a 10 percent tax penalty.

Furthermore, there is the hidden 83 percent tax that can occur if you die with funds left in these plans. This is discussed in Chapter 15 later in this part and explained in full detail in Chapter 57; and solutions are offered in Chapter 58.

CHAPTER TEN

GETTING DEDUCTIONS FOR BUYING INSURANCE— WELFARE BENEFIT PLANS (419s)

Do you have your own business, share one with partners, or work for a small company? If so, you might be able to take advantage of a welfare benefit plan (WBP), a tool that can significantly reduce your taxable income and provide a tremendous benefit for your family's Financial Fortress.

BACKGROUND INFORMATION

The WBP, also called a 419 plan, is governed by section 419A of the Internal Revenue Code (IRC) and was enacted by Congress in 1984. Virtually any type of business can participate in a WBP, but the simplest way to benefit is to join a multiple-employer plan authorized by IRC section 419A(f)(6). This plan allows tax-deductible contributions by an employer for the benefit of certain employees.

Because of its flexible rules and favorable tax treatment, the WBP is an ideal planning tool for taxpayers who own their own business or work for a small business.

PLAN BENEFITS

Contributions to WBPs are *tax deductible.* That is the key for reduction of income taxes—any amount contributed to the plan is deductible for the business. This is similar to a retirement plan, such as a pension or a profit-sharing plan.

Unlike a pension, though, WBP contributions are used to purchase certain benefits, typically life or disability insurance, for the participant(s). In some cases, employee-owners have contributed up to $500,000 annually to a WBP—saving them about $250,000 in income taxes. By purchasing insurance with pretax dollars, the client can lower his cost of insurance by 50 percent.

By utilizing other tools in conjunction with the WBP (including a life insurance trust—see Chapter 55), it is possible to eliminate the 50 percent estate tax burden on those insurance proceeds as well. In this way, the income tax deduction and the estate tax avoidance combine to make life insurance *75 percent less expensive* for clients utilizing WBPs.

For more on WBPs, including a case study of how the WBP works, see Chapter 63.

Important Note: At the time this book went to press there were a number of fundamental changes to the potential tax treatment of WBPs. Be sure to consult a licensed tax professional when examining a WBP as a planning option.

CHAPTER ELEVEN

HOW TO BORROW YOUR CHILDREN'S LOWER TAX RATES WITH FLPs/ LLCs

TWO CENTERPIECES OF WEALTH PROTECTION PLANNING

Of all the legal tools we use as part of a Wealth Protection plan, by far the two we use most are family limited partnerships (FLPs) and family limited liability companies (LLCs). Of course, having family members play a role in these tools is typical—that's why we use the word *family* in front of the LP or LLC. However, using family members in this way is *not* required. Whether you use family members or not, these tools can provide you with extraordinary asset protection. Nonetheless, we will use the abbreviations FLPs and LLCs throughout this chapter and others that deal with these two tools in Parts V and VIII on asset protection and estate planning, respectively.

You can think of these plans as closely related, like brothers or sisters, because they share many of their best characteristics. In fact, unless we make the point otherwise, we will use these tools interchangeably—if a case study refers to a FLP, you can assume that an LLC could have been used and vice versa.

Key characteristics of FLPs and LLCs for income tax planning

There are two key characteristics of the FLP and LLC in terms of income tax planning. (For more detail on the FLP and LLC, see Chapter 29 in Part V.)

1. *They have two levels of ownership.* Both the FLP and the LLC allow for two levels of ownership: (1) active owners and (2) passive owners. Active owners have 100 percent control of the entity and its assets. In the FLP, active owners are called "general partners," and in the LLC they are called "managing members." Passive owners have little control of the entity and have only limited rights. These owners are called "limited partners" in the FLP and "members" in the LLC. This bilevel structure allows a host of planning possibilities because clients can then use FLPs and LLCs to share ownership with family members without having to give away any practical control.

2. *They both have "pass through" tax treatment.* In terms of income taxes, both the FLP and the LLC can elect for "pass through" taxation—meaning neither entity will pay any taxes; the income will "pass through" to the owners. Thus, if the assets of an LLC make $100 in income this year, and you own 80 percent of the LLC interests, you will be liable for $80 of income. Whoever owns the other 20 percent will be taxed on $20 of income.

How FLPs and LLCs can help you reduce income taxes

FLPs and LLCs can save you tens of thousands of dollars, or more, each year in income taxes. This is accomplished by what is called "income sharing." This means spreading the income created by FLP or LLC assets to the limited partners or members who are in lower tax brackets. Typically, these are children or grandchildren. In this way, the client gifts ownership of the LLC or the FLP to children and grandchildren over time. As long as the child is over 14 (IRS rules), then their share of the income will be taxed at their tax brackets. Let's see how this works.

CASE STUDY: DOUG AND SHEILA'S LLC REDUCES INCOME TAXES

Doug and Sheila had annual taxable income of $100,000 from their rental real estate, which was worth $1 million. In a 40 percent combined state and federal tax bracket, their total tax on this income came to $40,000. To reduce their taxes, they set up an LLC.

The LLC was funded with the real estate. Doug and Sheila set themselves as managing members, so they had 100 percent control. They gifted their four children 3 percent member interests (12 percent total). Because each child's interest would be valued at about $20,000 (3% × $1,000,000, minus the minority valuation discount [see Chapter 56]), no gift tax applied to the transfers to the children. Doug and Sheila made these 12 percent transfers to their children annually for five years.

Under the LLC agreement, the children were taxed on their share of the LLC's income, which, after five years, grew to 60 percent. In year five, 60 percent of the LLC's taxable income was taxed at the children's lower tax rate. When the LLC assets then earned $100,000 in income, 60 percent of that income was taxed at the children's rate—15 percent. Thus, their tax bill with the LLC was $25,000: 40 percent of $40,000 (the parents' share), or $16,000, plus 15 percent of $60,000 (the children's share), or $9,000. Doug's family's tax savings?

Total tax with the LLC, year 5:	$25,000
Total tax without the LLC, year 5:	$40,000
Year 5 family income tax savings with the LLC:	$15,000

Keep in mind that there were taxes saved in years 1 through 4 and this $15,000 will continue every year (or increase if they continue to gift interest to the children). Also, under the LLC agreement, the managing members did not have to distribute any LLC income to the members. This was totally within the discretion of Doug and Sheila, as managing members. Thus, Doug and Sheila could pay all LLC taxes with the income and reinvest the remaining proceeds.

Note: At the time of publication, there are current tax court cases that may result in changes in the way gifts of LLC and FLP interests will be treated for tax purposes. Be sure to check with a licensed tax advisor to guide you in this planning area.

LAST WORD

FLPs and LLCs are some of the most powerful Wealth Protection tools available. Read Chapters 29 and 56 for more on FLPs and LLCs and how they can shield assets from lawsuits and save estate taxes, all while allowing you to maintain control of the underlying assets.

CHAPTER TWELVE

DEDUCTING LONG-TERM-CARE INSURANCE

You're reading this chapter, and the other chapters in Part IV, Tax Planning, because you want to reduce your income taxes. In this chapter, you'll learn about how to reduce those taxes while providing an important Wealth Protection tool for your family—long-term-care insurance (LTCI).

Conventional financial planning wisdom offers three reasons for buying LTCI: (1) to make sure you have enough money to pay for potentially outrageous medical costs later in life, (2) to protect your inheritance from high medical costs so you can leave what you had planned to your children and grandchildren, and (3) to make sure those high medical costs don't destroy your retirement funds.

LTCI is a type of health insurance that pays for a variety of health costs that may or may not be covered by Social Security, Medicare, Medicaid, or your state plan. The details of LTCI and our recommendations on what to look for in an LTCI contract are covered in Part VI, Chapter 38. The purpose of this brief chapter is to explain why LTCI is an important part of any retirement plan and how purchasing LTCI in the proper way can save you taxes.

THE IRS GIVES YOU A BREAK

As a reult of HIPAA (Health Insurance Portability and Accountability Act of 1996), long-term-care insurance premiums are treated like health insurance premiums for the self-employed. That means that an owner of an S-corporation, a professional corporation (PC), or an LLC can now take a tax deduction of 70 percent for 2002 and 100 percent for tax years 2003 and beyond (this might be new information for those of you who thought health insurance premiums were always 100 percent deductible). There is no good reason for any business owner or professional to pay for LTCI on an after-tax basis under these laws. Moreover, premiums for LTCI that are paid by a *C-corporation* are *100 percent tax deductible.* Thus, if you have the use of a corporation or LLC and are paying for LTCI with after-tax dollars, you are paying twice as much as you have to for your LTCI.

WOULD YOU PURCHASE LONG-TERM-CARE INSURANCE IF IT WERE *FREE*?

If you have a return-of-premium rider, LTCI can literally be free. An example is the best way to illustrate the point.

CASE STUDY: "FREE" LTCI FOR GINA

Gina, a 45-year-old attorney, has an estate of $1,000,000 and an income of $150,000 a year. She is worried about having to pay more than $100,000 over her lifetime for LTCI coverage for her and her nurse husband, Michael. Gina also doesn't like buying insurance and doesn't want to pay LTCI premiums for the next 30 years while she waits to become sick. Gina's solution is to purchase a tax-deductible, limited-pay LTCI policy with a return-of-premium rider.

- Gina pays a premium of $8,985 per year for 10 years.
- Because she works for a C-corporation, she can deduct 100 percent of her LTCI premiums.
- She is in a 40 percent combined-income tax bracket, so her tax refund is $3,594 per year.
- Her after-tax cost of the LTCI is $5,391.

(continued)

Gina becomes disabled at age 75 and needs home health care at $200 a day until death at age 85. Total LTCI benefit for 10 years = 365 × $200 × 10, or $730,000.

Because of the return-of-premium rider, when Gina dies at age 85, her heirs receive the entire premium paid—$89,850.

Bottom line. The LTCI cost for Gina was $53,910 out of pocket over the 10-year pay period. Her heirs received $89,850 in cash (income-tax free) from the LTCI carrier because of the return-of-premium rider and her estate did not have to pay for the $730,000 in long-term-care costs incurred from age 75 to 85. Total cost $89,850; total benefit—$730,000 + $89,850, or $819,850.

By purchasing LTCI through the corporation with pretax dollars, Gina was able to protect her estate from long-term-care (LTC) costs and was also able to return the entire premium to her heirs income-tax free at her death. If you are serious about asset protection and would rather leave assets to children than to the IRS, you should closely look at this option as a way to shield family assets from the devastating costs of LTC.

CHAPTER THIRTEEN

USING CHARITABLE GIVING TO REDUCE INCOME TAXES

CHARITABLE INTENT

As a society, Americans cherish the right to give to the charitable institutions of their choice. The will to give is what we refer to as "charitable intent." We want to give. The problem, many times, is that we do not know how to give or that we assume that our family will suffer as a result of our giving. Our goal here, and in Chapter 61 in Part VIII on estate planning, is to show you some of the many ways you can make charitable gifts while benefiting your family as well. This is possible because of the tremendous tax benefits the IRS grants for charitable gifts. Before we examine a few options for using charitable giving to reduce income taxes, let's take a look at the basic tax rules regarding charitable giving.

TAX BACKGROUND

DIRECT GIFTS

The federal tax code provides for current income tax deductions for gifts to any charity that has qualified under 501(c)(3) as a charitable organization. Furthermore, the IRS distinguishes between "public charities" (universities, hospitals, churches, etc.) and "private charities" (private family foundations are most common). *What's the difference?* If the gift is to a public charity, you can deduct the amount of the gift against your adjusted gross income (AGI) to a maximum of 50 percent of your AGI. If the gift exceeds this amount, you can apply the excess to future year's income for five years.

If the gift is to a private charity, then you can only deduct to a maximum of 30 percent of AGI, but this also can be applied forward five years. Here is an example.

PHILANTHROPIST PHIL: GIVE TO THE FOUNDATION OR TO THE MUSEUM?

Phil is a retired executive who set up a small private family foundation a few years ago to give something back to the community, while involving his children in the foundation and taking some significant tax benefits. Now Phil has $90,000 worth of highly appreciated stock he doesn't need, which he would like to gift to charity. His annual AGI is only $30,000 per year from the consulting work he does. Phil is considering whether to give the stock to his family foundation or to the local art museum, where he sits on the board.

If he gifts the stock to the foundation, he will only be able to deduct $9,000 per year from his tax return (30 percent of AGI); but if he gifts to the museum, he will be able to deduct $15,000 (50 percent of AGI). Because he can carry the deduction forward only five years, he'll only be able to apply $54,000 ($9,000 this year and for five more years) worth of deductions using the foundation; but he'll be able to use all $90,000 ($15,000 this year and for five more years) of deductions if he gifts to the museum.

INDIRECT GIFTS

The real beauty of charitable giving from the family perspective is that the IRS also allows tremendous tax benefits for "indirect gifts," those left to charity through a trust or an annuity. In fact, the IRS allows deductions for indirect gifts through irrevocable charitable remainder or lead trusts and even charitable gift annuities. By using an indirect gift, charitable planning can truly be a win-win-win situation: You win, your family wins, and your favorite charities win.

COMMON CHARITABLE GIVING SCENARIOS

The following are the most common scenarios where it makes sense for a family to consider charitable planning.

SALE OF A HIGHLY APPRECIATED ASSET

Many people, especially those over age 50, hold highly appreciated assets—real estate or stocks that have grown enormously in value over time. Even more problematic is a situation in which there are just a few assets making up the bulk of the client's net worth. This is often the case where the client owns a closely held family business or a family farm. Regardless of the asset, the client may want to sell the asset but doesn't want to take the capital gains hit, which reduces the value by up to 25 or 30 percent because of taxes. Through the use of charitable planning strategies, that client may be able to unlock some of the appreciation and to eliminate the capital gains tax while benefiting his or her favorite charity as well.

NEED TO GENERATE FAMILY INCOME FROM INVESTMENT ASSETS

The past 25 years have seen unprecedented growth of personal wealth in the form of portfolio appreciation. However, when clients seek to reshuffle their asset allocation to produce more income and to diversify their portfolios, they are often hit with a substantial tax on their gains. Charitable planning affords the client a chance to be creative in his or her approach to converting paper gains to cash flow and to turning nondeductible items into tax-deductible charitable gifts.

ESTATE PLANNING

The most powerful benefits of charitable planning can be enjoyed when using it as part of a Wealth Protection estate plan. As you'll learn in Part VIII, when you die, your family could pay as much as 50 percent in federal estate taxes, plus income tax on IRD assets, such as pensions and IRAs. In Chapter 61, we'll address charitable planning specifically in the estate planning context.

The most common charitable tool: The charitable remainder trust

Suppose you have one highly appreciated asset that you would like to sell, but you are reluctant to do so because of the significant capital gains taxes you would owe. At the same time, you are looking for ways to reduce your current year's taxable income. Finally, you would like to diversify your overall investment portfolio. Usually, that would mean selling that highly appreciated asset, paying the high taxes, and reinvesting with a substantially reduced amount. In this situation, the charitable remainder trust (CRT) may be an ideal option for you.

Effects of a CRT

Used properly, a CRT can potentially:

- Reduce current income taxes with a sizable income tax deduction.
- Eliminate immediate capital gains taxes on the sale of appreciated assets, such as stocks, bonds, real estate, shares of a business, and just about any other asset.
- Increase your disposable income throughout the remainder of your life.
- Create a significant charitable gift.
- Reduce estate taxes that your heirs might have to pay after your death.
- Avoid probate and maximize the assets your family will receive after your death.

Think of a CRT as a tax-exempt trust that provides benefits to two different parties. The two different parties are (1) the individuals receiving income and (2) the chosen charity or charities. The first set of individuals, known as "income beneficiaries" (usually, you or your family members), typically receive income from the trust either for their lifetimes or for a specified number of years (20 years or less). At the end of the trust term, the chosen charity will receive the remaining principal to utilize for their charitable purposes.

How a CRT Works

A CRT is an irrevocable trust that makes annual or more frequent payments to you (or to you and a family member), typically until you die. What remains in the trust then passes to a qualified charity of your choice.

A number of advantages may flow from the CRT. First, you will obtain a current income tax deduction for the value of the charity's interest in the trust. The deduction is permitted when the trust is created, even though the charity may have to wait until your death to receive anything. Second, the CRT is a vehicle that can enhance your investment return. Because the CRT pays no income taxes, the CRT can generally sell an appreciated asset without recognizing any gain. This enables the trustee to reinvest the full amount of the proceeds from a sale and thus generate larger payments to you for your life.

The trust will be eligible for the estate tax deduction if it passes to one or more qualified charities at your death. If you wish to replace the value of the contributed property for heirs who might otherwise have received it, you could use some of your cash savings from the charitable income tax deduction to purchase a life insurance policy on your life to be held in an irrevocable life insurance trust for the benefit of your heirs. This is called a "wealth replacement trust."

Often, through the leveraging effect of life insurance, it is possible to pass on assets of greater value than those contributed to the trust. In this way, your heirs are not deprived of property they had expected to inherit. Let's see how this works.

- You gift a highly appreciated asset to the CRT—there will be no capital gains tax when the asset is sold. You can then reduce your current income taxes with an income tax deduction.
- Utilization of a CRT enables you to receive more income over your lifetime than if you had sold the highly appreciated asset yourself.
- After the death of all income beneficiaries, the remaining assets from the CRT go to your selected charity.
- A "wealth replacement trust" can be funded with life insurance to replace those assets given to charity and to give the family even more than they would have received had no charitable planning been done.

FIGURE 13.1 CHARITABLE REMAINDER TRUST WITH WEALTH REPLACEMENT TRUST

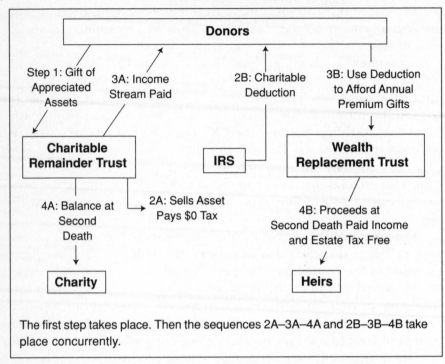

The first step takes place. Then the sequences 2A–3A–4A and 2B–3B–4B take place concurrently.

THE CRT'S "COUSIN": THE CHARITABLE LEAD TRUST (CLT)

When it comes to charitable trusts, CRTs seem to get all the attention. But the cousin of the CRT, the charitable lead trust (CLT), also can provide significant charitable and tax benefits, particularly in an environment of lower interest rates.

With a CLT, sometimes called a "charitable income trust," you transfer cash or income-producing assets to the trust. The trust then pays out income earned by the assets to a designated charity or charities. The payout can be an annual fixed-dollar amount set at the time of the transfer—called "an annuity trust"—or an amount based on a percentage of the assets in the trust at the time of each annual payout—called a "unitrust."

At the end of a specified number of years, the remaining assets in the trust are distributed to the noncharitable beneficiary, usually someone other than you or your spouse. It could be your children, your grandchildren, or other family members. This timing is, in effect, the opposite of the CRT, in which the donor receives current income from the trust assets and the assets go to the charity at the end of the designated time.

A gift tax or an estate tax may be due at the time the assets are transferred to the trust because noncharitable beneficiaries (your family) will ultimately receive the assets. However, this can often be planned so that no gift tax will be due. This is because (1) the gift is discounted, as the beneficiaries won't receive the gift for some time; and (2) you receive a gift tax deduction because a charity is receiving the income from the assets (the deduction is based on the amount transferred into the trust and the amount of time the assets are to remain in the trust). Furthermore, the gift won't be taxed at all if its discounted value is less than the $1,000,000 gift tax exemption.

Projected Estate Tax Exemption by Year

Year	Exemption
2002–2003	$1,000,000
2004–2005	$1,500,000
2006–2008	$2,000,000
2009	$3,500,000
2010	No estate tax.
2011–	???

Note: Gift tax exemption remains at $1,000,000 for all years.

LAST WORD

If you have any charitable intent whatsoever and want to reduce current income taxes, capital gains taxes, or even estate taxes, then you should seriously consider charitable planning techniques.

CHAPTER FOURTEEN

THE TAX-ADVANTAGED TOOL FOR COLLEGE SAVINGS—529 PLANS

U ndoubtedly, you or your parents paid a lot less for your college education than you will pay for your kids' education. The average cost of a four-year education at a private college for a student graduating in 2000 was $85,356. With a 6 percent inflation estimate, the estimated cost of a four-year private education for the graduating class of 2020 will be over $273,000. Of course, if your child goes to an Ivy League school, the total cost of the undergraduate degree could be over $500,000. If you consider that you may pay almost 50 percent in income taxes *and* between 20 percent and 50 percent on your capital gains and dividends, it may seem almost impossible to save for a child's or a grandchild's education while also putting away funds for your own retirement.

If you have children or grandchildren who might go to college, graduate school, medical school, or law school, recent tax laws make the 529 College Savings Plan the ideal vehicle if you wish to make providing for educational expenses much easier on your pocketbook. Though these plans are actually over five years old, the recent changes in the tax code have made them far more attractive. What are the benefits of the 529 Plan?

- Contributions over $22,000 per year are allowed—gift-tax free.
- You receive the tax benefits.
- You direct the type of investments.
- You may change the beneficiaries.

- You, the donor, control the withdrawals.
- The money grows tax free.

See Table 14.1 for a comparison of the 529 savings plans to other savings plans and for the advantages of 529 plans.

CONTRIBUTIONS OVER $22,000 PER YEAR ARE ALLOWED— GIFT-TAX FREE

You may already know that an individual can make annual tax-free "gifts" of $11,000 to any person and that a couple can make such gifts of up to $22,000. With the 529 College Savings Plan, an individual can make five years' worth of gifts in one year without paying a gift tax. The 529 Plan allows you to allocate those gifts over the next five years. Thus, a couple can gift $110,000 tax-free in one year to a 529 Plan for each child or grandchild.

Total proceeds in a 529 Plan are capped at approximately $220,000 to $280,000, depending on which plan you utilize. This means that a set of parents could gift $110,000 to a 529 Plan *and* a set of grandparents could gift an additional $110,000 to the same child's 529 Plan, and no gift taxes would be paid. Larger amounts could be gifted, but gift taxes would apply.

When you compare the 529 Plan to the old Education IRA, which had an annual contribution limit of $2,000, there was no comparison. Now, there is a new plan, the Coverdell Education Savings Account that was new at the time of this writing. It appears to improve upon the old Education IRA. Please check with your advisor to confirm our information.

YOU, THE DONOR, CONTROL THE WITHDRAWALS

Unlike Uniform Gift to Minors Act (UGMA) trust funds where the child has access to the funds in the plan when he or she reaches the "age of majority," the 529 funds can only be withdrawn by you, the owner. This is a very important point as most clients agree that an 18-

TABLE 14.1 COMPARISON OF 529 SAVINGS PLANS TO OTHER EDUCATIONAL FUNDING ALTERNATIVES

	529 SAVINGS PLAN	COVERDELL EDUCATION IRA	UGMA/UTMA	529 PREPAID PLAN
Income limitations	None.	AGI limits apply.	None.	None.
Maximum yearly contribution per beneficiary (all numbers double, except IRA, when gifts come from two parents or grandparents)	$55,000 in the first year of five-year period, without exceeding the annual federal gift-tax exclusion.	$2,000	$11,000 without exceeding the annual federal gift-tax exclusion.	$55,000 in the first year of a five-year period, without exceeding the annual federal gift-tax exclusion.
Account earnings	*Tax free,* if used for qualified expenses.	*Tax free,* if used for qualified expenses.	Taxable.	*Tax free,* if used for qualified expenses.
Ability to change beneficiaries	Yes.	Yes.	No.	Yes.
Control of withdrawals	Owner of account.	Transfers to child when child reaches legal age.	Transfers to child when child reaches legal age.	Owner of account.

	529 SAVINGS PLAN	COVERDELL EDUCATION IRA	UGMA/ UTMA	529 PRE-PAID PLAN
Investment options	Ready-made portfolios of mutual funds.	Wide range of securities.	Wide range of securities.	Tuition units guaranteed to match tuition inflation.
State-tax-deductible contributions	Varies by state.	No.	No.	Varies by state.
Qualified use of proceeds	Any accredited post-secondary school in the United States.	Any accredited school in the United States.	Unlimited.	Varies by state.
Penalties for nonqualified withdrawals	10% penalty withheld on earnings.	10% penalty withheld on earnings.	No.	10% penalty withheld on earnings.
Taxation of qualified withdrawals	Tax free.	Tax free.	A portion may be exempt; income may be taxed at child's rate.	Tax free.
Ownership of assets for financial aid purposes (may vary by institution)	Account owner.	Account owner.	Student.	Student.

or 21-year-old with a $100,000 account in his or her control may be more dangerous than a 16-year-old with a car. Some clients even liken it to a loaded gun. Why test their maturity at that age if you don't have to?

YOU RECEIVE THE TAX BENEFITS

You may be able to reduce estate taxes by using a 529 Plan. The plan's high contribution limit provides a convenient way to effectively lower the taxable value of your estate. As you'll learn in Part VIII on estate planning, federal estate taxes start at 37 percent and quickly rise to 50 percent. Given this, the ability to reduce your taxable estate while providing educational funding for family members should be very attractive.

> *Special note:* Tax-deductible contributions can be enjoyed in some states. That's right! Some states actually allow an income tax deduction for contributions. That's a tax deduction to go along with the tax deferral that accompanies the plan. If you're not sure if your state offers a deduction, feel free to visit www.savingforcollege.com.

YOU DIRECT THE TYPE OF INVESTMENTS

Some 529 Plans allow you to invest in a variety of stock, bond, and money market funds. You may have a choice of a growth portfolio or a balanced portfolio. There's even a company that offers an "Age-Based Portfolio" that focuses on growth in the early years of the child and automatically rebalances every few years to focus more on capital preservation as college approaches. There is no extra fee for this added service.

YOU MAY CHANGE THE BENEFICIARIES

Unlike a Uniform Gift to Minors Act (UGMA) account, in a 529 Plan you may change the beneficiaries. If one child doesn't go to college

or receives a scholarship, you may change the plan to benefit someone else. You can also make these changes as often as you like, as long
as the beneficiaries are related. In fact, you can even name yourself
the beneficiary if you plan to go back to school.

If you change your mind about the beneficiary and want to withdraw the funds and use them yourself, you may do so. But you will
have to pay a 10 percent penalty.

THE MONEY GROWS TAX FREE

Like an education IRA, the funds grow on a tax-free basis—while
invested in mutual funds. Because annual capital gains and dividends
are not taxed in the 529 Plan, the account balance has the potential
to grow faster than it would if invested in comparable taxable investments. If you consider that dividends and short-term capital gains are
taxed at rates that may be as high as 50 percent in some states, the
529 Plan could grow twice as quickly as an UGMA.

THOSE OF YOU WITH UGMA ACCOUNTS

If you already have an UGMA, there's no need to fret. Congress has
allowed for UGMA funds to be placed into 529 Plans, and those funds
will be treated with the same tax benefits as all other 529 Plans.

SHORTFALL OF THE 529 PLAN

If you make your scheduled contributions, don't mind the risk of the
stock market, and don't die, the 529 Plan is as good a plan as there
is. However, there is no guarantee that you will live to see all of your
children go to college or graduate school, nor can you invest in a 529
Plan without subjecting your funds to market risk. For these reasons,
you may want to consider some type of life insurance as part of your
college savings plan. There are two plans to consider. If you are going to invest in a 529 Plan, you should also invest in a decreasing term
life insurance policy. If you need $1,000,000 because your two young
children will someday attend Ivy League schools, then you should buy
a $1,000,000 decreasing term policy that reduces by your annual
contribution amounts. See Table 14.2.

**TABLE 14.2   529 PLANS AND TERM
                  INSURANCE**

YEAR	CHILD'S AGES	AMOUNT IN 529 PLANS	AMOUNT OF TERM INSURANCE
1	2 and 4	$40,000	$1,000,000
2	3 and 5	$84,000	$950,000
3	4 and 6	$132,400	$900,000
5	6 and 8	$244,200	$800,000
10	11 and 13	$637,500	$500,000
15	16 and 19	$1,279,000	$0

If you are very concerned about the stock market's volatility and don't want it to have a significant impact on your children's educational funds, you should consider a whole life policy with a AAA-rated or AA-rated insurance company. This is a very stable investment and will grow at a steady rate. Even in 2001, one of the worst years in recent stock market history, one AAA insurance company paid over 8.2 percent on its whole life policies. In addition to the tax-free cash accumulation inside such a policy, there is also a minimum death benefit to protect against an early death. When your children eventually attend college, you can then use tax-free loans to withdraw money from the policy and keep the death benefit intact.

LAST WORD

If you have children, grandchildren, nieces, or nephews whom you would like to assist in their educational funding, or if you or your spouse might go back to school, you should seriously consider a 529 College Savings Plan for its tax benefits and flexibility. In many cases, a 529 Plan along with a life insurance component is an ideal strategy.

CHAPTER FIFTEEN

INCOME IN RESPECT OF A DECEDENT

No tax discussion is complete without mentioning income in respect of a decedent (IRD). This is income that would have been taxable to the decedent (a deceased person) had the decedent lived long enough to receive it. These items include unpaid salaries, bonuses, and commissions (that the decedent would have been taxed on had he or she lived) as well as retirement plan (pensions, 401(k)s, etc.) and IRA balances and variable annuity appreciation. Statistically, retirement plan and IRA balances are by far the most significant IRD assets.

Figure 15.1 shows how the funds in a retirement plan may be distributed at the time of death.

FIGURE 15.1   IRD DISTRIBUTION

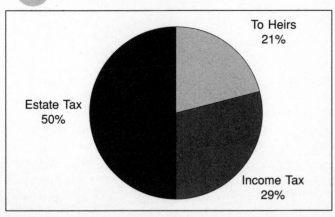

To Heirs
21%

Estate Tax
50%

Income Tax
29%

You can see that the combination of estate and income taxes may cause 79 percent of the retirement plan to be lost to taxes. Estate taxes are first levied because the plan balance was owned by the taxpayer when he died. Income taxes are then imposed on the amount left, which is then paid to beneficiaries. However, as you will see in Chapter 57, because of a harsh quirk in the tax law, your family will pay tax on money they never received.

Because you don't know when you will die, you will probably die with some IRD—unless you implement a plan to avoid this problem well in advance of your death. Read Chapter 57 to better understand IRD and Chapter 58 to learn how to avoid this terrible problem.

CHAPTER SIXTEEN

Is Your Tax Advisor Helping You or Hurting You?

Don't make a $5 million mistake.

As professionals who work with clients throughout the country, we create Wealth Protection plans that are often reviewed by the client's *local* advisors, who may help implement the client's plan. Coordinating our planning recommendations with those of a local accountant, attorney, or financial planner often makes sense, so we are happy to work as part of a team.

Unfortunately, however, this often proves impossible when the local advisor rejects our recommendations. Sometimes, local advisors simply will not go along with any strategy other than their own. As we have seen this hundreds of times over our careers, we know this problem is most prevalent in the tax area. Repeatedly, we watch local advisors reject recommendations or strategies when they truly don't understand what they are rejecting. Whether the advisor didn't want to take the time to research the new strategy for the client or won't accept the fact that someone else had a better idea for the client is irrelevant. The end result is that the client suffers.

Though your present tax advisor may be very good at what he or she does, keep in mind that he or she cannot be an expert in all areas of tax planning. For this reason, you may wish to get a second opinion from an expert so you get the most effective Wealth Protection plan.

Would you like to overpay $5 million in taxes? Here's an unforgettable true story.

David's law firm was recently retained to perform a tax audit by a long-term client. The client, an extremely successful businessman, was concerned when one of his business colleagues was found liable for back taxes and penalties because of some mistakes by his accounting firm. Nervous that he might become an IRS target soon, this client hired David's firm to do an audit of his personal and business income taxes for the past five years. What they found was shocking.

Although this client had used five different accounting firms for his various returns (including a large regional firm), his tax bill was off by millions of dollars! Lucky for him, it was an overpayment. Although David can't divulge the exact numbers, this client will now be able to legitimately avoid $20 million worth of reportable gains, providing a $5 million tax savings.

Because of the self-imposed audit that David's firm oversaw, the client will file for a seven-figure refund from the IRS and the state tax agency. It is fortunate that the client was concerned about poor tax advice . . . and spent the money to hire David's firm to perform the audit (thinking he would owe more taxes, not less taxes).

This anecdote demonstrates the two ways millions of taxpayers get into trouble with tax planning—by relying on tax professionals (1) who incompetently cause unjustified underpayments of tax or (2) who are so conservative or closed-minded that they actually "cost" the client through gross overpayments of tax.

As a potential Wealth Protection client, you may pay income taxes at rates from 40 percent to 50 percent, when federal, state, and even municipal taxes are considered. At these rates, the following questions become very important: Does your tax advisor—CPA, attorney, or other professional—lack proper knowledge or experience? Is he or she too conservative? As advisors who deal with clients across the country (as well as with *their* existing advisors), we see the problems of incompetence and overconservativeness every day.

Ask yourself how likely you would be to pay an outside tax attorney or accounting firm thousands of dollars to perform a self-audit for you. If the answer is "Not very likely," how can you really know whether you're getting accurate tax advice?

INCOMPETENCE: ADVISORS NOT ADMITTING WHEN AN AREA IS BEYOND THEIR EXPERTISE

This is the most obvious but crucial issue. Do the advisors actually know what they are doing? Of course, you want to avoid the incompetent advisor, but the signs of incompetence are not so apparent.

A more common situation occurs when the client's advisor is skilled in one area of practice but not knowledgeable about other tax areas. This is understandable. Tax planning is like medicine; each area has become so complex that it is difficult to become an expert in all areas. In the medical arena, most physicians refer cases to other specialists. A gastroenterologist would no sooner make diagnoses of skin conditions than a dermatologist would of stomach problems. Yet this is what happens all the time in the tax arena.

OVERCONSERVATIVENESS: IF EVERYONE ISN'T DOING IT, THEN IT ISN'T WISE PLANNING

Although they may be competent in their field, many tax advisors are so conservative that they will not consider a strategy unless it has been around for decades or unless it is so common that every Tom, Dick, and Sally employ it. Although we are certainly not advocating an approach on the other end of the spectrum (following every tax strategy that comes along), it is important to realize that either extreme position ends up hurting the client at the end of the day.

This pitfall, we believe, was the one that caused the aforementioned client to mistakenly report $20 million in gains. His previous advisors simply did not utilize planning techniques that could have legitimately reduced his overall tax bill by over $5 million. How can you tell whether a tax strategy has any merit and whether an advisor should be considering it for you?

In our tax law, there is a concept called *substantial authority*. This means that, when the IRS examines all of the authority on a certain tax issue (statutes, cases, memoranda, etc.), a taxpayer who has more than 50 percent of that authority supporting his position is said to have "substantial authority" on his side. This is the litmus test for a tax strategy and one that your tax advisor should examine when evaluating a particular technique, not whether everyone else in the neighborhood is doing it or not.

Solving the problem: Take an active role and get a second opinion

There is no easy answer to the dilemma of how to choose a tax advisor—one who is not overly aggressive but also competent and who is not too conservative or closed-minded. However, it makes sense to take an active role in your tax planning, bringing new solutions to your advisor and asking them, or better yet, paying them, to review these solutions for you. Only then can you force your advisor to take the time to research these solutions and give you an informed opinion.

Furthermore, you should not hesitate to seek a second opinion by speaking to other professionals who have subspecialties within the tax arena, especially those who are experts on several topics. For example, we use an attorney who is one of the country's experts on several tax structures, including the welfare benefit plan (see Chapters 10, 59, 63). When we think a client may be a good candidate for such a plan, we call in that expert and defer to his analysis. You should do the same for your planning.

Last word

Because you will ultimately pay for the planning, or lack of it, by your advisors, it behooves you to make sure that your tax planning fits your needs and goals. Don't hesitate to bring in new advisors and to get a second opinion on your current planning.

PART IV

INVESTING

CHAPTER SEVENTEEN

YOUR MONEY DOESN'T COME WITH INSTRUCTIONS

I n the mid-1990s, many Americans decided that it was time to "jump into the pool" and try to invest on their own. They began investing their money in the stock market, through mutual funds and then directly into stocks and bonds. For a few years, many of these new investors were probably quite pleased. After all, it was pretty easy to make money in the stock market from 1993 to 1999—almost every stock seemed on a perpetual increase.

However, the year 2000 brought a rude awakening. The Dow Jones Industrial Average went from 12,000 to below 10,000 by 2001 (and close to 9,000 by July of 2002), and the Nasdaq fell from a high of over 5,000 to below 2,000 over the same period. Trillions of dollars of wealth were lost as many of these "new" investors were left holding the bag. As a result, investors now realize that the stock market is hardly a "free lunch."

It may seem incongruous to discuss investing in a book on Wealth Protection planning. Part III, Tax Planning, showed you how to reduce taxes on your income. Part V, Asset Protection, will show you how to protect your investments from lawsuits. Part VIII, Estate Planning, will show you how to pass your wealth onto your heirs with as little tax and as few complications as possible. This part, Part IV, Investing, is going to help you avoid the most prevalent investment mistakes by teaching you some basic investment fundamentals and by explaining some common and some not-so-common investment alternatives.

Specifically, this part will teach you the basic risk versus return theory of all investments, why taxes and inflation are important factors in your investment plan, why you need more than a Nobel Prize-winning strategy to invest wisely, and how and when to get back into the market. Finally, we'll introduce to you the ideas of using insurance, annuities, and other less common investment tools.

Like every other part of this book, you should consult other chapters to which you are referred to get a complete and fully integrated Wealth Protection plan tailored specifically to your situation.

CHAPTER EIGHTEEN

UNDERSTANDING INVESTING

Many investment advisors may boast that their strategy is based on a Nobel prize–winning theory. Unfortunately, this means that nearly everyone's strategy is based on that same theory, and the theory itself has a number of limitations.

The purpose of this chapter is threefold. First, we will give you a very basic understanding of the aforementioned Nobel prize–winning investment theory. Second, we will point out the limitations of the theory. Third, we will suggest how to make the theory work for your particular Wealth Protection plan.

In 1990, the Nobel prize in Economics was awarded to Harry Markowitz, Merton Miller, and William Sharpe for their Modern Portfolio Theory (MPT) and Capital Asset Pricing Model (CAPM). We would like to offer simplistic summaries of the CAPM and MPT (with apologies to Markowitz, Miller, and Sharpe). There are three concepts you must be able to grasp, before putting them together to form the CAPM and MPT:

1. Types of risk.
2. Risk versus reward.
3. Diversification of investments.

TYPES OF RISK

The CAPM divides the risk of any investment into *specific risk* and *market* (or systematic) *risk*. Specific risk is unique to an individual investment, whereas market risk affects all investments in the market. Let's look at examples of each:

- Do you remember the Tylenol scare in the fall of 1982? Someone had tainted a number of bottles of Tylenol with cyanide. This obviously affected the stock price of Johnson & Johnson (J&J), the maker of Tylenol. The risk of something like that happening is specific risk, as it didn't have an effect on all investments in the market, just on J&J.
- Do you recall the stock market crash of 1929? That incident affected all investments in the market. The risk of a crash is certainly the most extreme example of market risk. The fall in 1987 wasn't nearly as severe, but was another example of market risk.

When you make an investment, that investment is subject to both market and specific risk. In a portfolio of investments, you are subject to market risk, which affects the whole portfolio, and a combination of specific risks that affect each asset distinctly.

RISK VERSUS REWARD

In a general sense, rewards are higher for those who take more risk. Individuals who start their own businesses and are ultimately successful will probably make considerably more money than those individuals who took the less risky route and went to work for someone else. Entrepreneurs risked their time and money. If successful, they will be rewarded handsomely for the risk they took. Of course, they have more risk and may very possibly end up with less.

Doctors and lawyers passed up the opportunity to make money right out of college. Instead, they spent more money going to medical school or law school and delayed their income-producing careers by another three to seven years. For this risk of time and money, these professionals are generally rewarded with generous salaries.

DIVERSIFICATION

Diversification is a business school term for "not putting all of your eggs in one basket." When applied to investments, it means investing in a combination of stocks, bonds, real estate, cash, and other investment classes. It also applies to investments made within each asset class—not investing in just a few stocks, not just a few bonds, not just one or two pieces of real estate, and so on.

We have explained that an investment portfolio is subject to (1) market risk and (2) all of the specific risks for all of the assets in the portfolio. One interesting finding of the CAPM and MPT is that in a well-diversified portfolio, all specific risks cancel each other out. In other words, specific risk can be diversified away. Investors can reduce the overall risk in their portfolios by spreading their risk across and within different asset classes. Though this may make perfect intuitive sense, the mathematical proof for this statement and the subsequent model for creating the "most efficient" set of portfolios was worthy of a Nobel prize.

How do the CAPM and MPT work for you?

The CAPM and MPT provide a mathematical model for minimizing market risk in any investment portfolio. Once an investor determines the level of risk with which he or she is comfortable (risk tolerance), he or she can follow the mathematical model to construct a portfolio that will optimize the risk-reward balance. In other words, by following this theory, the investor can maximize expected returns for any level of risk. All such "maximized" portfolios exist on what the finance people call the "efficient frontier."

All of this, however, is just theoretical. While we're not saying that the findings of three Nobel laureates are incorrect, we are going to point out their acknowledged limitations in the theory and offer additional insights that might help you.

As acknowledged by the laureates, the CAPM and MPT are designed to work in a simplified world where:

- There are no taxes or transaction costs.
- All investors have identical investment horizons.
- All investors have identical perceptions regarding the expected returns, volatilities, and correlations of available risky investments.

PROBLEM 1—TAXATION AND TRANSACTION COSTS EXIST.

We consider taxation to be a significant concern of yours. If all of your stock investments were in a nontaxable account, like an individual retirement account (IRA), you wouldn't have to worry about taxes. You would maximize the returns on your portfolio for a given amount of risk—and taxes would not come into the picture until you withdrew the funds. Chapter 57 describes the tax dilemma you will then encounter.

Clients frequently have one portion of a stock portfolio in a retirement account (or other tax-favored entity like those discussed in Chapters 42 and 43) and the other portion in a taxable environment. If this applies to you, you will need to determine which investments will be made in the tax-favored accounts and which investments will be made in taxable accounts. If you are in prime earning years and are in the 35 percent to 38.6 percent federal income tax brackets, the following two rules of thumb help you:

1. Hold all interest-bearing and dividend-producing assets within a tax-favored account. Otherwise, as much as 50 percent of the earnings will go to paying income taxes each year. You are better off deferring the tax and earning money on the government's dime.

2. Hold all long-term-growth assets in your taxable accounts. If you don't intend to sell these assets for at least one year, you will only pay 20 percent capital gains taxes when you sell. If you hold these assets in a pension account, you would be taxed at 38.6 percent federal (plus state) when you make withdrawals.

These are just basic strategies to supplement the CAPM and MPT relative to taxes. There is much more to be learned about taxes in Part III.

PROBLEM 2—ALL INVESTORS DO *NOT* HAVE IDENTICAL INVESTMENT HORIZONS.

Varying investment horizons are obviously a problem with the CAPM and MPT. Some investors need their money in 30 days, and some don't need it for 30 years. The investor who needs his money in less than a month would be well served by a certificate of deposit (CD) or a money market account. The investor who doesn't need the money for 30 years should have nearly 100 percent of his or her investments in equities (stocks).

If you have assets that you don't expect to need for five years, you can afford to take significant risks with those assets and should seriously consider investing in the stock market. If you anticipate needing the money in less than a year, cash equivalents are your best option. For the assets that need to be accessed in one to five years, some combination of investments may work well.

PROBLEM 3—ALL INVESTORS HAVE VERY DIFFERENT PERCEPTIONS REGARDING THE EXPECTED RETURNS, VOLATILITIES, AND CORRELATIONS OF AVAILABLE RISKY INVESTMENTS.

In plain English, the environment where the CAPM and MPT work best is one where everyone has the same knowledge of all assets and the same access to purchasing assets. For stocks and bonds, where there is more research available than you could possibly read, perceptions of the risk of any given stock are across the board. People can't even agree on the value or the risk of certain stocks. How else can you explain a stock dropping 2% to 10% in a day?

As far as availability, there is a very wide gap. If you are investing only $100,000, you may be restricted to mutual funds that have very high transaction costs and taxes (see Problem 1). If you have more than $500,000, you have access to unique products, and your transaction costs are considerably lower relative to the smaller investor. If you have $5 million or more, you can access products that others can only dream of buying. These may include small businesses, private equity, and initial public offerings (IPOs), to name a few.

For those of you who have experimented with or who are experts in real estate investing, you know the knowledge gap to be the key competitive advantage. Many professional real estate investors have admitted that over 50 percent of their profits are a direct result of a buyer not understanding the real estate market. The CAPM and MPT call for a percentage of your portfolio to be invested in real estate assets. However, for real estate experts, who know this market better than most, we would deviate from the strategy and recommend that they stick with what they know best and profit from their advantage in this arena.

For the investor with little knowledge of real estate, we advise against investing in real estate (other than your home). The time necessary to manage the property or the costs to pay someone else to do it will decimate the earnings the property generates unless you are lucky and we don't want to rely on luck. You probably don't either. That's why you bought this book and not 25 lottery tickets. Furthermore, there is no reason to jump into a market where you have a distinct disadvantage. This is adding risk to your portfolio, not reducing risk as you had hoped by utilizing the CAPM and MPT.

LAST WORD

The CAPM and MPT have contributed greatly to the field of portfolio selection. In fact, these theories are the basis for a significant percentage of institutional investors and mutual fund managers. However, there are problems with the practical application of these theories. You should consult a financial planner who has experience as an investment advisor for help with applying these theories to your individual situation. As you will learn in later chapters, you may wish to invest in a vehicle that offers you other benefits (like asset protection, tax deferral, or protection against a premature death) in addition to capital appreciation.

CHAPTER NINETEEN

TAXES, INFLATION, AND YOUR INVESTMENTS

"XYZ fund returned 18.6 percent last year." "My money manager has beaten the Standard and Poor's (S&P) Index consistently for five years." "In this magazine, we'll profile the 'best returning' mutual funds." As financial professionals, we read and hear these types of statements constantly. Everyone looks at the investment returns as the "currency" of investing, as a way of comparing money managers, mutual funds, CDs, bonds, and so on. However, what most people fail to consider is the impact of taxes and inflation on those investments. When you consider that investment and financial professionals report their preinflation and pretax returns, it's easy to see why some people achieve no added purchasing power from their investments. They simply don't understand what they are really getting.

In Chapter 18, we discussed how taxes were not considered in Markowitz, Miller, and Sharpe's Nobel prize–winning Capital Asset Pricing Model (CAPM) of investments. This is a serious limitation for any of us concerned about paying taxes. Add to this the fact that nearly every money manager and mutual fund publishes returns without regard to taxes, and it's no wonder than many investors are confused. Fortunately, a new development in the mutual fund arena is that mutual funds may have to report after-tax gains, not pretax gains. This would dramatically change the numbers in fund marketing materials as the average federal income tax liability on a mutual fund was 32 percent in 2000.

How much tax do mutual funds cost you?

Without boring you with the math, this high tax rate of 32 percent means that mutual funds sell most of the stocks they have purchased within one year. Therefore, you get much more short-term capital gains tax treatment (likely 27 percent to 38.6 percent for most of us) on your appreciation than long-term capital gains tax treatment (20 percent). For example, if your mutual fund appreciated by 11 percent in the preceding year, it probably cost you close to 4 percent in taxes. Which number is more important to you, the 11 percent it boasts in its advertising or the 7 percent that you actually take home after taxes?

Taxes also impact CDs, money markets, and bonds. All of the income from these vehicles is taxed as ordinary income. This will likely be taxed at federal rates between 27 percent and 38.6 percent, and at state rates of up to 10 percent. For this reason, 5 percent to 6 percent in dividend or interest income may only be worth 2.5 percent to 4.0 percent after taxes. Although this is depressing, it isn't the end of your problems.

What is inflation?

You would always rather have a dollar today than a dollar tomorrow, right? There is a concept in finance and economics that deals with this simple idea. It is called "present value of money." When determining the present value of future dollars, many people want to know what a dollar in the future will buy them—what tomorrow's dollar is worth in today's dollars. What they are really talking about is inflation.

Obviously, things become more expensive as we get older. We all heard our parents talk about a Coke (or soda pop) costing a nickel or a movie costing a quarter. The fact that seeing a movie today costs close to $10 is because of inflation (though many might call it highway robbery, given the quality, or lack thereof, of the films today). The average annual inflation rate over the past 70 years has been approximately 3.1 percent. This means that approximately every 22 years, things cost twice as much.

HOW DO YOU CALCULATE THE IMPACT OF INFLATION?

The after-tax return that an investment achieves is called the *nominal return*. This does not take inflation into account. When you divide the nominal return of an investment over time by the inflation over that same period of time, you get the *real* rate of return, or inflation-adjusted rate of return.

Think back to the mutual fund mentioned earlier—where an 11 percent pretax return meant a take-home return of 7 percent after taxes. That 7 percent return is actually more like a 3.8 percent *real* return (1.07 / 1.031 = 1.038), after inflation is factored into the results.

HOW DO YOU INVEST TO PLAN FOR INFLATION?

If they want to reduce taxes, most savvy investors invest in the stock market through tax-managed investment accounts (Chapter 23), variable annuities (Chapter 21), or variable universal life insurance (Chapter 22); or through mutual funds or managed accounts if the funds are inside tax-deferred retirement plans.

However, if you want the most accurate hedge against inflation, then real estate would be the ideal investment because real estate almost always moves directly with inflation. Now, most people own a home, and the home represents a significant portion of their net worth. This is usually enough to fill up the real estate portion of their diversified portfolio. However, if you have significant wealth or like real estate, you may want to purchase more real estate than simply a home. If you do, you should read Chapters 11 and 29 in Part III, Tax Planning, and Part V, Asset Protection, respectively, to make sure you don't unnecessarily spend too much in taxes or expose yourself to lawsuit risk.

LAST WORD

When it comes to investing, there is no sure-fire method of avoiding
inflation or taxes. However, there are a number of strategies that can
help you avoid unnecessary taxes and serve as a hedge against inflation. The more you know about these strategies, the easier it will be
for you to understand what you are really getting from your investments and what alternative investments may offer. Once you understand the true value of each type of investment to your overall portfolio, you will better appreciate the service that a qualified investment
advisor or financial planner can provide you.

CHAPTER TWENTY

WHEN (AND HOW) TO GET BACK INTO THE MARKET

I n the opening of this part, we discussed how many of the investors who poured their family savings into the stock market in the 1990s have pulled their money out (or at least not invested more funds) in the new decade. If you are one of these investors, you may be asking the question: "When should I get back into the market?" The truth is that we really cannot say for certain. Rather, your investing strategy should be determined by your answer to this question: "When do I need the money?"

WHEN DO I NEED THE MONEY?

If you are saving your money to buy a house, to cover the tab for a child's education, or to pay for a vacation in the next few years, then you have a short time horizon. With this time frame, you can't afford to lose money because you don't have time to wait for the market to turn. In these situations, you'll have to stick to CDs and money markets. If you are investing for events more than five years away, like retirement, you have a long time horizon. Obviously, the longer your time horizon, the more risk you can take because you can afford to weather the storm and to ride out the tough times of the stock market.

WHAT ARE MY OPTIONS?

To lessen some risk in your longer-term investments, consider these strategies:

- Get a second opinion if you wish to ride out the storm.
- Lock in your retirement income.
- Use dollar cost averaging (with securities or with variable annuities).

GET A SECOND OPINION

If you are just going to wait out the down market, consider getting an objective second opinion of your current holdings. We have seen many investors who believe they are in diversified portfolios because they have 25 stocks or 10 mutual funds. Unfortunately, all of their funds are heavily weighted toward the same sectors or stocks so they are not diversified well enough in terms of sector risk. Review the top-10 holdings of all of your funds. If there is overlap, you may not be diversified enough and may be subjecting yourself to too much risk with your investments.

LOCK IN YOUR RETIREMENT INCOME

If you are systematically selling a portion of your stock portfolio to pay your bills or are living on the dividend income of your stocks, on the coupon payments of your bonds, or on the interest from your CDs or money markets, you may be exposing yourself to too much risk. If the stocks don't perform or don't give you a large enough dividend, you will find yourself cutting into your principal. If interest rates drop, the bonds and CDs (as well as money markets) that you intend to purchase in the future may not pay enough. If interest rates go up, the value of your bonds will go down. One popular alternative to this dilemma is the Single Premium Immediate Annuity (SPIA). The SPIA, unlike life insurance or variable annuities, can pay you (and/ or your spouse) a fixed income for the rest of your life.[*] It does not change when the market does. SPIAs generally are used when the client wants a portion of his or her retirement income to be "fixed." This is usually the amount needed to cover costs of living or insur-

---

[*]Both the income guarantees and the death benefit are dependent on the claims-paying ability of the issuing company.

ance premiums. If you would like to "lock-in" income for you and your spouse or for your parents or in-laws, then you should consider a SPIA.

DOLLAR COST AVERAGING

Dollar cost averaging (DCA) is not new. It is a strategy that has been used for years. The idea is to systematically spend the exact same amount per month to buy the same investment (stock, bond, mutual fund). By spending the same amount each month, and not by purchasing the same number of shares, you effectively reduce the average price paid for the investment. For example, if you spend $1,000 per month to buy shares of XYZ Company and it is trading at $50 one month, you will buy 20 shares that month. If the stock goes up to $60 another month, you will only buy 16.7 shares at that higher price. If the price falls to $40 per share in a third month, you will buy 25 shares at that price (see Table 20.1). This is a good way to ease back into the market because you will reduce your average price of the stock and mitigate your risk of "getting in" at too high of a price. Almost all mutual fund companies offer a DCA program, and most insurance companies offer DCA on their variable annuities. (See below.)

Of course, dollar cost averaging does not guarantee a profit and does not protect against loss in declining markets, and it involves continuous investing in securities regardless of fluctuating prices. An investor should consider his or her ability to continue investing even in periods of low price levels.

DCA WITH VARIABLE ANNUITIES

A variable annuity is an insurance contract that offers a variety of investment options, including cash equivalents, stocks, and bonds. The insurance contract protects the value of your initial investment at death. If you contribute $500,000 to a variable annuity and your investment drops 20 percent (to $400,000) at the time of your death, your family still gets $500,000, less any withdrawals you may have made. This is important for families who want to make sure their heirs have assets if the breadwinner passes away. Also the variable annuity can offer a DCA program. If you put $500,000 into a variable annuity with a DCA strategy now, the company will put your money into the investment you have selected systematically over a 6- or a 12-month period. While the money is waiting to be invested, these com-

TABLE 20.1   BUYING STOCKS

Shares per Month Method

MONTH	SHARE PRICE	SHARES PURCHASED	TOTAL SPENT
1	$50.00	20	$1,000
2	$60.00	20	$1,200
3	$40.00	20	$800
Average Share Price $50.00		60	$3,000

Dollar Cost Averaging Method

MONTH	SHARE PRICE	SHARES PURCHASED	TOTAL SPENT
1	$50.00	20	$1,000
2	$60.00	16.7	$1,000
3	$40.00	25	$1,000
Average Share Price $48.65		61.7	$3,000

panies will pay a fixed rate of return that changes periodically. If you want to ease back into the market, you may want to consider a DCA variable annuity strategy.

Variable annuities usually have mortality and expense charges, administrative fees, and sales charges. Investments in a variable annuity will fluctuate, so your shares may be worth more or less than the original cost when redeemed.

LAST WORD

If you have funds that are "on the sideline" earning a very low 2–3% and you don't need the funds for five years, then you should consider a DCA strategy to ease your money back into the market.

CHAPTER TWENTY-ONE

◆

VARIABLE ANNUITIES

Variable annuities have their place in a Financial Fortress or Wealth Protection plan. Typically, it is not because of their nominal investment returns but because of their other benefits, particularly their flexibility. The more flexible the components of your total Wealth Protection plan, the more flexible your overall plan— *the whole is greater than the sum of its parts!*

WHAT IS A VARIABLE ANNUITY?

A variable annuity is a personal retirement vehicle that brings together the features of investments and insurance. Money is invested in various investment options of your choosing, with potential growth treated on a tax-deferred basis. At retirement, the money in a variable annuity can be converted into income that is guaranteed to last for life. (The payment of income for life depends on the claims-paying ability of the issuer of the annuity. For this reason, you should research the insurance company issuing the annuity.)

Variable means that the return on your investment depends on the composition and the performance of the investment portfolios you choose. These investment options, including stock- and bond-based alternatives, give your assets the potential to grow more quickly than traditional fixed annuities; but they also provide for greater downside risk.

How do you like those 1099s and k-1s?

You undoubtedly receive one of these forms from one of your investment providers each year. With mutual funds, money management accounts, and investment limited partnerships, a significant portion of your earnings may be subject to taxes even if you do not take any distributions. In fact, you may even see realized capital gains during a year where your mutual fund investment *depreciates*. This is always a bitter pill to swallow.

With a variable annuity, on the other hand, all investment earnings grow tax-deferred until you access the money. This means you can feel free to move your money from one investment option to another without incurring a current tax liability.

You may already be in a high combined marginal tax bracket (31 percent to 50 percent). If so, the last thing you need is to pay additional taxes in April without seeing any cash flow. The variable annuity can help mitigate this tax risk.

Are you stuck investing in one company's funds?

The variable annuities that we use and recommend for our clients offer 35 to 45 investment choices. These choices include a few in-house funds, but they also offer 10 or more outside mutual fund families. Part of what your investment advisor should do is to help you create a portfolio that meets your level of risk tolerance and your investment goals, without being tied to one company's products.

How does a variable annuity protect my investment?

As stated earlier, the variable annuity is a combination of investments and insurance. Generally, the insurance company issuing the annuity "insures" your heirs against lost capital at the time of your death. For example, if you put $500,000 into an annuity and the account is worth only $400,000 when you die, your heirs will receive the full $500,000 less any withdrawals taken. There are even ways to increase the insured amount each year, as will be explained later.

What additional options or features are typically available with variable annuities?

- *Automatic dollar cost averaging (DCA).* DCA is a popular investment strategy. It buys the same dollar amount of an investment each month. This means more units will be purchased when the price is lower and fewer units will be purchased when the price is higher. Covered in Chapter 20.

- *Interest sweep option.* For individuals with money invested in a fixed account option within a variable annuity contract, they can have any earnings automatically transferred to one or more variable investment options on a regular basis.

- *Choice of payment method.* In retirement, you can receive scheduled income payments for life, or you can choose to take out money as you need it. It's entirely up to you.

- *Access to your money before retirement.* You may withdraw up to 10 percent of your premiums or all of your accumulation in a given year without a surrender charge. Of course, you will still have to pay income tax on your withdrawals and a 10 percent federal income tax penalty if you take distributions prior to age 59½.

- *Automatic portfolio rebalancing.* If you diversify your investments in a number of portfolios, their performance may vary, which can take your strategy off track. This option automatically rebalances your investment for you.

- *Annual ratchet protection.* If you purchase this death benefit option and your investment increases in a given year, the greater amount is then protected from that year forward. This reflects only positive performance, and the insured amount never decreases. This is available for an extra charge.

WHICH FUNDS ARE BEST SUITED FOR A VARIABLE ANNUITY?

Before we tell you what funds to use, let us tell you what funds *not* to use. First, we wouldn't invest in any variable annuity within a retirement plan because you are already getting tax deferral. With an annuity, you are paying for tax deferral and the death benefit. Unless your main concern is the death benefit, we wouldn't recommend paying for the tax deferral twice. Second, we would not invest money that you foresee needing before retirement or before age $59^1/2$, because there are penalties for early withdrawal.

The best funds to use to purchase variable annuities are those funds, not in retirement plans, that you would like to use for retirement. If you don't foresee needing these funds before age $59^1/2$, then you should consider using a variable annuity. Additionally, we would consider rolling IRA funds into variable annuities in states where annuities are asset protected and IRAs are not. (Because this list changes periodically, please visit our web site at www.mywealth protection.com for more information.) In this way, you will maintain your tax deferral and also get asset protection. Like every tool and strategy we present, the variable annuity has its rightful place in financial planning—the key is using each tool when it makes sense.

Please keep in mind that every financial planning tool has its dangers. If you have over $1 million of variable annuities and are worth more than $2 million, you may be subject to the 80 percent tax at your death. This problem is explained in Chapter 57. If you have a large variable annuity portfolio and you want to avoid that tax trap, you should contact a professional who is experienced in dealing with issues of IRD.

HOW MUCH DO VARIABLE ANNUITIES COST?

Before you look at how much they cost, you must know exactly what you are paying for. First, if your investments decline below your initial investment at the time of your death, your heirs are protected by the death benefit. Second, because of this insurance element, you get tax deferral on all short- and long-term capital gains, dividends, and interest payments. If you are in a 38.6 percent tax bracket now and anticipate being in a 27 percent or 30 percent federal tax bracket in retirement, you may realize great tax savings from the variable annuity. Third, you may get excellent asset protection benefits from the variable annuity. If you consider that an asset protection plan may cost upward of $10,000, this may be a significant benefit that you can get for $0 in legal fees (though there are mortality and administration fees with the variable annuity).

With these benefits in mind, you can gauge what they may be worth to you. The costs of a variable annuity include the cost of the insurance element (and additional administrative charges) and the cost of the investment management. According to one firm in the industry, as of mid-1998, the average investment management fee was about 0.82 percent and the average administrative charges were 0.14 percent. The insurance charge (or mortality and expense charge) averages around 1.1 percent. Additionally, there is a contract fee of $25 to $40, which may be waived if your account size meets the threshold. Lastly, annuities have something called a surrender charge. This is like a back-load for a mutual fund and can be as high as 7 percent to 10 percent in the first year (and decreasing over time).

Generally, if your premiums remain in the annuity for more than 7 years (some companies have 10-year surrender periods), the surrender charge is eliminated. However, some variable annuities have rolling surrender charges that apply a new schedule of surrender charges to each additional payment. Finally, some firms may have transfer fees, which may be applied if the client is making numerous investment changes.

LAST WORD

In general, variable annuities make sense if you are looking at one as a long-term investment and if you don't plan on making excessive fund transfers. If it is worth paying a little bit more for the tax deferral, insurance, and potential asset protection, then you should consider utilizing variable annuities as part of your investment portfolio and retirement planing.

CHAPTER TWENTY-TWO

◆

LIFE INSURANCE AS AN INVESTMENT

You may have read or heard that "life insurance is a terrible investment" or that "mutual funds are better investments than life insurance." However, because we espouse "flexible planning" or "integrated planning," we believe life insurance often has a major role in a fully integrated Wealth Protection plan.

Chapters 36 and 46 in Parts VI and VII on insurance and retirement planning, respectively, will explain in great detail all the benefits of life insurance. Also, you may want to reread this chapter after you have read the recommended chapters on asset protection and retirement, insurance, and estate planning to which the RFA directs you. Then, you will truly realize why you need flexible investment tools.

In a nutshell, life insurance is a very powerful investment because:

- It grows tax free.
- It is available to you later without taxes.
- Rather than reducing in value by 50 percent when you die because of estate taxes (like every other asset you have), it appreciates when you die.
- It is the only asset that protects your family against your untimely death.
- It is asset-protected in many states.

If these benefits appeal to you, consider life insurance as part of your portfolio.

CHAPTER TWENTY-THREE

HAVE YOU OUTGROWN MUTUAL FUNDS?

I f you are reading this chapter, you probably have more than $100,000 in mutual funds. These holdings may be inside or outside of your tax-deferred retirement plans. In Chapters 21 and 22, we discussed alternatives to taxable mutual fund accounts that are ideal for your nonretirement plan accounts. Some of these alternatives offer asset protection, tax deferral, and death protection. In this chapter, we will discuss an alternative to mutual funds both inside and outside of retirement plans. Before we compare mutual funds and individually managed accounts, we'll first define each type of investment.

Mutual funds (MFs) and individually managed accounts (IMAs) represent two of the most popular investment programs designed to create wealth. On the surface, at least, one could argue that they are not all that dissimilar. Both offer investors a professionally managed portfolio of securities—generally stocks, bonds, or a combination of the two—designed to provide ample diversification. However, they use two distinct approaches. Each offers particular advantages, depending on one's needs. Which is the more prudent choice, a MF or a IMA? This is a question properly answered only by the individual investor. The information in this chapter will help you make an informed decision, one with which you are comfortable, and one that, we hope, will prove over time to be the right choice.

WHAT ARE MUTUAL FUNDS?

A *mutual fund* is a company that invests in stocks, bonds, and other securities on behalf of individual investors with similar financial goals. A no-load mutual fund is one whose shares are sold directly to investors without an initial sales charge, or "load."

Many financial advisors now provide access to no-load MFs as part of a comprehensive range of services. However, you will pay a charge for the advisor's assistance, a charge that tends to offset the lack of an initial sales charge, effectively minimizing any cost differences between load and no-load MFs. For the purposes of this discussion, therefore, *no-load mutual funds* will refer to funds whose shares are purchased directly from the MF company without the help of an advisor.

Both load and no-load MFs are essentially "cooperatives" of investors who pool their money for a common purpose. Investors contribute to the pool by buying shares in the fund. Each share represents an equal percentage of ownership in the fund's assets.

The MF draws from the pool not only to make investments but also to pay for the services of a fund manager (who decides when and if to buy and sell securities for the fund—based on its stated objective), for marketing and distribution costs, for custodian fees, and for transaction costs. Mutual funds are not limited; they generally hold several hundred different securities. No matter how many shares of the MF you, the investor, hold, you cannot control the buying and selling of these securities inside the MF. You can only buy or sell the basket of securities the MF has by buying or selling your shares of the MF.

WHAT ARE INDIVIDUALLY
MANAGED ACCOUNTS?

An IMA is an account that is individually managed by a professional investment manager who decides when to buy and sell securities based on your stated investment strategy or goal.

Unlike MF investors, IMA investors do not pool their money. Instead, they own the securities in their account directly. Investment managers may have many similar holdings with a number of their clients, but each portfolio is separate. You, the investor, can direct the manager to buy only certain types of stocks or to avoid certain stocks (perhaps no tobacco stocks for moral reasons or no airline stocks because you work in the airline industry). This obviously gives you greater flexibility and control than you would have with a mutual fund.

ARE MANAGED ACCOUNTS
WORTH THE MONEY?

One of the most common problems we see with clients is that they are obsessed with the fee associated with any type of planning. If you took this approach to everything you bought, you'd eat only 99 cent Big Macs for every meal. There is truth to the saying "You get what you pay for." Don't immediately dismiss the advantages of one investment strategy over another simply because of price. The recent popularity of no-load MFs is proof that many investors, particularly those who like a no-frills, hands-on approach to investing, are doing just that.

You paid for this book in the hopes you would benefit from reading it. You are considering asset protection, insurance, estate planning, and retirement strategies that undoubtedly will cost you something. Why? Because those strategies will offer you something valuable in return. A prudent investor should consider these important factors when comparing investment options:

- The quality of service provided in return for the fee.
- How the accounts treat capital gains and losses relative to your situation.
- The effect that other investors may have on an investment manager's decisions.
- The methods used to report information.
- The way in which fees are handled.
- Whether your fees are tax deductible or they just reduce your gross return.

IS YOUR TAX SITUATION COVERED?

With IMAs, you pay taxes only on the capital gains you actually realize. Because you own the securities in your account directly, you can
work with your tax advisor to implement planning strategies that MF
investors may not be able to duplicate. There are actually IMA firms
that call you to ask you how you want to end the year tax-wise in your
portfolio (more gains, more losses, balance to $0 tax).

With MFs, investors pay taxes on their pro rata share of capital
gains experienced by the MF, whether or not they benefited from the
securities' sale. A hypothetical example illustrates this point:

> Assume that a mutual fund purchases stock at the beginning of
> the year for $25 per share. Over the next few months, the stock's
> price rises to $50 per share. Coincidentally, an investor buys shares
> in the MF just as the stock's price reaches this peak.

> Later in the year, the stock's price falls to $40 per share, and the
> MF sells its position at a gain of $15 (the difference between the
> purchase price of $25 and the sale price of $40). At the end of
> the year, even though the investor did not benefit from the gain—
> in fact, the stock actually declined in value after the investor
> purchased shares in the MF—the investor is allocated a pro rata
> share of the MF's gain on the stock.

Over time, IMA investors and MF investors who hold their investments for the same period and whose portfolio managers follow identical strategies will report little, if any, difference in capital gains taxes,
at least on those particular investments. For the MF investor, however,
the point at which the gains are realized may be moved forward—
and that can affect the investor's tax planning strategy. To see the
differences between IMAs and MFs, refer to Table 23.1.

SO, WHAT DO THEY REALLY COST?

Investors who open IMAs usually do so with a minimum investment
of at least $100,000. At that time, the money in the account—less the

initial quarter's fees, which typically equal 0.75 percent or less of the opening balance—is invested by the portfolio manager.

Subsequent transaction costs are paid either by paying commissions on individual trades or by paying an asset-based fee on a quarterly basis. In addition to covering transactions, these fees encompass reporting, custody, and the services of a financial advisor. For a stock-based portfolio, on average, total fees range annually from 1.3 percent to 3 percent of the assets under management. There are no additional charges.

MFs have lower minimum investment requirements, often $1,000 or less. With a no-load mutual fund bought directly from the company, the entire investment is placed in the fund at the time of initial purchase. With a front-end load fund, the investor's money is placed in the fund only after deducting a sales charge. In the case of a 3.5 percent load fund, the fund would invest $965 of the investor's initial $1,000.

Beyond the initial sales charge or lack thereof, the difference in fee structure between load and no-load MFs virtually disappears. Management fees, transaction costs, custody fees, and distribution and marketing costs (known as 12b-1 fees) are deducted automatically from the fund's assets. These fees are usually not seen directly by investors but instead are specified in the fund's prospectus and statements of additional information.

MF expenses for stock-based portfolios typically range from 1.5 percent to 2 percent per year for no-load funds and from 2 percent to 3 percent per year for load funds.

According to a third-party research publication that follows open-end mutual funds, the average diversified domestic equities fund incurs about 1.63 percent in annual costs, including a 1.32 percent expense ratio and 0.31 percent in transaction costs. Tack on an additional 0.94 percent annual sales charge on average for load funds or an estimated 1 percent annual charge for no-load funds purchased through a financial advisor, and that annual cost figure rises to approximately 2.6 percent.

Investors should note that transaction costs tend to vary depending on the type of securities in the fund. Trading foreign securities, for instance, can cost almost twice as much as trading domestic securities.

TABLE 23.1 COMPARING INDIVIDUALLY MANAGED ACCOUNTS AND MUTUAL FUNDS

	INDIVIDUALLY MANAGED ACCOUNT	FRONT-END LOAD MUTUAL FUND	NO-LOAD MUTUAL FUND
Investment portfolio	Tailored to meet investor's particular needs.	Two-way communication, including in-person discussions with financial advisor. Can also call toll-free number.	One-way communication, call toll-free phone number and talk to sales representative.
Establishing investor's goals	Investor benefits from financial advisor's help.	Investor benefits from financial advisor's help.	Investors determine on their own.
Investment manager selection	Chosen by investor with financial advisor's help.	Chosen by mutual fund.	Chosen by mutual fund.
Investment manager evaluation	Screened and evaluated by investor and financial advisor.	Screened and evaluated by investor and financial advisor.	Investors must screen and evaluate on their own.
Performance monitoring	Financial advisor monitors on investor's behalf.	Financial advisor monitors on investor's behalf.	Investors must monitor on their own.

	INDIVIDUALLY MANAGED ACCOUNT	FRONT-END LOAD MUTUAL FUND	NO-LOAD MUTUAL FUND
Tax planning	Investors have some control over the timing of capital gains.	Investors have little control over the timing of capital gains.	Investors have little control over the timing of capital gains.
Redemption requests	Investors are not affected by the actions of others who use the same manager.	Manager may be forced to sell securities at undesirable prices to raise cash to meet redemption requests.	Manager may be forced to sell securities at undesirable prices to raise cash to meet redemption requests.
Reporting	Detailed monthly or quarterly statements; monthly letters; quarterly newsletters; periodic investment literature from manager.	General quarterly statements; semiannual investment reports; possibly periodic newsletters.	General quarterly statements; semiannual investment reports; possibly periodic newsletters.
Up-front costs	$0	Up to 6 percent of investment or an additional 1 percent per year added to the annual cost.	$0
Annual costs	On average for a stock-based portfolio, between 1.3 percent and 3 percent of total investment.	On average for a stock-based portfolio, between 2 percent and 3 percent of total investment.	On average for a stock-based portfolio, between 1.5 percent and 2 percent of total investment.

THE FINAL DECISION

Only the individual investor can decide which investment program is the most appropriate for him or her.

Those who work with a financial advisor will find only modest cost differences between no-load MFs, load MFs and IMAs, with IMAs providing the highest degree of service in relation to cost.

Although you can save money by purchasing no-load MFs directly from the company, such savings may not be enough to offset the loss of the value-added services—investment planning, monitoring, communication, and so on—that a financial advisor can provide.

Beyond cost differences, both load and no-load MFs require a lower initial investment than IMAs do. However, MFs limit investors' tax planning choices and offer individual investors no control over securities in the fund. Additionally, fund performance can be affected by the redemption requests of other investors.

IMAs require a higher initial investment but, in return, provide more service, customization, and flexibility. Furthermore, IMA investors are not affected by the actions of others who use the same manager.

Ultimately, IMAs and MFs should both be considered for your portfolio. What portion of your investment plan they should be is a decision best made only by you and your financial advisor.

CHAPTER TWENTY-FOUR

CONVERTIBLE BONDS

A s a true disciple of Wealth Protection planning, you are moving toward reducing risk and adding flexibility to your fully integrated Wealth Protection plan. You're concerned with risk to your principal, and/or you want the flexibility of income and appreciation in your investments.

In our professional experience, there are generally two types of investors who are most concerned with stock market risk and who, therefore, find these solutions extremely attractive. These investors are:

1. Those who have highly appreciated portfolios, want to remain in the market, but want to lock in their present gains.

2. Those who have not yet jumped into the market because they feel more secure in less risky investment classes, such as certificates of deposit (CDs) or money market accounts (MMs).

CERTIFICATES OF DEPOSIT AND MONEY MARKETS: THE NONALTERNATIVES

If you have not invested in the stock market because of its inherent risk, you probably own CDs or MMs. Similarly, if you want to lock in your gains, you might consider cashing out and putting your funds into these vehicles. Either way, you probably see CDs and MMs as safe investments because they are federally insured and offer a guaranteed return each year.

The first thing to consider is that CDs and MMs do not appreciate in a "real" economic sense (see Chapter 19 on inflation). Generally, CDs and MMs return 3 percent to 5 percent, more during times
of inflation. When you consider that the inflation rate has been approximately 3.1 percent over the past 50+ years, inflation-adjusted
returns of CDs and MMs become a mere 0 percent to 2 percent.
Furthermore, when CDs and MMs enjoy higher returns, this is generally due to an inflationary economy in which the higher inflation
eats away at those larger returns. Thus, you gain no real dollars, or
purchasing power, by investing in these vehicles. Consider this example: $1 million invested in CDs in 2000 may grow to $2 million in
12 to 15 years. However, $2 million in 2012 or 2015 will buy almost
exactly what $1 million would buy you in 2000, gaining you nothing
in a raw economic sense. Remember that the goal of investing is to
increase, not maintain, your purchasing power.

Therefore, CDs and MMs make little sense for most investors who
are looking for real appreciation, especially those investing for the
long or even the medium term. Nonetheless, if principal security is
an important issue for you, consider the following alternatives, all of
which allow for the upside of the market, while protecting against
downside risk as well.

PROGRESSIVE IDEAS: THREE
INVESTMENT ALTERNATIVES

The three tools that allow investors reduced risk and increased upside potential are:

1. Principal protected mutual funds (PPMFs).
2. Convertible bonds (CBs).
3. Indexed/variable annuities.

Because we have discussed variable annuities at length in other
chapters (Chapters 21, 28, and 45) and because PPMFs are investments that are only available sporadically (they must regularly close
the funds so they can acquire insurance on the investors' principal)

we will limit our discussion in this chapter to convertible bonds. (See Table 24.1 for a comparison of CBs, PPMFs, and variable annuities.)

STOCKS AND BONDS

If you cringe at the idea of buying bonds, you must take a few moments to learn about an underutilized investment class—the convertible bond. The convertible bond offers the safety, security, and income of a bond and the upside appreciation you can get from stock investments. In essence, it is the best of both worlds.

Stocks, also called equities, are ownership shares of a company. When you own a share of a company, you are an owner of that company. As an owner, you will participate in any earnings or losses the company experiences during your period of ownership. If the firm makes money during a given year, they can decide to pay you a dividend or to retain the earnings to fund future programs, product launches, or similar opportunities.

As a stockholder, you have no say as to whether or not the firm pays a dividend. Typically, the blue chip companies offer dividends and the hi-tech companies plow their earnings back into their growing companies. For this reason, common stocks are not a good investment if you need annual income (preferred stocks may offer dividends, but they are more commonly an institutional investment). With stocks, there is no guarantee of returns; and though most stocks have done well over the past decade, there have been many periods where equities have performed poorly (like 2000 to 2002).

A *bond* is a debt instrument issued by a company (or a governmental body). The debt issuer takes your money, generally in increments of $1,000 (face value), and promises to pay you back at some specified time in the future. In the interim, the debt issuer (company) pays you (the bond holder) a semiannual or annual dividend. This dividend is often called a *coupon*. For example, suppose a company's bond pays a 5 percent dividend, or coupon, on a $1,000 face value bond. The bondholder would receive $50 every year, or $25 each six months, until the bond is retired at some time in the future. This date is referred to as the "maturity date." The coupon is guaranteed by the company; and in the event the company goes bankrupt, the bondholders receive their dividend and principal before any stockholders receive a single dollar.

Because of this "preferred" treatment, bonds are less risky and generally have lower returns than stocks. Bonds are very popular for (1) investors near or in retirement, (2) those who need annual income, (3) those who are concerned with protecting their principal, and (4) risk-averse investors who find the stock market too risky. They are also very popular with companies and other institutions that have certain investment restrictions.

This look at two investment situations should clarify any confusion.

CASE STUDY: BRUIN Co. VERSUS TROJAN TECH

Steve buys stock in BRUIN Co.—5,000 shares at a price of $20 per share. The total value of his investment is $100,000. At the same time, Bonnie buys 100 five-year bonds of BRUIN Co. ($1,000 face value) at par with an 8 percent coupon. She also pays $100,000 for her investment in BRUIN.

As one would expect, BRUIN does very well over the next five years, and the share price appreciates to $40. How does this affect Steve and Bonnie?

Steve now has 5,000 × $40, or $200,000, worth of BRUIN, a 100 percent increase over five years, roughly a 14 percent annual return. Bonnie received $8,000 annually for five years and was returned her $100,000 principal at the end of the five years when her bonds were "called" by BRUIN. She earned an 8 percent annual return on her investment.

Who did better? Well, obviously Steve did better under this scenario. That's because they invested in a winner—a company whose stock appreciated at a rate greater than the coupon rate on the bonds. What would have happened had they chosen to invest in a dog, rather than a winner?

Suppose Steve had bought 2,500 shares in the overly hyped TROJAN Tech at a share price of $40 and Bonnie had bought 100 bonds ($1,000 face value) of TROJAN Tech. They still would have started with the same $100,000 investments. Steve would have had his stocks and Bonnie her bonds. However, this situation is much different.

After five years, as you would expect, TROJAN Tech has lost all of its smartest customers to BRUIN. Despite the constant influx of capital from their investors, it appears to be a case of throwing good money after bad. TROJAN's stock ends the five-year term at a value of $12. How does this affect Steve and Bonnie?

Steve now has 2,500 shares of stock with a share price of $12. The total value of his investment is $30,000, for a loss of $70,000. Bonnie has continued to receive her dividends. She has been paid $8,000 per year *and* received her $100,000 principal back when the bonds were finally called. In this scenario, Steve lost 70 percent of his investment (−21 percent per year) while Bonnie earned 8 percent per year. In this case, Bonnie definitely did better. As you can see, Steve is taking all the risk with the stocks, and Bonnie has much less risk with her investments in bonds.

It is not always as easy as choosing between a BRUIN and a TROJAN. In the investment arena, the choices are not obvious. You will not know the outcome before you make your investment. Understandably, you would like to have a chance at the upside potential of the stock market, but you may not be very comfortable with the risk. This is where the convertible bond makes an excellent choice.

WHAT IS A CONVERTIBLE BOND?

A convertible bond has a face value (principal amount) and a coupon (dividend). However, it is a bond with a special feature. It can be converted, at the debt holder's request, to a specified number of shares.

In financial terms, this feature means you have a bond and a call (or swap) option. You can keep the bond and receive your annual dividends and have the security of the principal. In addition, if the stock price appreciates considerably, you can trade in your bonds for a specified number of shares of the company, thus significantly increasing the value of your investment.

How does this work? Let's consider a variation of Steve's and Bonnie's investments.

CASE STUDY: CONVERTIBLE BONDS

Bonnie bought 100 convertible bonds of BRUIN with a coupon of 4.5 percent. She was also given a conversion option of five shares for every bond. The coupon rate is less for the convertible bond than for the standard bond. If the stock appreciated to $40 before the end of year five, Bonnie could have received all of her annual interest payments of $4,500. Furthermore, right before the bonds were called, she could have redeemed them for $200,000 in stock (5 shares × 100 convertible bonds = 500 shares at $40 each, or $200,000 worth of stock). In this case, Bonnie received income during the life of the bond, had the security of the bond, *and* benefited from all of the appreciation of the stock.

In the TROJAN case, Steve could have purchased convertible bonds and protected his investment. In this situation, Steve would have happily received his annual interest payments. Then, when he saw that the stock was doing very poorly and that the shares were worth less than the face value of his bonds, he would have let his bonds be called and he would have received his $100,000 back from TROJAN. This would have saved him $70,000 and provided him with some income each year as well.

The best way to describe a convertible bond is to say that the value of the investment in the convertible bond is, at worst, the value of the company's slightly-reduced coupon bond. At best, if the company stock appreciates significantly over time, the investor in convertible bonds could reap excellent returns on his or her investment. Because the investment was made through a bond with a convertible feature, there was reduced equity risk to the investor. Although convertibles are underutilized today, this may be because many advisors simply don't make clients aware of this potential. This is unfortunate.

TIMING IS EVERYTHING: WHEN TO USE EACH VEHICLE

Each investment solution has its place in proper planning; and in some cases two or three of the solutions may be used. It all depends on the client's situation, net worth, income, age, and goals. Table 24.1 may help you determine which tool(s) will work best for you.

TABLE 24.1 FEATURES OF MUTUAL FUNDS, CONVERTIBLE BONDS, AND INDEXED/ VARIABLE ANNUITIES

	PRINCIPAL PROTECTED MUTUAL FUNDS	CONVERTIBLE BONDS	INDEXED/ VARIABLE ANNUITIES
Nature of protection	Insurance on account.	Bond's preferential treatment.	Insurance companies' guarantee.
Nature of upside potential	As good as the underlying mutual funds.	Ability to convert to the stock of the companies you invest in.	As good as the underlying mutual funds.
Cost of $1 million portfolio	2.5%, including insurance.	0.5%–0.8%, depending on size.	1%–10% if withdrawn in first 5 to 7 years, 0% after; 1%–2% management fees per year.
Tax benefits	None.	None.	Complete deferral.
Principal available for withdrawal	10% per year, 100%—no insurance, no penalties.	100% with taxation.	10% per year; more with penalties in first 7–10 years.
Estate planning benefits	None, unless part of insurance product.	None, unless part of insurance product.	Yes.

(continued)

TABLE 24.1   (CONTINUED)

	PRINCIPAL PROTECTED MUTUAL FUNDS	**CONVERTIBLE BONDS**	**INDEXED/ VARIABLE ANNUITIES**
Ideal for what vehicle?	Pensions or brokerage accounts.	Pensions or brokerage accounts.	Anywhere *but* in retirement accounts.
Ideal for what investor?	Near or in retirement or risk averse.	Near or in retirement or risk averse.	High earner, to reduce tax burden, or young.

LAST WORD

Like all tools, convertible bonds and variable annuities (and even PPMFs) have their place in a Wealth Protection plan. Now that you understand the basics of each of these tools, you can move forward through this book and learn about asset protection, insurance, retirement, and estate planning. When you have done that, you (and possibly your Wealth Planning advisor) can put together a plan that addresses all of your needs.

PART V

ASSET PROTECTION

CHAPTER TWENTY-FIVE

WHY ASSET PROTECTION IS SO IMPORTANT TODAY

I n previous generations, most clients did not see the need to shield assets from potential lawsuits. But today, after seeing the explosion of litigation in this country, you should understand such a need, especially since the results of your risk factor analysis (RFA) show that you have asset protection risk. Nevertheless, in case you are still skeptical about the need for asset protection in your Wealth Protection plan, we want to introduce this part of the book by answering one key question: "Why is asset protection so important for you?"

MORE LAWSUITS THAN EVER BEFORE

The number of civil lawsuits in this country has skyrocketed in the past few decades, with no sign of slowing. *Millions of new lawsuits* will be filed this year alone—almost triple the number filed 30 years ago. One new lawsuit is filed every 1.3 seconds. Any of us could be the next target.

YOUR ODDS OF BECOMING A
LAWSUIT VICTIM

In California, in 1998 and 1999, there were 1.5 million civil lawsuits filed—nearly one lawsuit for every 20 people. If you factor out the children and elderly (who generally don't get sued), you are looking at some very unattractive odds. Odds are that your state isn't much better than California.

YOU ARE MORE LIKELY TO BE SUED
THAN TO . . .

1. *Be injured in a car accident.* Almost 20 million new lawsuits will be filed this year. Yet only 5.7 million injuries and deaths will result from car accidents. Thus, you are nearly four times as likely to be sued than to be injured or killed in a car accident. If you think going without car insurance is foolish, you are four times as foolish to ignore lawsuit protection.

2. *Lose your home to fire.* The number of new civil lawsuits filed this year will be nearly 80 times the number of residential fires nationwide. You surely have insurance to protect your home against fire loss and even floods. But have you taken the simple steps to safeguard your home from lawsuits and creditors? We hope that after reading this book, you will.

The simple truth is that being sued is more likely than many of the losses against which we typically protect ourselves. Protecting our valuable savings and possessions from lawsuits and other creditor problems is possible. More important, it need not be overly expensive, especially when the protection is established sooner rather than later.

PEOPLE ABUSE THE LEGAL SYSTEM

Another factor adds to the lawsuit explosion: Many people simply abuse the legal system for their own personal gain. This trend is so severe in California that its legislature passed the Vexatious Litigant Act, creating a list of people who, in a judge's opinion, abuse the legal system by repeatedly filing meritless lawsuits without attorneys or who engage in other frivolous tactics. Of course, these same individuals cannot be denied their "constitutional right" to sue; but they cannot file suits without attorneys unless they have a judge's permission. This list is available to every lawyer in the state.

Here are two awful examples of who is on this list.

1. One Los Angeles claimant filed over 200 lawsuits in seven years. Very few were successful.

2. A court clerk recommended certain individuals for this list. These individuals then made the clerk a lawsuit target and sued the clerk 11 times in two years—unsuccessfully. The clerk's reaction: "I do not exaggerate when I say I am extremely frightened by these people." (*The Sacramento Bee*, November 26, 1995)

In California, an estimated two-thirds of medical claims from auto accidents are phony or exaggerated.

ENORMOUS AWARDS FOR NEGLIGIBLE DAMAGES

There are so many more lawsuits today because the lawsuit has become a way to "get rich quick," not a method to achieve justice. Some people now believe that whenever something goes wrong, someone should pay, regardless of who is at fault. Unfortunately, juries routinely adopt this idea and often disregard the facts of the case. Through emotion and bias, juries can give away large sums of money . . . whether or not the defendant was at fault.

You read about these cases in your daily newspaper. A woman receives $2.6 million because her coffee was too hot. A homeowner pays thousands of dollars to a trespasser injured while burglarizing the homeowner's property. People see these same awards and ask, "Why not me?" They want to win the lawsuit lottery, too. Their first step is to spot a target and manufacture a reason to sue. It is only a matter of time until that target is you.

Between 1994 and 2002, the average jury award in tort cases tripled
to $1.2 million.

- One Chicago law firm proudly announced to its many clients
  and prospects that it obtained the *largest verdict ever for an arm
  amputation: $7.8 million.* (*U.S. News and World Report,* January
  30, 1995)
- An auditor won over $2.5 million when fired from a $52,000-
  a-year job after being employed by the company for $2\frac{1}{2}$
  months.
- A college student was awarded $75,000 for a broken arm suf-
  fered at a friend's house.
- Nationally, 12 percent of all jury awards are $1 million or more.
- A mugger shot by the police won $4.5 million from New York
  City after claiming excessive force.
- A small construction company in Washington State saw its insurance policy premiums rise from $92,000 to $580,000 in one
  year!

Such awards were once the exception, but now they are common-
place. Juries today routinely dole out millions of dollars, frequently
even more than the plaintiff demands.

In a study of over 23,000 Illinois jury trials, the Institute for Civil Justice found that the average punitive damages award increased, in
inflation-adjusted dollars from $43,000 in the 1965–1969 period to
$729,000 in the 1980–1984 period. Those figures are even higher
today!

THE RULES OF ASSET PROTECTION: FRAUDULENT TRANSFER LAWS

Now that you have seen why asset protection is so important today,
you must understand the basic rules for asset protection. Essentially,

you must protect assets before any lawsuit or creditor claim arises. That's because, once a claim has arisen, the person suing you can always ask the court to undo any transfers you make to hinder his or her collection of the debt. The court can do this under what are called "fraudulent transfer" or "fraudulent conveyance" laws.

Think of asset protection planning as a vaccine, not a cure. Once a lawsuit or a claim is threatened, many protective strategies can no longer be used, just as a vaccine is not effective once you are afflicted with a disease. Proper asset protection is always preventative planning. For more on fraudulent transfer laws and how proper asset protection complies with these laws, see Appendix 2.

Last word

At this point, we hope you realize a cold hard fact: In our litigious society, asset protection planning is an integral part of any Wealth Protection plan. In Chapters 26 through 34, you'll learn the various tools and techniques you can implement to shield your wealth from lawsuits and other claims.

CHAPTER TWENTY-SIX

OWNERSHIP FORMS YOU MUST AVOID: YOUR OWN NAME, JOINT OWNERSHIP, AND GENERAL PARTNERSHIPS

A comprehensive Wealth Protection plan should not only protect your assets from outside threats, but also should steer you away from the many dangerous liability traps that exist. If you have been directed to this chapter by the RFA, it means that these traps are in your plan right now. If you can avoid these dangerous types of ownership, you will have done a better job than most people to shield your wealth, even before you explore the more advanced topics discussed later in this part. Let's review the forms of ownership that can be so treacherous.

DO NOT HOLD ASSETS IN YOUR OWN NAME

If you hold property in your name, you have absolutely no asset protection against your creditors or against lawsuits. Unless homestead or other state or federal exemptions protect the asset, an asset held in your name is wide open for attack (for a list of state and federal exemptions, visit www.mywealthprotection.com). Although owning assets in your own name does provide you with maximum flexibility, flexibility is not enough of an advantage to justify exposing your wealth to all of the lawsuit and creditor risks. This is especially true because other tools can provide you with flexibility while also protecting your assets.

WHY JOINT OWNERSHIP IS SO DANGEROUS

Joint ownership is the most popular form of ownership in the United States for stocks, bonds, real estate, and bank accounts. In this ownership form, when one joint owner dies, property owned in joint ownership may automatically pass to the surviving joint owner(s). This is called "joint ownership with right of survivorship," which may be the joint form assumed under the law of your state. In this common interpretation, jointly owned property passes outside of a will and avoids the expense of probate (see Chapter 52 for more on the pitfalls of probate). Because it avoids probate, many financial and legal advisors recommend joint ownership as a form of ownership. However, these advisors may not warn you of the disadvantages of keeping assets in joint ownership.

Here we will examine the two major asset protection risks of joint ownership. Later, in Part VIII on estate planning, you will learn how joint ownership can ruin your intended estate plan as well.

JOINT OWNERSHIP CREATES LAWSUIT AND CREDITOR RISKS

If you own property (personal property or real estate) jointly, you face even more lawsuit and creditor risks than if you owned the property in your own name. Let's examine these risks through the following case study.

CASE STUDY: THE BUILDING YOU AND FRANK OWN

You and your friend Frank are joint owners of a residential apartment building—each of you can sell, give away, or mortgage your half share of the building without consent of the other person. You are partners in the business of renting the apartments, collecting the rents, maintaining the premises, and so on, and you plan to use the building to provide you both with an income. You both agree that, given the right market conditions, you should sell the building for a hefty profit.

If Frank is ever sued for a reason unrelated to the building, Frank's creditors can only come after his half of the building. Do you think your half is safe from Frank's creditors? This arrangement may seem like an asset protection advantage, but if you are the safe joint owner, it is not. That is because Frank's creditors can ask the court to sell the entire property, including your share, to satisfy the outstanding debt. This is called *forced liquidation*. Here, the court can sell the entire property on the open market. You lose your share of the property, but you get to keep your share of the proceeds.

Returning to the case study, Frank's financial problems could cause any number of problems for you, even though you are supposedly *safe*. Consider these scenarios:

- Frank's creditors force a sale of the entire building during a terrible market for sellers. The creditors know even a rock-bottom price will pay off their debt, so they do not care what the building sells for. Because you cannot come up with the cash to buy Frank's share, the building is sold well below its fair market value. Frank's creditors are paid, and you get half of the proceeds. However, you lose a building that provided you a steady cash flow and that you know is worth much more than its selling price.

- Frank's creditors like the apartment building. They decide they should keep the building themselves. Now you have a new partner—someone (or likely some*thing*, like a bank or a credit union) you don't know, trust, or understand. This is not an ideal partner for a business venture going forward.

• Frank's creditors like the apartment building. They take Frank's half share. When the market turns into a strong seller's market, you want to sell the building and make your profit. However, Frank's creditors, now your partners, disagree. You end up selling your half, which gets much less on the market than half of the whole building would yield. It turns out that few others also want to accept Frank's creditors as their partners.

Joint Ownership Creates a "Winner-Take-All" Game

Joint ownership puts you in a winner-take-all waiting game, where you are gambling that you survive longer than your fellow joint owner(s). Jointly owned property typically passes automatically to the surviving joint owner(s) at death. If the safe owner dies before the debtor owner(s) the whole property belongs to the debtor(s) and can be taken by creditors. Returning to the case study, if you and Frank owned the building in joint ownership and you died before Frank, Frank would own the building outright. Frank's creditors could then seize the entire building. Your family would have no rights whatsoever.

The other outcome of the winner-take-all game is that the safe joint owner (assume that is you for now) survives longer than the debtor owner (assume that is Frank). Does this mean that you take the building free and clear of Frank's creditor problems? In most cases, yes. This is the one asset protection aspect of joint ownership—winning the winner-take-all game. This victory, however, is not absolute. There are three situations, even if you survive and take the entire building, in which Frank's half share may still be vulnerable:

1. Frank owed federal or state taxes.
2. Frank declared bankruptcy. The bankruptcy trustee can sell any property Frank owned, even if he is now dead. You must then claim a share of the sale proceeds.
3. The situation occurs in a limited number of states that allow a dead joint owner's creditors to come after the surviving joint owner's property.

GENERAL PARTNERSHIPS: A LIABILITY NIGHTMARE FOR BUSINESSES

In a general partnership, two or more people join together to run a business or venture for profit without registering the business as a corporation, a limited partnership, or any other legal entity. The law assumes that any business involving more than one person is a general partnership unless the partners prove otherwise. Similarly, the law assumes that a business run by one person is a proprietorship unless proven otherwise. A proprietorship provides no asset protection whatsoever because the person is, for all legal purposes, the business.

Like the proprietorship, general partners have the right to manage partnership affairs and are personally liable for the debts and the liabilities of the partnership. The general partnership is even more of a liability trap than the proprietorship, however, because general partners can incur liability because of their own acts, the acts of their employees, and the acts of their fellow partners.

THREE REASONS NOT TO OPERATE ANY BUSINESS AS A GENERAL PARTNERSHIP

Never operate any business or practice as a general partnership! A general partnership is a creditor's or a plaintiff's dream and a partner's liability nightmare. It should not be part of anyone's asset protection plan. Why is a general partnership so dangerous? Consider the three hidden dangers of a general partnership:

1. *Partners have unlimited liability for partnership debts.* This tragic fact goes unrealized by many businesspeople, professionals, and other entrepreneurs who are involved in general partnerships. They, in effect, personally guarantee every partnership debt, personally assuming the risk for malpractice, accidents, and other liability sources of the entire partnership. These businesspeople fail to consider that their liability as partners is "joint and several" with other partners. This means that a plaintiff who successfully sues the partnership can collect the full judgment from any one partner.

CASE STUDY: JANE AND TED'S REAL ESTATE VENTURE

Jane and Ted were friends who decided to go into a real estate venture together to refurbish old three-family homes and then sell them as condominiums. Events went well for a while, but the real estate market went sour, and Jane and Ted defaulted on a $650,000 bank loan. Jane was much wealthier than Ted, so the bank pursued Jane for the full amount, ignoring Ted. Jane ended up having to pay over $600,000 to the bank. Of course, she could have sued Ted for his share of the debt, but Ted didn't have the money anyway, so Jane didn't see the point.

2. *Partners have unlimited liability for their partners' acts.* With a partner in a general partnership, you assume all the risk that the partner will cause a lawsuit. When the lawsuit arises from one partner's act or omission in the ordinary course of business, every other partner is personally liable. The dreaded "joint and several liability" then applies! If one of your partners gets into trouble and causes a lawsuit, you can be personally liable for the entire amount of the lawsuit judgment—even if you were neither involved in the alleged incident nor aware of it.

Think of the many ways a partner could get you into trouble: He or she commits malpractice, gets into a car accident while on partnership business, defrauds someone through the business, sexually harasses an employee, wrongfully fires an employee, and so on. Multiply this risk by the number of partners in your partnership, and you have a lawsuit liability nightmare! Here is a real-world example.

CASE STUDY: MICHAEL GETS BURNED BY HIS PARTNERS

Michael was the founding partner in a successful three-partner software development firm near Portland, Oregon. One of the firm's

(continued)

customers sued the firm when a program did not perform as one of his partners had erroneously promised, causing a loss of valuable data. The lawsuit alleged breach of contract and product liability and sought punitive damages.

Settlement negotiations were unsuccessful, and the trial jury awarded an extremely large verdict against the partnership, exceeding its liability policy limit. Because Michael was the wealthiest of the partners, the plaintiff's lawyer pursued him first, forcing Michael to pay the entire amount above the insurance policy limit—$250,000— from his personal savings. Although Michael had less contact with this customer than his partners, he now understands the risks of a general partnership.

3. *You may be an "unaware" general partner.* A general partnership does not require a formal written agreement, as does a limited partnership. You can verbally agree to start a venture with another person and create a general partnership, with all of its liability problems. Think about this whenever you start a new business venture with someone.

Even if you make no agreement to partner with another person, the law may impose general partnership liability on you if the general public reasonably perceives you as partners. You may already be part of a liability-ridden general partnership and not even know it.

CASE STUDY: ROGER INADVERTENTLY HAS PARTNERS

Roger was one of four accountants who used a common office arrangement. They each had their own clients, whom they did not share. However, they did share a common waiting area, support staff, and bookkeeping. Each professional had his own practice methods, set his own hours, and was not otherwise accountable to the others.

When a client sued one of the accountants for professional misconduct, Roger and the two others had a rude awakening. Although only the client's accountant was negligent, all four were defendants in the lawsuit. The court found that the client could reasonably conclude that the four professionals were partners together because of their office setup and common support staff. Therefore, the court allowed the plaintiff to proceed with the suit against all four—as a general partnership, with each jointly and severally liable for the plaintiff's losses.

How to Protect Yourself in a General Partnership

We repeat our warning: *Do not run any business as a general partnership!* It is too risky. Rather, convert the business into a limited partnership, a C- or an S-corporation, or a limited liability company. Because of certain ownership restrictions in some states, you may have to use a general partnership.

If you must use a general partnership, each partner should set up corporations or limited liability companies (LLCs); then the corporations or LLCs should become the partners in the general partnership. This advice is followed by many medical professionals and attorneys using professional corporations (PCs). Each doctor or lawyer sets up a PC, and the PC, not the professional, is the official partner in the partnership. By structuring the partnership in this way, the underlying corporate owner's personal assets remain protected from claims against the partnership. However, as with any corporation, the corporate formalities must be followed to achieve the asset protection.

Last word

The first step in any asset protection plan is to avoid dangerous ownership forms to the maximum extent possible. Once this is accomplished, you can move to the next stage of the planning: using insurance and legal tools to proactively shield assets going forward.

CHAPTER TWENTY-SEVEN

◆

USING INSURANCE AS AN ASSET PROTECTOR: A MIXED BLESSING

As licensed insurance professionals, we both strongly believe that various types of insurance are required components of every Wealth Protection plan. Certainly, property and casualty insurance is one of these tools for asset protection.

WHAT PROPERTY AND CASUALTY INSURANCE IS

To begin with, there are two categories of insurance: (1) life and health (L&H) and (2) property and casualty (P&C). In addition to all life insurance and health insurance, L&H includes disability insurance and long-term-care insurance, among others. The purpose of P&C insurance is to protect against property and casualty losses. Often P&C is referred to as "property and liability" insurance because it protects people from all types of liabilities. Examples of P&C coverages are automobile, homeowner's and renter's, umbrella liability, professional liability, medical malpractice, general liability, flood, earthquake, premises liability, errors and omissions, and products liability.

Property and casualty insurance is designed to "indemnify" the insured. The insurance industry's definition of *indemnify* is "to make whole." If you suffer a loss and have the proper coverage, you should be put back in the same place you were before the loss (minus any applicable deductibles or copayments). In addition to the actual loss, P&C coverage covers your legal bills and other loss adjustment expenses. This may include the costs of adjusters, estimates, expert testimony, or other associated costs.

This is very important because, as you know from earlier chapters, the nuisance lawsuit is more popular than ever. As long as there is one ambulance-chasing attorney who is willing to take the case, there is no out-of-pocket cost (or deterrent) to the plaintiff. If you didn't have insurance but still won your case, you still might have tens of thousands, if not hundreds of thousands, of dollars in legal fees and related expenses. It is usually worth buying insurance to avoid these costs and the inconvenience and aggravation, let alone the potential judgment or loss.

BEST USES OF PROPERTY AND CASUALTY INSURANCE

As mentioned earlier, there are various types of insurance that fall under the P&C category. The most common of these are homeowner's (or renter's) and automobile. You probably have these coverages if you have a mortgage on your home or a loan or a lease on your car. In a way, you do not own your home or car yet—the bank or credit department does. They require, as collateral, that you insure their asset while you are paying for it. Once you pay off your home or car, you are no longer required to have insurance, although most states require you to maintain liability insurance if you drive a car. Of course, we would *never* recommend dropping the insurance on your home. The odds are very slim that you will suffer a house fire or a burglary, but if you do, you would be very upset knowing that you lost so much and could have avoided that loss by paying a few hundred or a few thousand dollars for insurance.

Another common P&C insurance is the umbrella liability policy. For a very reasonable premium, you can get an additional $1 million to $2 million of excess liability insurance on top of the liability protection you may have from your homeowner's or auto policies. If you are a high-net-worth individual or are in a high-liability profession, you should seriously consider an umbrella policy.

Other popular P&C coverages are for professional liability and for premises and products liability. Depending on your occupation, you may have medical or legal malpractice insurance. If you own your place of business, you should have premises liability insurance. If your business makes a product (toy, part, widget, etc.), then you should have products liability. This will protect you from claims that a part malfunctioned and caused damages.

FIVE LIMITATIONS OF PROPERTY AND CASUALTY INSURANCE

Although some P&C insurance always makes sense as part of a Wealth Protection plan, there are significant limitations to this tool. That is why we typically recommend using the legal asset protection tools we describe in this part, in addition to any insurance. Let's examine these limitations individually.

1. *Policy exclusions.* Often we find that clients are completely unaware of the "fine print" exclusions and policy limitations. Of course, they often become aware of such exclusions after it is too late. For example, many clients fail to realize that their umbrella policy only picks up if certain underlying insurance coverage amounts are in effect. If your liability limits on your homeowner's policy or auto policy are too low, then you'll have to be paying out of pocket before the umbrella kicks in. You must know your policy.

CASE STUDY: ALAN'S DAUGHTER'S CAR ACCIDENT

Alan was sued for over $150,000 when his teenaged daughter, who was using his car, was involved in a car accident. Alan was certain that his insurance policy covered his daughter. However, Alan's insurance agent told him that the policy no longer covered his daughter because she had recently moved out of the house. There was an exclusion for coverage of children drivers if they did not reside in the same residence as the parents. Now, Alan alone faced a lawsuit that cost him over $150,000.

Note: As of this writing there is a significant debate regarding the September 11, 2001 tragedy. A very common exclusion to nearly all P&C policies is that losses will not be paid in the event of war or civil commotion. The debate is whether or not the insurance companies can rely on this exclusion to avoid paying claims on September 11 losses. We doubt the issue will be resolved expediently because there is simply too much money at stake.

2. *Inadequate policy limits.* Even if your insurance policy does provide some coverage for losses from a particular lawsuit, the policy coverage may be well below what a jury will award. You must pay any excess above the coverage out of your own pocket. Juries routinely hand out awards in excess of the coverage limits of traditional auto, medical malpractice, employee harassment, and other common P&C insurances. You should get sufficient coverage to protect against a large judgment. Do not skimp on coverage; consider an umbrella policy and utilize other asset protection tools.

3. *Your insurer no longer exists.* There is no guarantee that your insurance company will exist if and when you finally get sued. Insurance companies are not invincible. Like other businesses, some go bankrupt or shut down and leave you without coverage when you most need it. This is exactly what happened to a large physician-owned malpractice carrier in California. Now, the physicians are being forced to pay the outstanding debts of their former insurer. That's why we recommend you use top-rated carriers.

4. *Insurance forces you to lose control of the defense.* Even if your insurance policy covers against a specific claim, consider the consequences. You have lost negotiating power because your insurance company will dictate whether the case is settled and for how much. Although this may not matter with a personal injury/car accident lawsuit, a claim against you professionally is another case. Here you may

not want to admit liability and settle, whereas your insurance company does.

If the claim involves your professional reputation, you may want to settle the case out of court and away from the public view. There is no guarantee that your insurer will see things the same way. In these situations, if you rely solely on insurance, you lose all ability to negotiate effectively.

> *Tip:* If you want to retain some control over a lawsuit where your defense is being handled by an insurance company's lawyer, hire your own attorney to review the case at key junctures. While this will cost you some money, it may be well worth it to see that your interests, not just those of the insurance company, are being served.

5. *Claims bring ever-higher premiums.* An additional consequence of relying solely on insurance to protect you from lawsuits is that once you make claims on the policy, your premiums rise. Given the dismal statistics, you will probably endure a number of lawsuits over your life—your cost of insurance will rise with every claim, even if you are not at fault. Consider the following solution for a construction company owner who, before protecting his assets, relied solely on insurance. After his insurance company defended four unsuccessful lawsuits against him, three of which went through trial, his insurance premiums rose to over $100,000 per year. Insurance cost him more over the next five years than any one lawsuit. This is not an extreme example. The point is clear: By relying solely on insurance, lawsuits cost you dearly, even if you win the trials.

LAST WORD

One part of everyone's Wealth Protection plan should be P&C insurance. Certain coverages, such as homeowner's, auto, and even umbrella, are musts. Beyond this, however, to adequately shield assets and to discourage claims from the outset, more must be done. In the next chapters, you'll learn about powerful legal tools that you can use to protect all your assets and to enjoy significant tax benefits as well.

CHAPTER TWENTY-EIGHT

INSURANCE AND ANNUITIES: PROTECTED INVESTMENTS

I f you're here in the asset protection part, shielding your wealth is an important part of building your Financial Fortress. In the next few chapters, you'll learn about several legal structures that can shield all types of assets. In this chapter, we will focus on the investments themselves—certain investments are given special creditor protection under the law. The important issue is then, if you have a choice between two fairly equal investments, why not use the one that is asset-protected under the law? Typically, the wise choice is to make use of the protected investment. Let's see how that works.

FEDERAL LAW GENERALLY DOES NOT SHIELD INVESTMENTS

In general, federal law does not protect particular investments from creditors. However, it is important to know that federal law does shield certain pensions, profit-sharing plans, 401(k)s, and other plans from creditors under its Employee Retirement Income Security Act (ERISA) rules. For more on these types of "qualified retirement plans," see Chapters 42 and 43.

STATE LAW DOES PROTECT CERTAIN INVESTMENTS

Every state has laws that shield certain assets from creditors. These are called "exempt assets"—they are exempt from seizure in a lawsuit or in bankruptcy. What types of assets are afforded this protection? Most common are the individual retirement account (IRA) and the home, through what is called a "homestead exemption." (The homestead exemption is important enough that we have covered it separately in Chapter 33.)

As far as the IRA goes, many states protect the entire amount in the IRA; others protect only "the amount reasonably necessary for support," leaving it up to a judge to decide how much should be shielded in any particular case. Do you want to leave the security of your retirement in the hands of a judge? To see what the level of IRA protection is in your state, see our web site at www.mywealth protection.com.

As you will see with the homestead exemption, there is tremendous variation among the states in terms of what and how much is protected under exemption laws. Nevertheless, along with the home, there are two important assets that are given significant protection in many states. These are life insurance and annuities.

LIFE INSURANCE: PROTECTED EVERYWHERE

All 50 states have laws protecting life insurance, but they each protect differing amounts. There are some general trends:

- Most states shield the entire policy proceeds from the creditors of the policyholder. Some also protect against the beneficiaries' creditors.

- States that do not protect the entire policy proceeds set amounts above which the creditor can take proceeds. For example, Arizona exempts the first $20,000 of proceeds.

- Many states protect the policy proceeds only if the policy beneficiaries are the policyholder's spouse, children, or other dependents.

- Most states also exempt term and group life policies.

- Some states protect a policy's cash surrender value in addition to the policy proceeds. If your life insurance has substantial cash value, be sure to consult your state exemptions to determine how well protected you are.

- No state can protect life insurance from the IRS—the IRS can take your insurance proceeds and cash value if you owe them money.

- If the policy is purchased as part of a fraudulent transfer, a court can undo the policy, like any other fraudulent transfer (see Appendix 2 for more on fraudulent transfers).

ANNUITIES ARE SHIELDED IN MANY STATES

As you will learn in Part 7, Retirement Planning, there are two types of annuities: (1) variable annuities and (2) life annuities. *Variable* annuities are insurance contracts that invest the contributions in investment vehicles on a tax-deferred basis. *Life* annuities are insurance contracts for which the investor pays a certain amount of money up front and the insurance company then pays the investor back at a fixed payment every month, quarter, or year for as long as the investor (or spouse) is alive. (See Chapter 45 for more on annuities.)

Some states protect annuities from creditor claims. In the states that do exempt them, annuities are an ideal tool to safeguard wealth.

CASE STUDY: SAM CHOOSES BETWEEN MUTUAL FUNDS AND A VARIABLE ANNUITY

Sam is a business owner with many employees, and he is concerned about asset protection. He has $50,000 to invest and is in a state where variable annuities are protected. Sam must decide whether to invest the money in mutual funds or in a variable annuity. In Part 4 on investing, you learned that annuities have higher charges than

(continued)

mutual funds. However, for that higher expense, you receive some life insurance, the value of tax deferral, and, for Sam, asset protection. Let's assume that the difference in charges is about 1.5 percent annually. Is it worth it for Sam to use the annuity when it is protected and grows tax-deferred rather than the mutual fund? We can't say for sure without knowing more about Sam's goals and portfolio; but in terms of asset protection, there is no doubt.

LAST WORD

To see which assets are given protection in your state, visit our web site at www.mywealthprotection.com. Once you know to what extent these investments are protected in your state, you can better evaluate the role they may play in your Wealth Protection plan.

CHAPTER TWENTY-NINE

FAMILY LIMITED PARTNERSHIPS AND LIMITED LIABILITY COMPANIES: TWIN ASSET PROTECTION POWERHOUSES

N ow that you're familiar with insurance coverage, the ownership forms that are liability traps, and the financial products that are protected in different states, you're ready to tackle the "meat" of any asset protection plan—the legal tools.

Of all the legal tools we use to shield assets, by far the two we use most are family limited partnerships (FLPs) and family limited liability companies (LLCs). Of course, having family members play a role in asset protection strategies utilizing these tools is typical—that's why we use the word *family* in front of the LP or LLC. However, using family members in this way is *not* required. Whether you use family members or not, these tools can provide you extraordinary asset protection. Nonetheless, we will use the abbreviations FLPs and LLCs throughout.

SIMILARITIES BETWEEN THE FLP AND THE LLC

1. *They both are legal entities certified under state law.* Both tools are legal entities governed by state law in the state in which the entity is formed. Many of these laws are identical, as they are modeled after the Uniform LP and LLC Acts, which have been adopted at least partially by every state. As state-certified legal entities, the owners of the FLP/LLC must pay the state fees for the structure to remain valid. For a list of state fees for LLCs and FLPs, contact your state's secretary of state office.

2. *They have two levels of ownership.* Both entities allow for two levels of ownership. We'll call one ownership level "active ownership." The active owners have 100 percent control of the entity and its assets. In the FLP, the active owners are called "general partners"; in the LLC, the active owners are called "managing members." As you may have already guessed, the second ownership level is passive ownership. The passive owners have little control of the entity and only limited rights. The passive owners are called "limited partners" in the FLP and "members" in the LLC. This bilevel structure allows a host of planning possibilities because clients can then use FLPs and LLCs to share ownership with family members without having to give away any practical control of the assets inside the structures. Why is it optimal to be able to give away ownership but still maintain control? The asset-protection reasons will be discussed in great detail in this chapter and the estate planning benefits will be explained in Chapter 56 in Part 8.

3. *They both have beneficial tax treatment.* In terms of income taxes, both tools can elect for "pass through" taxation—neither the FLP nor the LLC is liable for income taxes. Rather, the tax liability for any and all income or capital gains on FLP/LLC assets "passes through" to the owners (partners or members). Also, as discussed in Parts 3 and 8, both entities allow the participants to take advantage of "income sharing" and "discounting" techniques in the same ways. See Chapters 11 and 56 for more on these tactics.

4. *They both have the beneficial charging order asset protection benefit.* Although state laws do vary slightly, those based on the Uniform Limited Partnership Act (ULPA) and the Uniform Limited

Liability Company Act (ULLCA) provide "charging order" protection to FLP and LLC owners. Continue reading this chapter for more on how this characteristic provides powerful asset protection.

5. *They both cost about the same in terms of legal fees.* To create the FLP or the LLC—designing how the entity will work in a client's plan, drafting the operating/partnership agreement, minutes, preparing tax forms, assignments, and so on, experienced attorneys in the field will charge between $2,000 and $5,000, depending on the complexity of the ownership and several other factors.

TWO BIG DIFFERENCES BETWEEN THE FLP AND THE LLC

The two significant differences between the FLP and the LLC are:

1. *Only the LLC can be used for a single owner.* Most states now allow single-member (owner) LLCs, whereas a limited partnership in every state must have at least two owners. Thus, for single clients, LLCs are often their only option. Also, if we are considering having an FLP or an LLC protect a home, then the single-member LLC is often the best alternative. (See Chapter 33 for further discussion on the home, also called "primary residence.")

2. *The FLP's general partner has liability for the FLP.* Whereas a general partner has personal liability for the acts and the debts of the FLP, a managing member has no such liability for his or her LLC. For this reason alone, asset-protection experts always recommend using an LLC rather than an FLP when the entity will own "dangerous" assets.

Dangerous assets are those with a relatively high likelihood of creating liability. Common dangerous assets include real estate (especially rental real estate), cars, recreational vehicles (RVs), trucks, boats, airplanes, and interests in closely held businesses.

Safe assets, conversely, are those that are unlikely to lead to lawsuits. Common safe assets include cash, stocks, bonds, mutual funds, certificates of deposit (CDs), life insurance policies, checking or savings accounts, antiques, artwork, jewelry, licenses, copyrights, trademarks, and patents.

Because FLP general partners have liability exposure and LLC managing members do not, it usually makes sense to use an LLC rather than an FLP to own dangerous assets.

How FLP/LLC powerfully protect assets

FLPs and LLCs are outstanding asset protectors because the law gives a very specific and limited remedy to creditors coming after assets in either entity. When a personal creditor pursues you and if your assets are owned by an FLP or an LLC, the creditor cannot seize the assets in the FLP/LLC. Under the Uniform Act provisions, a creditor of a partner (or LLC member) cannot reach into the FLP/LLC and take specific partnership assets.

Of course, assets owned in your name are vulnerable. But when assets are owned by the FLP/LLC, the best the creditor can do is to obtain a charging order—a very weak remedy indeed.

This discussion assumes that in transferring assets to an FLP or an LLC, you do not run afoul of fraudulent transfer laws. We introduced the concept of these laws in the introduction of this part. For more on fraudulent transfer laws, see Appendix 2.

The weaknesses of the charging order

The charging order is a court order that instructs the FLP/LLC to pay the debtor's share of distributions to his or her creditor until the creditor's judgment is paid in full. You should know that the charging order does not give the creditor FLP/LLC voting rights; nor does it force the FLP general partner or LLC managing member to pay out any distributions to partners/members.

While this may seem like a powerful remedy, consider its limitations:

1. *The charging order is available only after a successful lawsuit.* Only after the creditor has successfully sued you and won a judgment can

he or she ask the court for the charging order. While there is a threat and even while a lawsuit is proceeding, FLP/LLC assets are completely untouchable and available for you to use (as long as you avoid fraudulent transfers—see Appendix 2).

2. *The charging order does not give voting rights, so you stay in complete control.* Despite the charging order, you remain the general partner of your FLP (or managing member of the LLC). You make all decisions about FLP/LLC assets—whether to sell, to distribute earnings to the partners or members, to shift ownership interests, and so on. Your judgment creditor cannot vote you out because it cannot vote your shares. Thus, even after the creditor has a judgment against you, you still make all decisions concerning the FLP/LLC, including the decision to refuse to pay distributions to the owners. Why would you decide to pay distributions when you know that the creditor will get them?

Perhaps you want to compensate yourself and your spouse as general partners (or managing members) by paying yourself a salary for running the FLP/LLC—this is 100 percent permissible. And your creditor will still not get one red cent! If your creditor wishes to get access to this income, he or she will have to file to have your wages garnished. Because you may not have received a salary before the initial judgment, the creditor wouldn't have known to ask to have your wages garnished. If the creditor does file for this remedy, you can stop paying yourself a salary or pay another family member to do this task.

Keep in mind that a charging order may have no impact on most FLP/LLCs. If your FLP/LLC simply owns cars, vacation homes, antiques, or other non-income-producing assets, your FLP/LLC may never have any income to distribute.

3. *The creditor pays the tax bill.* The real kicker is how the charging order backfires on creditors for income tax purposes. Because taxes on FLP/LLC income are passed through to the parties who are entitled to the income, the FLP/LLC does not pay tax. Each partner/member is responsible for his or her share of the FLP/LLC income. This income is taxable, whether or not the income is actually paid out. Because a creditor who gets a charging order against you "steps into your shoes" for income tax purposes with respect to the FLP/LLC, your creditor will get your tax bill and owe income taxes on your share of the FLP/LLC income. This tax liability exists even

though the creditor never received the income. (Remember, you and your spouse decide if and when to make distributions, and you certainly won't make any when there is a creditor with a charging order.) With this extraordinary "poison pill," you may ask the creditor to sue your wife and your kids, too, so your family never pays any tax again!

If a creditor thinks he will get more money out of a cheap settlement than from elusive FLP/LLC distributions, he will settle.

CASE STUDY: WOODY AND MARGE ARE PROTECTED BY THEIR FLP

Return to the example of spouses Woody and Marge. Assume that Woody is an auto dealer. After two years of employment, Woody's assistant, Maribel, sues Woody for sexual harassment and wins an award of $750,000. Woody's general business insurance package does not cover this type of lawsuit. Once Maribel discovers, through a debtor's examination, that Woody and Marge's assets are owned through their FLP, what can she do?

She cannot seize the vacation home, stocks, and cars owned by the FLP. The ULPA provisions prohibit that. She also has no fraudulent transfer claim to cling to in an attempt to undo the FLP because the FLP was created in advance of her claim. She can get a charging order on Woody's 39 percent share of the FLP, but Woody and Marge still control the FLP. Maribel would probably end up with no distributed profits, only a tax bill on dividends paid out by the stocks, which Woody and Marge never distributed. The charging order will not sound too inviting to Maribel, will it?

Maribel could look only to Woody's assets not owned by the FLP. As Woody had an incomplete asset protection plan, he did have assets exposed—copyrights and business interests in a film company worth about $75,000. Woody settled the judgment for just that— $75,000 cash. Woody and Marge's FLP helped them to avoid financial disaster and to settle the claim for pennies on the dollar. And they never lost control of their assets.

You may wonder why we have such protective laws for limited partnerships and limited liability companies. The charging order law, which can be traced back to the English Partnership Act of 1890, is aimed at achieving a particular public policy objective—that business activities of a partnership should not be disrupted because of nonpartnership-related debts of one or more of the partners. The justification? Because nondebtor partners and the partnership were not at fault, the entire partnership should not suffer. United States law adopted this policy over the past hundred years, culminating in the charging order law of the Uniform acts.

Two tactics for maximizing FLP/LLC protection

You now understand the basic strategy for using FLPs/LLCs—put your assets into the FLP/LLC so they will be protected from your personal creditors. This is basic *outside* asset protection. Assets *inside* the FLP/LLC are protected against outside threats to you. Beyond this, consider these two basic rules:

1. *Don't put all your eggs in one basket.* If any asset within a single FLP/LLC causes a lawsuit, all assets owned by that FLP/LLC are vulnerable. By using multiple FLP/LLC "baskets," you will better protect each of your eggs. This also makes it more difficult for any creditor to come after your entire wealth. Practically speaking, they must conduct more investigation, file more motions with the court, and perhaps even travel to different states. The more entities used, the more difficult it will be for your creditors to attack your wealth. The result? Creditors negotiate more favorable settlements.

2. *Segregate the dangerous eggs from the safe ones.* This increases your inside asset protection. Whereas outside protection focuses on shielding your wealth from claims against you, inside protection concerns shielding your total wealth from liability created by one of your own assets. As we explained in the beginning of the chapter, dangerous assets should be owned by an LLC rather than by an FLP because LLCs give better inside protection. Continuing with this logic, it

makes sense to isolate the dangerous assets from the safe ones, keeping them apart in separate LLCs. We'll see this in the Gump case study.

CASE STUDY: PUTTING IT TOGETHER

Harry Gump, a 53-year-old co-owner of a retail company, and his wife Wilma, a day school teacher, have two teenaged children and the following assets:

Safe Assets

Asset	Equity
Home	$550,000
Cash	50,000
Mutual funds	550,000
Interest in business	600,000
Antiques	20,000
Total safe equity	$1,770,000

Dangerous Assets

Rental condo #1	$275,000
Rental condo #2	255,000
Cars	20,000
Powerboat	30,000
Total dangerous equity	$580,000
TOTAL EQUITY	**$2,350,000**

To provide the Gumps with maximum financial security using FLPs/LLCs, we use between two and four entities/tools. Let us examine each.

Tool #1: Gump Safe Asset FLP

Owns: Cash, mutual funds, business interest, and antiques. Total value: $1,220,000.

Interests: Mr. and Mrs. Gump—2% as general partners.
Mr. and Mrs. Gump—96% as limited partners.
Each child—1% limited partner.

Strategy: The family home is not included because of the special tax consequences noted later (see Chapter 33). By isolating safe assets from dangerous assets, we ensure their security. Furthermore, because Mr. and Mrs. Gump are general partners, they have 100 percent control of the FLP and all FLP assets. They are more comfortable with this ownership arrangement.

Result: All $1,220,000 is now safe from creditors or lawsuits. The Gumps may decide to gift more to the children for estate and income tax reduction. (See Chapters 11 and 56.)

Tool #2: Gump Dangerous Asset LLC

Owns: Condo #1 and Condo #2.
                  Total value: $530,000.
Interests: Mr. Gump—50% owner as managing member.
                  Mrs. Gump—50% owner as managing member.

Strategy: These assets are dangerous because of the likelihood of lawsuits from tenants, guests, or neighbors. Although one LLC owned both condominiums, a strong argument can be made to set up separate LLCs for each condo.

Result: Any lawsuit arising from the condos is isolated to the condos. All other wealth is shielded.

Tool #3: Gump Dangerous Asset LLC 2

Owns: Cars and the powerboat.
                  Total value: $50,000.
Interests: Mr. Gump—50% owner as managing member.
                  Mrs. Gump—50% owner as managing member.

Strategy: These assets are extremely dangerous, especially because the children drive both cars and the boat regularly. With an LLC, we protect the Gump's personal wealth from liability caused by the cars or boat. Yet Mr. and Mrs. Gump still completely control the boat and cars.

Result: All other wealth is shielded from lawsuits arising from car and powerboat ownership. Also, Mr. and Mrs. Gump achieve personal protection through the LLC.

Without the FLPs and the LLCs, the Gump family had assets worth over $2.3 million exposed to lawsuits. Now, Mr. Gump has shielded over 75 percent of that wealth, and we haven't even addressed the home yet. Furthermore, they have the tools now to reduce income taxes and perhaps even to eliminate estate taxes. And they have relinquished no control of any of their assets in the process.

LAST WORD

FLPs and LLCs are the two most utilized and most powerful asset protection tools we use. Chapters 11 and 56 explain how FLPs and LLCs also can reduce income and estate taxes.

CHAPTER THIRTY

USING TRUSTS TO SHIELD WEALTH: FLEXIBLE TOOLS FOR EXCELLENT ASSET PROTECTION

A trust is a legal entity. This chapter explains how a trust works and the asset protection role that a trust can play in your Wealth Protection plan. A number of different trusts used in asset protection planning are covered, each with its own place and use in specific situations.

DEFINITIONS

1. *Trust:* The trust is essentially a legal arrangement by which one person, the *trustee*, holds property for the benefit of another, the *beneficiary*.

A trust is created by a trust document that specifies that the trustee holds property owned by the trust for the benefit of the beneficiary of the trust. The trust document also establishes the terms of how the trust should be administered and how the trust assets should be distributed during the lifetime of the trust as well as after the trust is terminated.

2. *Grantor:* The grantor is the person who sets up the trust, usually the person who transfers property into the trust. The grantor is also called the *trustor* or *settlor*.

3. *Trustee:* The trustee is the legal owner of the trust property. The trustee is responsible for administering and carrying out the terms of the trust. The trustee owes a fiduciary duty to the beneficiaries—an utmost duty of care that he or she will follow the terms of the trust document and manage the trust property as the document specifies. A trustee may be a person, such as a family member or a trusted friend, or an institution, such as a professional trust company or a trust department of a bank. When there is more than one trustee, they are called *co-trustees.*

The trustee, as the legal owner of any assets owned by the trust, has "legal title" to the assets owned by the trust. For example, assume that Dad wants to set up a trust for his children, Son and Daughter. Dad wants his brother, Uncle, to serve as trustee. If Dad transfers his house into the trust, the title to that house will be with "Uncle, as trustee of the Dad trust."

4. *Beneficiary:* The beneficiary (or beneficiaries) is the person for whom the trust was set up. Although the trustee has legal title to assets owned by the trust, the beneficiary has *equitable title,* or the rights, to the trust property. The beneficiary can sue the trustee if the trustee mismanages the trust property or disobeys specific instructions in the trust.

The beneficiary may be the same person as the grantor and can possibly be the same person as the trustee. For asset protection purposes, the trustee, the beneficiary, and the grantor cannot all be the same person.

5. *Funding:* Funding the trust means transferring assets to the trust. A trust that is "unfunded" has no property transferred to it. It is completely ineffective. As with any other legal entity/asset protection tool, you must title assets to the trust if you want trust protection.

To title real estate to the trust, you must execute and record a deed to the property to the trust. Bank and brokerage accounts can be transferred by simply changing the name on the accounts. Registered stocks and bonds are changed by notifying the transfer agent or issuing company and requesting that the certificates be reissued to the trust. Other assets, such as household items, furniture, jewelry, and artwork, are transferred by a simple legal document called an *assignment* or *bill of sale.* Your asset protection attorney can draft such a document.

TRUST CLASSIFICATIONS

Trusts follow these four classifications:

1. *Revocable:* A revocable trust is one that you, the grantor, can revoke and undo at any time.
2. *Irrevocable:* An irrevocable trust is one that you cannot revoke or undo once established.
3. *Inter vivos:* An inter vivos trust takes effect during your lifetime.
4. *Testamentary:* A testamentary trust takes effect at your death. Testamentary trusts are usually created in wills, living trusts, or other documents taking effect at death. All testamentary trusts are irrevocable.

LIVING TRUSTS: ILLUSORY ASSET PROTECTION

Living trusts are excellent devices for avoiding probate. They also effectively sidestep the hidden dangers of joint tenancy. However, *living trusts provide no asset protection!*

REVOCABLE TRUSTS DO NOT PROTECT ASSETS

Living trusts provide absolutely no asset protection because they are revocable. As a revocable trust, the grantor of the living trust can undo the trust at any time during her or his lifetime. This is a great benefit of the living trust for probate avoidance and estate planning purposes. You, the grantor, can change the trust whenever you wish to change who receives your savings when you die. This greatly comforts those setting up living trusts—to know that they can change their living trust at any time, just as they could a will. However, while revocability is good for estate planning goals, it renders a trust useless for asset protection. Remember this simple rule: *Revocable trusts are vulnerable trusts!*

CREDITORS CAN STEP INTO YOUR SHOES AND REVOKE THE TRUST

Revocable trusts are useless for asset protection because revocable trusts allow the grantor to undo the trust. If the grantor's creditors want to seize assets owned by a revocable trust, they simply need to petition the court to "step into the shoes" of the grantor. If you have a living trust or any other revocable trust to shield assets from creditors, your creditors can easily ask the court to step into your shoes and revoke the trust themselves. The trust's assets will no longer be owned by the trust but by you personally. The creditors then have all the rights and privileges to seize these assets, now owned by you.

OTHER BENEFITS OF LIVING TRUSTS

Despite its weakness for asset protection planning, the living trust is still commonly used in asset protection plans. It is the ideal way to own FLP interests, LLC membership interests, or other interests in entities that will provide protection.

With these legal entities owned by your living trusts, rather than by you, you will save estate taxes and expensive probate fees later on. You get the best of both worlds: protecting your assets while alive and saving your family estate taxes and probate fees when you die. (For more about using living trusts, see Chapter 52.)

IRREVOCABLE TRUSTS: THE ASSET PROTECTORS

Whereas revocable trusts offer no asset protection, *irrevocable* trusts are important for asset protection. Once you establish an irrevocable trust, you forever abandon the ability to undo the trust and to reclaim property transferred to the trust. With an irrevocable trust, you lose both control of the trust assets and ownership.

Of course, this discussion assumes that in transferring assets to any irrevocable trust, you do not run afoul of fraudulent transfer laws.

We introduced the concept of these laws in the introduction to this part. (For more on fraudulent transfer laws, see Appendix 2.)

WHY IRREVOCABLE TRUSTS PROTECT YOUR ASSETS

Irrevocable trusts protect assets for the same reason that revocable trusts do not. Revocable living trusts do not provide asset protection because creditors can step into your shoes with such a trust. Assets owned by a revocable living trust are vulnerable to lawsuits and creditors.

The opposite is true of an irrevocable trust. Because an established irrevocable trust cannot be altered or undone, your creditors cannot step into your shoes and undo the trust, any more than you can. Assets in an irrevocable trust are immune from creditor attack, lawsuits, and other threats. An irrevocable trust carries a heavy price— you give up control and ownership of the asset to gain protection.

When does this severe price make sense? It should be considered when you would inevitably gift the assets to the beneficiaries and do not foresee needing the assets for your own financial security. When both factors are satisfied, your "price" is not particularly heavy. You do not personally need the assets and the trust will accomplish what you would do yourself—distribute the assets to your beneficiaries (usually children) at some future time.

THREE PITFALLS TO AVOID WITH IRREVOCABLE TRUSTS

Keep these considerations in mind:

1. You cannot reserve any power to revoke, rescind, or amend the trust or retain any rights, either directly or indirectly, to reclaim property transferred to the trust. Simply, there can be no strings attached.

2. Gifts to trusts are given the most scrutiny under fraudulent transfer laws—because there is no "for value" exchange as there is with LLCs or FLPs. Often, for asset protection purposes, these tools are superior. (Again, for more on fraudulent transfers, see Appendix 2.)

3. You, as the trust's grantor, cannot be its trustee. Nor can you appoint a trustee not considered at arm's length. Those who do not qualify for "arm's length" include your spouse, any close relative, or even a close personal friend. Courts closely examine the relationship between the grantor and the trustee to determine whether the trustee is only the grantor's "alter ego." If there is such a relationship, courts will ignore the trust and allow creditors to reach the trust assets.

> *Tip:* A corporate trustee, such as a bank or a trust company, is much less likely to be judged as an alter ego, thereby giving your trust an added layer of security.

THREE CLAUSES YOUR IRREVOCABLE TRUST SHOULD HAVE

For an irrevocable trust intended for rock-solid protection, you must include three significant clauses. These clauses are important not necessarily to protect you, the trust creator, but to shield your beneficiaries from their creditors.

1. *Spendthrift Clause.* The spendthrift clause allows the trustee to withhold income and principal, which would ordinarily be paid to the beneficiary, if the trustee feels the money could or would be wasted or seized by the beneficiary's creditors. This clause accomplishes two goals: (1) It prevents a wasteful beneficiary from spending trust funds or wasting trust assets. This is especially important to many grantors who set up trusts with their children as beneficiaries. If you worry that money in trust for your children would be wasted if not controlled, then use a spendthrift clause. The trustee can then stop payments if your child spends too quickly or unwisely. (2) It protects trust assets from creditors of the beneficiaries. Beneficiaries may now be young, but as adults they will face the same risks we all face: lawsuits, debt problems, divorce, a failing business, and so on. The spendthrift clause protects trust assets from your children's creditors by granting the trustee the authority to withhold payments to a beneficiary who has an outstanding creditor. If the beneficiary and the trustee are at arm's length, the creditor has no power to force the trustee to pay the beneficiary. The creditor only has a right to payments actually paid by the trustee. The creditor cannot force the trustee to make disbursements.

2. *Anti-alienation Clause.* The anti-alienation clause also protects trust assets from the beneficiary's creditors. Whereas the spendthrift clause allows the trustee to withhold payments if a creditor lurks, the anti-alienation clause goes one step further—it prohibits the trustee from paying trust income or principal to anyone but the named beneficiaries, which, of course, includes creditors of the trust beneficiary.

3. *Generation-Skipping Language.* While not technically an asset protection item, this language is crucial if the goal of the trust is to provide benefits to more than two generations. Because the IRS imposes a harsh generation-skipping tax in addition to the estate tax on gifts to grandchildren (or younger generations), this language is necessary to minimize those taxes and to make full use of the special exemption value for that tax. (For more on generation-skipping taxes and "dynasty trusts" that deal with them, visit our web site at www.mywealthprotection.com.)

CASE STUDY: JERRY AND HIS KIDS

Jerry, an investment banker, had a sizable investment portfolio, including $200,000 in mutual funds that he planned on leaving to his two children, Steve and Stephanie. Jerry knew that he and his wife could live quite comfortably without these mutual funds, and he wanted to save estate taxes and to provide security to his children. Jerry, however, was concerned that his kids would unwisely spend the funds.

We established an irrevocable trust for Jerry and named his local bank trust department as trustee. Jerry told the trust officer about his concerns for the funds. Jerry's wishes were incorporated into the trust document.

Although Steve and Stephanie were only 12 years old at the time, Jerry and his wife funded the trust with $20,000 worth of mutual fund interests each year, making the gifts to the trust completely tax free. The trust was made irrevocable so if Jerry or his wife were sued, their creditors could not seize these funds. The trust also had anti-alien-

(continued)

ation and spendthrift clauses so the funds would be protected from his children's possible poor spending habits as well as from their potential future creditors.

Jerry realized that the trust would eventually be substantial in value. He also recognized the possibility that his children will someday have creditor or divorce problems. With this irrevocable trust, Jerry protected these funds from his creditors, gifted them tax free to the trust, provided for his children's future (which he intended to do through his will or living trust), and did so in a way that fully protects the funds from his children's creditors as well.

FIVE STRATEGIES TO CREATE AN IRONCLAD IRREVOCABLE TRUST

You can greatly increase the asset protection for your irrevocable trust by using these five tactics:

1. *Fund the trust early.* As with any asset protection strategy, avoid fraudulent transfers. Set up the trust and fund it before a lawsuit arises. Thus, you ensure that your trust cannot be undone by a creditor crying "fraudulent transfer."

2. *Use an independent trustee.* Don't be the trustee of your own trust. The best trustees are completely independent: a bank or a professional, such as an attorney or an accountant. Less desirable are close family friends.

3. *State a nonprotection purpose for the trust.* It is usually desirable to state a nonprotection reason in the trust document. Courts are less likely to set aside a legal entity, such as a trust, established for estate planning purposes or to provide support for a family member. Often, we write this nonprotection purpose in the trust Preamble.

4. *The beneficiary should not be the grantor.* If the beneficiary is the grantor, courts will likely disregard the trust and allow the grantor's creditors to seize the trust assets.

5. *Keep accurate records.* Operate the trust in a businesslike way. Keep accurate records of all transfers to the trust, as well as disbursements of income and principal to beneficiaries. This is another benefit of a corporate trustee. They keep accurate records.

CHAPTER THIRTY-ONE

USING OFFSHORE PLANNING TO PROTECT ASSETS

W hether you were directed to this chapter or to the asset protection chapters in general, you have a need to shield your
wealth from potential claims and lawsuits. This chapter and the next
are extremely important parts of any Wealth Protection asset protection plan, if only for the reason that the leading work in the field of
asset protection for the past decade has been offshore planning.
You'll learn what to do (and what to avoid) in offshore planning and
about specific tools you can utilize in your plan.

OFFSHORE PLANNING: A WORLDWIDE PHENOMENON

Using foreign jurisdictions to protect wealth has been a popular strategy for estate and family-wealth planning since the early Roman days
when emperors attempted to preserve their riches for their descendants. Nevertheless, offshore planning has never been as popular as
it is today. For tens of thousands of Americans each year, offshore
structures become part of their Wealth Protection plan. There are
tremendous benefits to be gained by using opportunities outside of
the 50 states, provided you make sure you use the appropriate
strategies.

There is over *5 trillion* U.S. dollars in foreign vehicles. Most of this
wealth is held in offshore financial centers, such as the Bahamas,

Bermuda, the British Virgin Islands, the Cayman Islands, the Cook Islands, the Isle of Mann, Jersey and Guernsey, Luxembourg, Nevis, Switzerland, and Turks and Caicos. Because they have favorable tax, banking, privacy, estate planning, and asset protection laws, these offshore havens are extremely desirable countries in which to set up a trust or other structure.

Wealthy individuals and families from around the world have established legal entities in these countries for decades. In fact, for much of the world, the United States is an "offshore financial center" itself, with numerous tax benefits offered to foreigners who want to invest here. Nonetheless, only in the past 10 years have middle-income professionals, entrepreneurs, and other savvy U.S. citizens started taking advantage of offshore planning.

THE THREE REASONS AMERICANS GO OFFSHORE

1. *Asset protection.* This is the goal on which we will focus in this chapter. Many Americans (and potential clients of ours) may initially indicate that they want to put some of their wealth offshore for "privacy" concerns. While there certainly are some high-profile clients who do hold this as a true objective, we have found that these clients almost always use the word *privacy* to mean either asset protection or tax planning. Thus, we will not address privacy concerns separately here.

2. *Tax planning.* A common—and extremely dangerous—misconception about offshore planning is that simply by going offshore, you can avoid paying U.S. taxes. This is dead wrong. Americans are liable for income taxes on income, wherever earned. The vast majority of solid offshore asset protection plans are tax neutral, although there may be significant tax advantages by captive insurance companies or foreign life insurance and annuities.

3. *Investing.* Consider that the U.S. market now represents a minority of the world's capital market (contrasted with over 60 percent around 1960) and that market share is declining. This means that if you only invest in the United States, you are missing out on the majority of the world's investment opportunities. You are also making a 100 percent bet on the stability of the U.S. currency, which presently

is excellent but, like all currencies, historically has its ups and downs.

Because the Securities and Exchange Commission (SEC) makes it almost impossible for foreign companies to sell their stock in the United States, many clients use an offshore entity to purchase foreign securities. In this way, the other two-thirds of the world's investments become available.

DUAL THREATS TO YOUR OFFSHORE PLAN: THE DEVIL WITHIN AND THE DEVIL WITHOUT

In every case where a client fails to "do it right" offshore, there are almost always one of two common culprits to be found: (1) the client's greed (the devil within) and (2) an inept or ethically challenged advisor (the devil without).

As you might imagine, we have seen many people go offshore for the wrong reasons and get burned in the process. Often, they are so anxious to avoid taxes, to shield assets improperly, or to get rich that their reasonable judgment is clouded . . . and they engage in planning that they would never use here in the United States. Combine these desires with the virtually unregulated areas offshore (i.e., no reporting to the IRS, no SEC or NASD disclosure requirements, no state attorneys general remedying fraud, etc.), and the potential for abuse is apparent. Let's see how most clients get in trouble.

THE DEVIL WITHIN: WHY GREED IS BAD

1. *Desire to "hide" money to protect it—will not work without perjury.* As explained in this section, asset protection can be achieved in the United States through the use of legal entities such as limited partnerships (FLPs), trusts, and limited liability companies (LLCs). The source of the asset protection qualities of these entities is the way the law treats them in terms of ownership, control, and the rights of creditors.

Offshore entities have many of those same asset protection vehicles—most common are the LLC and the trust. Thus, the "right" way to protect assets offshore is to use the same structures and strategies one would use in the United States. However, using offshore planning adds the difficulty of having those entities located in foreign nations, where U.S. attorneys are unfamiliar with the local laws.

Unfortunately, while creating legitimate offshore asset protection plans is not difficult for experienced advisors, many Americans forgo such planning and try to hide wealth in these offshore centers. Rather than use an entity like an LLC, they simply set up a bank or brokerage account in countries where there is little, if any, reporting.

The problem with this "no entity" approach is that in any litigation—civil lawsuit, divorce, or even governmental case—there will eventually be some type of formal inquiry of assets. The inquiry might be a "debtor's exam" after a successful lawsuit, a bankruptcy filing, a list of assets for a divorce settlement, and so on. For the "no entity" approach to work, the client would have to omit the offshore assets or lie about their existence. This amounts to perjury, bankruptcy fraud, or obstruction of justice, depending on the forum of the case. You do not want to go down that road.

2. *Desire to avoid U.S. taxes offshore—leads to tax evasion.* Americans are liable for taxes on all income earned offshore. However, it is true that many offshore banks, mutual funds, and other financial institutions will not report earnings/interest to the IRS. This is the chasm where many greedy clients—or unscrupulous advisors—operate. This is also where tax evasion—a federal crime—is sometimes committed.

Although the client is required under U.S. law to make the necessary tax reporting on income earned offshore (and his or her advisors should instruct the client to do so), many clients will keep quiet, in the hope that they are never caught. This "hide the ball" strategy is used not only by knowing clients but also by shady advisors, who concoct ever more sophisticated schemes—moving money from one trust to another company to a third foundation and on and on.

Although an advisor's pitch may seem complex and impressive, you can always ask him or her the following question: If the income will eventually accrue to my benefit, how come I don't have to report it to the IRS? Unless a licensed U.S. advisor will go on the record (i.e., write an opinion letter) as to the tax treatment of a particular entity, steer clear, unless you want the cloud of a possible tax evasion indictment hanging over you for years to come.

3. *Desire to get rich offshore—leads to scams and frauds.* The type of greediness that leads clients into problems is most pervasive in the investment arena. Here, scam artists and fraudsters abound, poised to take advantage of the next client who wants to "get rich offshore."

Here are just a few of the numerous scams and frauds that we and our fellow advisors have seen attract clients over the years. (For an updated list of common traps in the world of offshore, see our web site at www.mywealthprotection.com.)

- *Offshore personal/private banks.* Often marketed with phrases like, "Open your own offshore private bank, and millions will start to walk into your life instantly!" In reality, you will see a six-figure legal and accounting nightmare walk into your life instantly.

- *Self-liquidating loans.* Borrow $500 million on Monday, and live on E-Z Street on Tuesday. Here, as you attempt to get nine-figure loans, the hucksters make a few thousand dollars and you get nothing.

- *Nigerian scam (a.k.a. 4-1-9 scam).* Marketing hook: If you help some wealthy Nigerians get $40 million out of their country, you will get a $12 million commission. Don't spend the money just yet . . . because it never arrives. However, there will be various costs along the way, which, of course, you will never recoup.

- *World Bank, or "leveraged" risk-free investment, scheme.* Banks identify inefficiencies in the currency exchanges across the country. They simultaneously buy and sell currencies so there is no risk to you! They can make a little here and a little there. Because your investment allows the bank to lend out four to five times as much money as they could otherwise, you get four to five times that "little bit here and there." Some investors have been convinced that they are getting 5 percent to 15 percent *per month.* We get this one all the time. This is impossible. We generally have to ask two questions of the poor victims who insist that they are getting great returns and that they have found the goose that lays the golden eggs. (1) How are the arbitrage departments of the world's largest investment banks, with dozens if not hundreds of employees in countries around the world, lucky to see 5 percent to 7 percent returns annually,

yet you found a bank that can get more than that monthly? (2)
If banks had found such a gold mine, would they market it to
small clients or to institutions with hundreds of millions to
invest?

THE DEVIL WITHOUT: WHY
YOUR ADVISOR MAY BE YOUR
WORST ENEMY

As common as the situation where a client's own motivations get him
or her in trouble is the scenario where a client with good intentions
is "up the creek" because of his or her advisors. Creating a viable
offshore plan requires expertise in such areas as international and
domestic taxation, conflicts of laws, asset protection, the law of corporations and partnerships, and estate planning. The bottom line?
While there are thousands of advisors in the United States holding
themselves as experts on offshore planning, probably only 1 in 50 is
truly knowledgeable and experienced.

What are the most common errors advisors make in offshore
planning? There are two that are always at the top of the list.

THE ADVISOR IS NOT EXPERIENCED IN
OFFSHORE, SO CLIENTS GET CAUGHT
IN SCAMS

A top offshore advisor should have experience in dealing with offshore havens and should have contacts in many of them. The advisor should keep abreast of up-to-the-minute developments in the
field, which, for those in the field, is not difficult through informal
professional contacts—not to mention professional journals and web
sites.

Furthermore, advisors should have existing relationships with top
fiduciary firms in the country where their structures are established,
including trust company or bank officers, insurance managers, actuaries, money managers, attorneys, and accountants. These contacts
can buttress the advisor's analysis of any offshore opportunities.

Advisors who are new to the field or who have not put in the years of due diligence required to be competent in offshore will not have these contacts and resources. Thus, when faced with tough judgment calls regarding whether to use a particular trustee firm or local accountant or trust investment, they cannot accurately evaluate the risks and rewards. Too often, these advisors put clients in structures or investments that a more resourceful advisor would have avoided. Inexperienced attorneys or CPAs (certified public accountants) may not even be aware of the popular scams. Unfortunately, the clients end up paying for the advisors' lack of knowledge.

THE ADVISOR IS NOT AN EXPERT IN INTERNATIONAL TAXATION

If you go offshore, you will need to use an attorney or a CPA who is an expert in international taxation. If your advisor does not have this specific knowledge, you risk tax fraud.

This is the most common failing of otherwise competent attorneys involved in offshore. They simply don't know all of the rules regarding U.S. taxpayers with investments and structures abroad. They may know most, but unless they are familiar with all, clients will pay a hefty price—either tax penalties for not reporting correctly or (like the case study of Michael, on the following page) paying too high a tax rate because of a lack of tax planning.

We frequently see this price paid by clients who have used another advisor and created an offshore structure that purchased offshore mutual funds. Often, these are very stable, recommended mutual funds from large European financial institutions, so there is no scam risk there. Nonetheless, in 99 percent of the cases, the client is looking at a tax nightmare—paying income taxes at effective rates of between 46 percent to 84 percent, depending on how long the client holds the investments! Investment returns become almost irrelevant when tax rates are this high.

Not too many advisors have heard of the PFIC QEF rules regarding the taxation of foreign mutual funds. These rules allow investors in "Passive Foreign Investment Company Qualifying Elective Funds" to use U.S. income tax rates on their income from the fund, including the most favorable long-term capital gains rates. Essentially, these rules require the fund companies to keep their books like U.S. fund companies do so that the U.S. investor receives the necessary data to compare with a 1099 from a U.S. mutual fund company. Less than 1 percent of offshore funds qualify under these rules, so many clients end up paying taxes under the complex excess distribution rules, which impose extremely high taxes, depending on the length of time the investor holds the asset (46 percent for a 4-year holding period to 84 percent for a 15-year holding period). This awful tax typically is taken for no reason other than the incompetence of the advisor. In fact, we have called more than one very reputable U.S. mutual fund family to discuss their offshore mutual funds, and the advisors with whom we spoke had never heard of the PFIC QEF issue. In fact, one of the advisors even told us that the clients won't have to pay taxes if they invest in the advisor's mutual funds. This could be disastrous for the client, and this came from one of the premium mutual fund companies in the world!

CASE STUDY: MICHAEL'S LAWYER GETS IN TROUBLE

Michael is a successful bond trader who was interested in shielding some of his liquid wealth from future lawsuits. He looked around locally for an attorney who might be able to help him, but he didn't find one who seemed to have experience in offshore planning. Eventually, he spoke to a colleague who had received an invitation to a seminar on offshore put on by a law firm. Michael attended the seminar, which was focused solely on asset protection. Soon after the seminar, Michael retained the firm to set up an offshore trust.

This law firm actually did a commendable job in creating the trust structure and making sure that Michael funded the trust, which he did with $500,000. However, when Michael asked what the trust should invest in, their only warning was that the funds remain offshore for asset protection purposes. They had a number of brochures from mutual fund companies in the jurisdiction where the trust was established, the Cook Islands.

Michael ended up researching the various funds for performance and for the size and stability of the company. However, he did not know the right questions to ask regarding the taxation of the funds under U.S. law; nor did his attorneys give him the questions to ask.

Two years later, Michael was audited. While the trust itself had made the proper filings (handled by the law firm), the gains from the funds were not reported in their proper form. Michael's trust (for which he had liability) was hit with back taxes, penalties, and fees of over $200,000. Michael felt cheated. He had only tried to do the right thing, but he had never been properly advised.

CHAPTER THIRTY-TWO

◆

OFFSHORE LLCS AND TRUSTS: THE DYNAMIC DUO OF OFFSHORE PLANNING

By using offshore planning as part of your Wealth Protection plan, you will have the most powerful asset protection tools at your disposal. In this chapter, we continue concentrating our discussion on two effective offshore tools: (1) the offshore limited liability company (LLC) and (2) the offshore trust (OT).

Of course, the following discussion assumes that in transferring assets to any offshore entity, you do not run afoul of fraudulent transfer laws. (We introduced the concept of these laws in Chapter 25. For more on fraudulent transfer laws, see Appendix 2.)

NEVIS: AN IMPORTANT JURISDICTION FOR LIMITED LIABILITY COMPANIES

When Nevis, a small Caribbean nation, part of a federation with St. Kitts, began to compete for the multibillion-dollar asset protection business earlier in the 1990s, it revised its trust and business entity laws. As part of this process, the lawmakers studied U.S. LLC statutes and improved on them, in terms of providing asset protection for U.S. citizens. Today, Nevis has the oldest and most stable LLC legislation outside of the United States, specifically modeled on the well-drafted Delaware legislation. The result is a superior asset protection tool used by many attorneys specializing in the field for years—the Nevis LLC.

THE NEVIS LIMITED LIABILITY COMPANY

As we explained in Chapter 29, domestic LLCs (those in the United States) protect your assets because your creditor can only obtain a "charging order" against your LLC interest after a successful lawsuit. This charging order entitles the creditor only to your share of any distributions actually made from the LLC (which you, as the manager of the LLC, control). The charging order does not allow the creditor to seize your interest in the LLC or to vote your interest. In this way, the assets within the LLC are shielded. Only when you decide to make distributions does the creditor get anything of value.

Paralleling the Delaware LLC law, the Nevis LLC has these same charging order protections drafted in its legislation. However, it adds a number of significant benefits that the domestic LLCs do not afford—the deterrence factors of Nevis law:

- *No contingency-fee attorneys—local attorneys only.* This means that any creditor attacking transfers to a Nevis entity (LLC or trust) must hire another lawyer in that country.
- *Bond required.* Nevis requires a bond to be posted by the party filing a lawsuit because the loser pays the winner's legal fees. This is the "British Rule." The bond is often required to cover tens of thousands of dollars for legal fees, making the prospect of suing even more expensive.
- *Tough burden of proof.* In many countries, as in Nevis, a plaintiff must prove that you fraudulently transferred assets beyond a reasonable doubt—an extremely difficult standard. In the U.S. legal system, this standard is only for criminal cases. In certain havens, however, any civil suit to get at your entity's assets may have to satisfy this difficult burden of proof.
- *Favorable statute of limitations period.* The *statute of limitations* is the time period within which a lawsuit must be brought. When the time expires, the lawsuit will not be allowed. In certain asset protection offshore havens, lawsuits against the entity must be commenced

in the haven's courts within two years after the legal right to sue arose, which, for many types of claims, is a much shorter time period than in the United States.

In this way, like all offshore tools, the Nevis LLC acts as a powerful litigation deterrent because most plaintiffs and their lawyers do not know how to approach getting to assets owned by foreign structures. Thus, in most cases, just by disclosing how the Nevis LLC protects a client's assets, we can deter a possible lawsuit or settle an outstanding claim. This works in the vast majority of cases, making the Nevis LLC more attractive than its U.S. counterparts.

Nonetheless, if a persistent creditor wants to attack the Nevis LLC, he might ask a U.S. court to dissolve the structure or to order assets back. However, because this entity is an LLC, with charging order protections like those in the United States, the courts do not have the same difficulties in evaluating foreign LLCs as they have with offshore trusts. Where offshore trusts take advantage of another country's laws that *differ* from those of the United States, the Nevis LLC laws were drafted to *replicate* U.S. laws. Clients with foreign LLCs are taking advantage of the same statutes as those in the states—an important factor in having U.S. courts respect such entities.

If a creditor cannot attack the Nevis LLC in the United States, she could attempt to do so in Nevis. To do this, Nevis procedural laws require that she must begin a new lawsuit on the underlying claim (e.g., malpractice), post a bond of at least $25,000, and hire a Nevis lawyer by the hour (another reason why Nevis LLCs deter lawsuits— U.S. attorneys would rather settle the case or drop it than face the prospect of losing the case to a foreign lawyer).

Suing in Nevis is a time-consuming, expensive, and unfamiliar process. It is not surprising, therefore, that we have yet to see a creditor make such a successful attack.

OTHER BENEFITS OF THE NEVIS LIMITED LIABILITY COMPANY

• *Tax neutral.* The Nevis LLC is tax neutral, like a domestic LLC. In terms of estate planning, the LLC can be used as part of a gifting program to move value out of a couple's estate by moving ownership units to children. This can be accomplished while the clients (parents) maintain 100 percent control.

- *Easy and inexpensive to maintain.* Unlike a foreign trust, a Nevis LLC has minimal tax-reporting requirements. Moreover, there are no conditions to keep minute books, to hold annual director or member meetings, or to observe other customary corporate formalities. Costs for maintaining the entity are around $500 per year.

CASE STUDY: "PROTECTED HOWARD" SETTLES CLAIMS FOR PENNIES

Howard, a geology consultant, is well respected in his scientific community. Although he had never been sued before, Howard recently learned that one of his colleagues has lost a judgment for $1 million over coverage limits. This was the result of the colleague's advice on a structure that was heavily damaged in an earthquake. Howard quickly decided to engage in asset protection planning.

Howard set up a Wealth Protection plan, part of which involved transferring his nonpension liquid assets to a Nevis LLC. The LLC then established a bank account, through which he then purchased a high-grade, tax-deferred variable annuity from a multibillion-dollar Swiss insurance company.

If Howard is ever threatened with a lawsuit, he won't be worried about losing what he has already earned. Instead, Howard now feels secure, knowing that his most important assets are safe from all creditors and that he is no longer at the mercy of the lawsuit and the legal system.

OFFSHORE TRUSTS: THE CLASSIC OFFSHORE TOOL

Many U.S. asset protection experts are using Nevis LLCs in place of offshore trusts, but there are still instances when the offshore trust (OT) may be preferable.

OWNING FOREIGN INSURANCE POLICIES

One of the leading offshore Wealth Protection strategies today is to have a client purchase a permanent (cash value) life insurance policy offshore. In terms of tax planning, if the policy is U.S. tax compliant, then all of the growth within the policy will accumulate tax free. Furthermore, the proceeds will pay out to the beneficiary income tax free, and the client can take loans against the accumulated cash values during his or her life tax free. This is similar to the benefits of a domestic cash value life insurance policy, which you can read more about in Part 3.

As in the United States, we would typically advise a client purchasing such a policy to do it through an irrevocable life insurance trust (ILIT), so that the proceeds of the policy pay out free of estate taxes and of income taxes. When dealing with a foreign insurance policy, we would use an OT to act as the ILIT. Often, the foreign insurers must sell their policy to some non–U.S. entity, even if that entity is completely disclosed and compliant with U.S. law. In this situation, we use an OT to purchase the policy and to act as a "foreign ILIT."

Why would a client want to use an offshore policy, rather than a domestic policy? Aside from the obvious asset protection benefit of having the asset offshore, one reason is that the cost of a foreign policy is typically much lower than a policy from U.S. companies. Furthermore, the client can enjoy the financial stability of the United States, by having the foreign insurance company use U.S.-based money managers to grow the cash in the policy and to reinsure the death benefit. In this way, the client gets the lower cost and the asset protection value of the offshore life insurance with the financial stability of U.S.-based financial institutions. It is not surprising that foreign life insurance is one of offshore's fastest growing segments.

MULTIGENERATIONAL PLANNING

Let's say your Wealth Protection goal is to create a nest egg for future generations—grandchildren and beyond. And let's say it was important to you that the nest egg be asset protected in an ironclad way. In this circumstance, an offshore trust would be an ideal tool for you, especially in countries where the law does not limit the duration of trusts under the "law against perpetuities," which is found in many of the states. By using an OT, you could literally ensure that your family enjoyed the fruits of your gift for hundreds of years, as long as other estate-planning tax issues were addressed.

LAST WORD

As with any area of Wealth Protection planning, using an expert advisor experienced in these matters is paramount. Nowhere is this more true than with offshore planning.

CHAPTER THIRTY-THREE

How to Protect Your Home: Turning Your Castle into a Lawsuit-Proof Fortress

Along with retirement accounts, your home is probably your most valuable asset. Even beyond its pure financial value, your home has large psychic value as well. In fact, we find that most of our clients who engage in asset protection planning often begin with the question: "How can I protect my home?" After all, what part of your Financial Fortress could be more important than your personal fortress?

In this chapter, we will cover the three leading methods of shielding your home from potential lawsuits. Each has its benefits and drawbacks. These three options are:

1. Using state homestead laws.
2. Owning your home in an LLC.
3. Using "friendly mortgages."

USING STATE HOMESTEAD LAWS TO SHIELD YOUR HOME

You may have already thought you knew about the laws that protect your home. Perhaps you have previously heard the term *homestead,*

186

and assumed that you could never lose your home to bad debts or other liabilities because of homestead protection. You would be wrong. Homestead laws are hot and cold—some give you total protection, while others are no shield whatsoever. Let's see why.

WHAT ARE HOMESTEAD LAWS?

Homestead laws are state laws that protect the home from certain creditors. Forty-five states have these laws. Each state declares a certain amount of equity (value) of the homestead to be protected against particular types of creditors. To understand whether these laws protect you, it is necessary to understand what the term "homestead" means.

WHAT IS A HOMESTEAD?

Defining *homestead* can be very tricky because not everything you might consider to be a "home" qualifies for homestead status. The homestead exemption only applies to real estate that serves as your primary residence and that you own and occupy. Beyond this, whether a certain piece of real estate can be considered your homestead depends completely on your state statute.

For example, many states extend homestead protection to condominiums, but some do not. Certain state statutes cover only single-family homes, not duplexes, triplexes, or larger structures. Some states even shield mobile homes, in the right circumstances, while others offer them no homestead protection.

HOW MUCH OF THE HOMESTEAD'S VALUE DO THESE LAWS PROTECT?

The value protected by homestead laws depends on your state, but in most cases the answer is "not enough." Given today's real estate values and the equity many people have in their homes, most state homestead exemptions provide inadequate protection—only between $10,000 and $50,000 of the homestead's equity! Some states, like New Jersey, provide no protection at all. But if you live in Texas or Florida, your homestead is protected up to an unlimited value. In Florida or Texas, you could keep a debt-free multimillion-dollar home, even when you file for bankruptcy! (For a list of each state's

homestead amount, please visit our website at www.mywealth
protection.com.)

*To determine how well a homestead law protects your home, compare the
protected value to the equity.* First, subtract the value of any mortgages
from the fair market value of your home. For example, if you live in
a home with a $300,000 fair market value and a $150,000 mortgage,
then your equity is $150,000. If your state protects only $20,000
through its homestead law, then you still have $130,000 equity vul-
nerable to lawsuits and other creditors.

> *Special note:* In 2001, federal bankruptcy legislation was intro-
> duced in both chambers of Congress. This proposed legisla-
> tion, if passed, would supercede any state homestead laws.
> Although the two bills differed slightly, each would have
> capped a state homestead protection to $150,000 or less.
> Thus, if either of these bills passed, states like Texas and
> Florida would lose their unlimited homestead protection. In
> the aftermath of September 11, 2001, this legislation was put
> on hold. However, it should be noted that if such legislation
> is proposed again, homestead protections could be uniform
> and (in some states) diminished.

Is Homestead Protection Automatic?

Homestead protection is often not automatic. Each state has specific
requirements for claiming homestead status. In some states, you must
file a declaration of homestead in a public office. Others set a time
requirement for residency before homestead protection is granted.
Never assume your home is protected and do nothing to protect this
valuable asset—your assumption may be wrong. Your asset protection
attorney can show you how to comply with the state law formalities.

Who Can Claim Homestead Protection?

Certain states allow only the head of household to make the homestead declaration. Others allow either spouse to do so. Beware: If both
spouses file a declaration, they could cancel each other out (in some
states). Once again, have your asset protection attorney determine
who can file the declaration.

WHOM DOES HOMESTEAD STATUS PROTECT AGAINST?

While it will again depend on your state's statute, the general rule is that homestead will protect your home from all debts (including judgments) that arose after the homestead status attached. Some states provide protection from debts incurred even before homestead status attached.

Homestead laws won't protect your home from certain types of creditor claims. These creditors can ignore homestead laws and take action against your home:

- The IRS and other federal agencies—if you owe federal taxes or are sued by the SEC or the Environmental Protection Agency (EPA), you can lose your home, no matter what state you live in. If you owe state taxes, homestead may protect you, depending on the state.
- Spouses in a divorce action and family members challenging inheritances.
- Plaintiffs with intentional tort claims—libel, fraud, deceit, and others.
- Creditors to whom you voluntarily gave interests in your home, such as mortgages or deeds of trust.

IS THERE ANY DOWNSIDE TO MAKING A HOMESTEAD DECLARATION?

The most significant downside to relying on state homestead laws is that you will be lulled into an illusory sense of security. For example, today you may have $30,000 worth of equity in your home. If you live in a state with a $30,000 homestead exemption, your home is fully protected today. But, what about in your future?

Lulled into a false sense of security, you believe your house is still fully protected. Yet, as the years move on, you build up more equity in your home. When you are eventually sued 5, 7, 10 years down the road, all the additional equity you have built in your home could be lost.

Wealth Protection planning clients never suffer this mistake. Their advisors analyze how homestead protects them today and how it will continue to do so in the future—using other tools to protect their savings wherever homestead comes up short.

Owning your home in a limited liability company

As we explained in Chapter 29, family limited partnerships (FLPs) and limited liability companies (LLCs) are extremely useful asset protection tools because of their "charging order" protections. The strategy here then simply involves owning your home through an LLC. This might seem simple, but there is another layer of complexity due to the special tax benefits afforded your home. This complexity also affects why we recommend an LLC, not an FLP.

Tax Rules

Under federal tax rules, your home—defined as your "primary residence"—has special benefits. These benefits can only apply to one home. Essentially, if you're single, you have a $250,000 capital gains tax exclusion on the sale of your home (i.e., there are no taxes on the first $250,000 in capital gains). If you're married, this exclusion is $500,000. At a 20 percent capital gains tax rate, this benefit is worth between $50,000 and $100,000!

This exclusion applies if both parts of a two-part test are met: (1) either spouse or both spouses have owned the home for at least two out of the five years prior to the sale, *and* (2) both spouses have lived there and treated it as their primary residence during the same period. If the taxpayer is single, then both conditions apply to that person.

Solutions

Because this tax benefit is so significant, we have to make sure that we won't violate tests (1) and (2) by protecting a home in an FLP or an LLC. If an FLP or an LLC owns the home for more than three of the past five years, that means that neither of the spouses (or the single client) have "owned" it for at least two of the past five years. This would violate test (1) and cause a loss of the tax benefit.

There are two ways to get around this problem: (1) The clients transfer the home to an LLC or an FLP for at most three years at a time. Then, they would retransfer the home back to their own names for two years. This is obviously not ideal—the transfer costs can be significant, and it's a practical headache. (2) Have a single-member LLC own the home. The LLC would only be owned by one spouse (if a married couple) or the single client. The single-member LLC is considered by the IRS to be a "disregarded entity" for tax purposes. Thus, if a single-member LLC owned the home, for purposes of the tax test, the home would be considered owned in the client's name directly and test (1) would be satisfied. The LLC would simply be "disregarded." As long as the client met the residency test (2), the tax benefits would be preserved. Be sure to check with a licensed tax advisor on this strategy, as this is the type of law that changes quite often.

DRAWBACKS

The main drawback to using an LLC to shield your home—or any real estate, for that matter—is that your existing bank/mortgage lender may not allow you to transfer the title out of your name(s). Almost every mortgage note today is drafted with a "due on transfer" clause, allowing the bank/mortgage lender to call the note if you transfer the title to your home out of your name. Typically, they have exceptions to this clause for transfers between spouses, to family members, to trusts, and so on. However, they typically do not have such an exception for transfers to FLPs and LLCs. Thus, you will often need the written permission of the bank/mortgage lender to make such a transfer. If they have sold the loan to Fannie Mae or some other mortgage investor, this is impossible. Even if they still hold the loan, it can be very difficult.

Often, many of our clients use this reason as an opportunity to shop around and refinance their home. When negotiating with a bank at the outset, it is a hundred times easier to arrange for a property to be owned initially by an FLP or an LLC than it is to transfer the property to such a tool after the loan has closed. If rates are low (as they are at the writing of this book), then it might make a lot of sense to refinance the property and to make the transfer to the LLC as part of the refinancing.

USING "FRIENDLY MORTGAGES" TO SHIELD ALL THE HOME EQUITY

Most people think of mortgages as a burdensome obligation. They believe that "the only good mortgage is one that is paid." But to turn your home into a creditor-proof fortress, you must see the silver lining in every mortgage—that it shields the secured assets from other creditors. After all, what creditor would want an asset already mortgaged for close to its full value to another creditor? The trick, of course, is to find a *friendly creditor* who can shield your home through his or her mortgage but who is unlikely to foreclose on the mortgage.

Where can you find such a friendly creditor? Look around. Do you have a relative who loaned you money to go to college or to begin a business? Our client Robert did, when he started his desktop publishing firm five years ago with a loan from his uncle. Now Robert has a home worth $500,000 and only $100,000 in debt. So, why not draw up a legitimate mortgage on his home in favor of his generous uncle? His uncle does not even care if he is paid back now, but the mortgage stands as a barrier against other creditors.

Beyond family members, there are actually financial institutions that can play a role here. We are familiar with several banks that have trust companies and that see an opportunity to provide asset protection "friendly mortgages" to their top clients for a fee. Although the details of the transaction are beyond the scope of this chapter, you can read more about it at www.mywealthprotection.com.

Suffice it to say here, at the end of the transaction, the client has a recorded mortgage for up to 90 percent of the value of the property from a third-party bank along with private legal documents that protect the client from the bank ever foreclosing on the loan. In this way, the client gets the debt shield from outside creditors without any foreclosure risk.

LAST WORD

For most of you, your home is one of your most valuable assets, financially and psychologically. Turning a vulnerable home into a literal "Fortress" is certainly a worthy Wealth Protection goal.

CHAPTER THIRTY-FOUR

PROTECTING WEALTH FROM DIVORCE

O
f all the risks to our assets, the most common threat to our financial security is divorce. Over 50 percent of all marriages in the United States end in divorce—and that percentage grows for second marriages. Undoubtedly an emotionally devastating experience, divorce can be a financially disastrous experience as well.

Divorce planning is not about hiding assets from a soon-to-be ex-spouse. Nor is it about cheating or lying to keep your wealth. Rather, it concerns resolving issues of property ownership and distribution before things go sour. By agreeing up front what will be yours and what will be your spouse's, you save money, time, and emotional distress in the long run. In fact, this type of asset protection planning inevitably benefits all parties, except the divorce lawyers, of course.

Divorce planning is also about shielding family assets from the potential divorces of children and grandchildren. Given the statistics about divorce, it is almost a certainty that either a child or a grandchild of yours will get divorced. Thus, for intergenerational Wealth Protection planning, this is a crucial topic, unless you want to give half your inheritance to the ex-spouses of your heirs. As you will learn, there are ways to protect your children and grandchildren without making their spouses even sign a prenuptial agreement!

WHY DIVORCE CAN BE A
FINANCIAL NIGHTMARE

Most Americans don't have to read newspapers to see how devastating a divorce can be financially. While high-profile divorces involving tens of millions of dollars illustrate the point dramatically, most of us need only look to family or friends to see how a divorce turns into a financial upheaval. The prevailing attitude toward divorce comes from a relatively recent movie. In the film, Ivana Trump explains her theory of divorce to three ex-wives, played by Goldie Hawn, Diane Keaton, and Bette Midler. "Don't get even," she says, "get everything!"

Combine this fight-for-everything attitude with the terrible odds of getting a divorce, and you have a very serious threat to financial security. In fact, a divorce threatens not only former spouses but also their families and possibly their business partners as well. To truly understand how a divorce affects the finances of the participants, you must first understand how property is divided when the marriage is dissolved.

COMMUNITY PROPERTY STATES

Nine states have community property laws: Arizona, California, Idaho, Louisiana, Nevada, New Mexico, Texas, Washington, and Wisconsin. If your divorce occurs in one of these states and there is no valid pre- or postmarital agreement, the court will divide equally any property acquired during the marriage, other than inheritances or gifts to one spouse. Even the appreciation of one spouse's separate property can be divided, if the spouse spent efforts during the marriage on that property. Obviously, how the asset is titled is not the controlling factor. When the asset was acquired and how it was treated are much more important factors in determining how the asset will be treated.

EQUITABLE DISTRIBUTION STATES

Non–community property states are called "equitable distribution" states because courts in these states have total discretion to divide the property equitably or fairly. The court will normally consider a number of factors in deciding what is "equitable," including the length of the marriage, the age and conducts of the parties, and the present earnings and future earning potential of each former spouse. The danger of equitable divorces is that courts often distribute both nonmarital assets (those acquired before the marriage) as well as marital assets (those acquired during marriage) in order to create a "fair" arrangement. In this way, courts often split up property in ways that the ex-spouses never wanted or expected.

CASE STUDIES: DISASTER DIVORCES

These case studies should help you decide whether you and your family are adequately prepared to divorce.

- A couple marries, each for the second time and each with adult children from their first marriages. Without any pre- or postmarital agreement, they title many of the wife's previously separate income-producing properties (such as her rental apartment units) into the name of the new husband to save income taxes. Within two years of the marriage, they divorce. The husband gets half the rental units (in addition to alimony and other property), even though both spouses understood that the wife intended them to go to her children. The court simply ignored their understanding, giving half the properties to each spouse.

- A couple marries, each for the first time. Over the next 20 years, the husband acquires more ownership in his family's bakery business. His father, the founder, gradually sold shares to him. At 42, he is the majority owner. Unfortunately, he and his wife then undergo a bitter divorce, with the ex-wife granted half the husband's bakery business as community property. She then forces (1) high dividends and (2) a sale of the company to a competitor.

- An internal medicine resident gets married. She and her husband discuss her medical education and agree that she should not have to later compensate him for his greater financial contribution in their early years. However, when they file for divorce eight years later, the husband considers the wife's professional degree as marital property, so he claims a share in her earning potential. The court agrees, even though the couple verbally agreed to the contrary.

CAN A "PRE-NUP" PROTECT YOU?

A premarital agreement (or prenuptial agreement [pre-nup], pre-marital contract, antenuptial agreement, etc.) is the foundation of any protection against a divorce in which you might be involved. The premarital agreement is a written contract between the intended spouses. It specifies the division of property and income upon divorce, including disposition to specific personal property, such as family heirlooms. It also states the responsibilities of each party and their children after divorce. Finally, these agreements lay out responsibilities during marriage, such as the financial support that each spouse can expect or the religion in which future children will be raised. The agreement cannot limit child support.

NOT ONLY FOR THE RICH

Premarital agreements are often perceived to be only for the wealthy, but this is not true. The three case studies given earlier didn't involve rich people, yet all could have benefited from a premarital agreement because these agreements deal both with current and future property. Such agreements help those who eventually acquire significant property, as they protect existing assets.

A premarital agreement, in fact, can be more important for the less wealthy spouse entering a second marriage. Why? Because that spouse typically gives up a major source of income—alimony from the first marriage. A premarital agreement can ensure that, if a divorce occurs, he or she will be at least as well-off as before remarriage.

COURT ENFORCED

A premarital agreement is properly drafted if it adequately discloses each party's financial condition and if other state law requirements are met. Courts will then abide by its terms. With a rock-solid premarital agreement, you can limit surprises in divorce. The court will simply allow you to split property as you both originally agreed. This not only ensures that you retain property, but it also saves you time, aggravation, and attorneys' fees. It can avoid a difficult process and a nasty fight.

REQUIREMENTS FOR A PREMARITAL AGREEMENT

Each state differs slightly on what is required for an enforceable premarital agreement. But there are some generally accepted requirements.

- The agreement must be in writing and signed.

  Every state requires that a premarital agreement be written and signed. Many also require that it be notarized or witnessed.

  Tip: Notarize your agreement, even if your state does not require it. This adds protection against claims of duress or forgery.

- There must be a reasonable disclosure.

  There must be a fair, accurate, and reasonable disclosure of each party's financial condition.

  Tip: Attach financial statements to the agreement, and have each spouse affirm knowledge of the other's financial condition.

- Each party must be advised by a separate attorney.

  Many states either require separate legal advice explicitly or use it as a factor in determining whether the agreement was fair.

  Tip: Hire separate lawyers, and give enough time between the agreement and the wedding to avoid any appearance of duress. Courts frown on last-second premarital agreements.

- The agreement must not be unconscionable.

  Courts will not enforce a one-sided agreement. Also, the contract must not be structured to encourage divorce, for example, by stating that one spouse has no rights to property except upon divorce.

  Tip: Avoid extremely one-sided agreements. It need not be a 50/50 split, but it should provide a fair balance.

- The couple must follow the agreement during the marriage.

  Courts disregard premarital agreements when the spouses bla-
  tantly disregarded it during their marriage, such as when property designated as the husband's separate property is retitled
  to the wife.

  Tip: Treat designated separate property as separate. If loans
  are made from one spouse's separate property to the marital unit, then those funds should not be commingled when
  repaid.

Special considerations for family business owners

Divorce commonly causes a major disruption to a family-owned business. Often, when a child of the founder of the business gets divorced
and the ex-spouse sues for half of that child's interest in the business,
it creates a terrible strain on the business.

The ex-spouse's demands can lead to a formal discovery process
in which information intended to be private is made available, such
as salaries for family members, benefits, and contracts. Dealing with
this process often injures the family and the business.

This is why family business owners are increasingly using lawyers
to protect against divorce before it occurs. The preferred tool to
prevent such disaster? The premarital agreement, of course. The *Wall
Street Journal* recently reported, "The number of premarital agreements drafted for members of family-owned businesses has skyrocketed in recent years." One New York attorney now drafts close to 300
agreements per year for family-owned businesses. Fifteen years ago
it was closer to 20.

Protect your business from the destruction that can result from
a bitter divorce. Have every owner of your family business create an
agreement (premarital or postmarital) that prevents any in-law from
claiming a stake in the business upon divorce. Specify a cash settlement instead. Should a divorce then occur, the ex-spouse will still be
fairly treated; but your business remains undisrupted and in the
family.

Irrevocable spendthrift trusts: Ideal tools to keep assets in the family

Irrevocable trusts are very effective asset protection tools because you no longer own the assets owned by the trust. You have transferred the property, with no strings attached. Because you neither own nor control the property, your creditors, including an ex-spouse, cannot claim the property.

Moreover, you can make children, grandchildren, and even future great-grandchildren beneficiaries of an irrevocable trust. However, even though the beneficiaries can benefit from trust assets, the trust can be drafted so that their creditors, including divorcing ex-spouses, cannot get to trust assets. As we explained in Chapter 30, these trusts have special "spendthrift" provisions.

Nonetheless, using an irrevocable trust should not be taken lightly. It means giving away those assets forever, with no strings attached. This is a serious consequence when protecting against divorce, lawsuit, or other threat. When would such a strategy make sense? When you would inevitably give the assets to certain beneficiaries. For example, the trust might be used for assets that you will leave to your children or grandchildren when you die and that you do not need for your financial security. Consider this case.

CASE STUDY: IRVING'S TRUST PROTECTS HIS SUMMER HOME

Irving, a plumber, bought a summer home on Cape Cod. He and his first wife had three small children. Unfortunately, they divorced after about six years. In the settlement, he received the summer home.

Fifteen years later, Irving was ready to marry again, now in Santa Fe. Both he and his prospective spouse had been married previously and understood divorce. Irving considered a premarital agreement

(continued)

to keep the summer home as his separate property. He had planned to give it to the three children of his first marriage and wondered whether working on the home would jeopardize this plan if he later divorced.

After speaking with Irving, we noted three important points: (1) his handiwork on the home might make it marital property; (2) his children and their families used the home throughout the year; and (3) Irving had a lawsuit from a failed real estate venture. It was clear that the best strategy for Irving was to have an irrevocable trust own the summer home, giving beneficial interests to use the home to all three children equally (which already occurred).

By using an irrevocable trust to own the summer home, Irving protected the home against possible future divorce and also shielded it from other creditors and lawsuits. By including spendthrift provisions, Irving protected the home from his children's creditors, as well. This will ensure that the Cape house stays in the family for generations.

PROTECT YOUR CHILDREN FROM DIVORCE

When your children or grandchildren come to you, giddy with exciting news about their recent engagements, the last thing they want to hear you ask is, "Are you going to sign a prenuptial agreement?" In fact, if you weren't paying for the wedding, you might lose your invitation for making such a statement.

As you learned earlier, the key to protecting assets from divorce is keeping the assets "separate property" and not commingling them with community or marital property. You can't trust your children to do this, so you are going to do it for them . . . without needing their or their spouses' consent.

By leaving assets to your children's irrevocable trusts with the appropriate spendthrift provisions, rather than to them personally, you can achieve this goal. Of course, if the children take money out of the trust and use it to buy a home or other property, that property will be subject to the rules in each state. Look at this case.

CASE STUDY: ROB AND JANELLE— COLLEGE SWEETHEARTS

Rob and Janelle got married right out of college. Their romance turned sour within a few years, and Rob could no longer handle the physical and emotional abuse he received from Janelle.

During their three-year marriage, Janelle had received a sizable inheritance and used it to pay off the couple's home. When they filed for divorce, Rob's attorney successfully argued that his time and labor on the house and the fact that he lived in it (except when Janelle occasionally kicked him out and he had to stay at his mother's) made half of the equity in the home (or $100,000) Rob's fair share. Though Rob and all of his friends will argue the $100,000 was small consolation for what he endured, Janelle's grandparents certainly didn't intend for Rob to receive their inheritance.

What could Janelle have done? Her grandparents could have left her the inheritance through an irrevocable trust that only allowed her to take out so much per year. In that case, she would have used the interest from the inheritance to pay the mortgage down each month, and the corpus of the inheritance would have remained separate property and would not have been part of the divorce settlement. In the three years of their marriage, they would have had next to no equity in their home, and Rob would have left the divorce with what he brought in and just his wounded pride . . . but none of Janelle's grandparents' life savings. It is left to the reader to determine what is equitable—we aren't marriage counselors. We are only trying to help you reach your desired objectives.

LAST WORD

In a nutshell, a little planning can go a long way to making sure that a divorce doesn't completely disrupt a family's financial situation. Whether you are a single person considering marriage or already have a family and are concerned about losing family assets to the divorces of younger generations, divorce protection planning is essential. Consider it an integral part of your family's Wealth Protection plan.

PART VI

INSURANCE PLANNING

CHAPTER THIRTY-FIVE

AVOID THE BIGGEST PITFALLS, HELP YOURSELF AND YOUR FAMILY, AND SAVE MONEY IN THE PROCESS

The insurance industry is a multitrillion-dollar industry. This shouldn't come as a surprise because insurance impacts you in many ways. You probably have auto insurance and health insurance. You more than likely have some form of homeowner's insurance and life insurance, as well as disability coverage. Even your bank accounts have insurance—banks are insured by the Federal Deposit Insurance Corporation (FDIC).

We, the authors, have life and health insurance licenses in almost every state in the country. We have reviewed or sold insurance policies from over a hundred insurance companies. David's law firm has analyzed insurance policies both in the United States and abroad, while also creating captive insurance companies for the firm's clients. Chris has worked in the actuarial departments of several insurance companies in the auto, homeowner, business liability, worker's compensation, and malpractice sectors. While in the actuarial departments, he assisted in the computation of insurance rates and rating mechanisms, before being hired by one of the world's largest auto manufacturers to help them create their two insurance captives.

Insurance planning can help protect your family, provide necessary benefits, and help you reduce your tax burdens. We will show you ways to achieve these goals and some "tricks of the trade" that may help you reduce costs and avoid unnecessary fees or commissions. In particular, we will cover:

- Ways to reduce your taxes with health insurance.
- What to look for in a disability policy.
- How to reduce your costs of life insurance.
- How to get a tax deduction for your insurance purchases.
- Why you need long-term-care (LTC) insurance and what to look for in an LTC policy.
- When to consider and how to create your own captive insurance company.

CHAPTER THIRTY-SIX

LIFE INSURANCE: THE BACKBONE OF WEALTH PROTECTION PLANNING

W ould you be surprised to know that, in our opinion, life insurance is the most important tool in your Wealth Protection plan? You shouldn't. No other financial, tax, insurance, or legal tool can play as many roles in a Wealth Protection plan as life insurance can.

Obviously, life insurance can provide death protection for a family. This is the role traditionally assigned to life insurance. However, beyond this, life insurance has several key characteristics that allow it to play other very important roles in your Wealth Protection plan.

Life insurance can also be a tax-free wealth accumulator and retirement vehicle (see Chapter 46), as well as an asset-protected investment tool (see Chapter 28). It can provide liquidity to pay estate taxes (Chapter 55). It can even be part of a solution to lower the 80 percent tax trap of pensions and individual retirement accounts (IRAs) (Chapter 58). In this chapter, we will introduce the basic concepts surrounding the tool of life insurance.

WHAT IS LIFE INSURANCE?

Life insurance is a contract between you and an insurance company whereby the insurance company pays your named beneficiaries the "face amount" of the policy when you die. Some life insurance policies accumulate cash over time (permanent policies) and some do not (term policies).

KEY CHARACTERISTICS THAT MAKE LIFE INSURANCE SO VALUABLE

These attributes apply to permanent (cash value) life insurance:

- *Amounts in life insurance policies grow tax deferred.* While investments outside of retirement plans and life insurance policies are taxed on income and realized capital gains, funds growing within a cash value life insurance policy grow completely tax free. Life insurance is very attractive as a wealth-accumulation and tax-reduction vehicle because it can serve as another retirement plan. (Read Chapter 46 for more information).

- *Cash values of life insurance policies can be accessed tax free.* When you take funds out of a retirement plan, such as a pension or an IRA, these withdrawals are always subject to income tax and may be subject to a penalty if they're withdrawn before you reach age 59^1/$_2$. With a cash value life insurance policy, you can take tax-free loans against the cash value at any time. There is never a tax penalty, and there is no tax on the loan as well, as long as you keep the policy in force and the policy is not a modified endowment contract (MEC).

- *Life insurance is asset-protected.* Most states give some measure of asset protection to cash value life insurance policies. Thus, this asset can play a role in your asset protection plan. See our web site at www.mywealthprotection.com to find out the protection for life insurance in your state.

- *Life insurance has beneficial tax valuation.* In dealing with the 80 percent tax trap facing pensions and IRAs, life insurance can play a very valuable role. See Chapter 58 for more on this important benefit.

Types of life insurance

Term Life Insurance

Given its affordability, term life insurance is the most common type of life insurance policy. However, because of its lack of a wealth accumulation component, term insurance can only play one role in your Wealth Protection plan—death protection for a limited time for the family.

The premium on a term policy is low compared to other types of life insurance policies because it carries no cash value. A term life insurance policy pays a specific lump sum to your designated beneficiary upon your death. The policy protects your family by providing money they can invest to replace your salary and covers immediate expenses incurred by your death. Term life insurance is best for young, growing families, when the need for death protection of the breadwinner is high and excess cash flow is especially low.

Pros: Affordable coverage that pays only a death benefit, term life insurance initially tends to cost less than other insurance policies mainly because, unlike other policies, it has no cash value.

Cons: Term life insurance premiums increase with age because the risk of death increases as people get older. Some term premiums may rise each year, or after 10, 20, or 30 years. Once you're over age 65, the cost of a new term insurance policy becomes very expensive, often unaffordable.

Whole Life Insurance

Whole life insurance pays a death benefit to the beneficiary you name and offers you a cash value account with tax-deferred cash accumulation. The policy remains in force during your entire lifetime and provides permanent protection for your dependents while building a cash value account. The insurance company manages your policy's cash accounts.

Pros: Whole life insurance has a savings element (cash value), which is tax deferred. You can borrow from or cash in the policy during your lifetime. It has a fixed premium that can't increase during your lifetime, as long as you pay the planned amount, and your premium is invested for you long term. Because it has the cash accumulation component, whole life insurance can play the roles of tax reduction, wealth accumulation, asset protection, estate planning, and even reduction of the retirement plan tax trap.

Cons: Whole life insurance does not allow you to invest in separate accounts, such as money market, stock, and bond funds. It also doesn't let you split your money among different accounts or move your money between accounts and allows no premium flexibility nor face amount flexibility.

UNIVERSAL LIFE INSURANCE

Universal life insurance is a variation of whole life. The insurance part of the policy is separated from the investment portion of the policy. The investment portion is invested by the insurance company in bonds, mortgages, and money market funds. This investment portion grows and is tax deferred. The cost of the death benefit is paid for out of the investment fund. A guaranteed minimum interest rate applied to the policy means that no matter how badly the investments perform, the insurance company guarantees a certain minimum return on the cash portion. If the insurance company does well with its investments, the interest return on the cash portion will increase.

Pros: The product is similar to whole life insurance, but it has more flexible premiums. It may be attractive to younger buyers who may have fluctuations in their ability to pay premiums. Because it is so flexible, universal life insurance can play the roles of tax reduction, wealth accumulation, asset protection, estate planning, and even reduction of the retirement plan tax trap. It is also usually less expensive than whole life.

Cons: If the insurance company does poorly with its investments, the interest return on the cash portion of the policy will decrease. In this case, less money would be available to pay the cost of the death benefit portion of the policy, or future premiums may be necessary in addition to the premiums originally illustrated.

VARIABLE LIFE INSURANCE

Variable life insurance provides permanent protection to your beneficiary upon your death. The term *variable life* means that you can allocate your dollars to various types of investment accounts within your insurer's portfolio, such as an equity fund, a money market fund, a bond fund, or some combination thereof. Hence, the value of the death benefit and the cash value may fluctuate up or down, depending on the performance of the investment portion of the policy.

Although most variable life insurance policies guarantee that the death benefit will not fall below a specified minimum, a minimum cash value is seldom guaranteed. Variable is a form of whole life insurance; and because of investment risks, it is also considered a securities contract and is regulated as securities under the Federal Securities Laws and must be sold with a prospectus.

Pros: Variable life insurance allows you to participate in various types of investment options without being taxed on your earnings until you surrender the policy. You can apply interest earned on these investments toward the premiums, potentially lowering the amount you pay.

Cons: You assume the investment risks. When the investment funds perform poorly, less money is available to pay the premiums, meaning that you then may have to pay more than you can afford to keep the policy in force. Poor fund performance also means that the cash and the death benefit may decline, though never below a defined level (if one exists). Also, you cannot withdraw from the cash value during your lifetime.

VARIABLE UNIVERSAL LIFE INSURANCE

Variable universal life insurance pays your beneficiary a death benefit. The amount of the benefit depends on the success of your investments. If the value of your investments decreases, there is a guaranteed minimum death benefit paid to your beneficiary upon your death. Variable universal gives you more control of the cash value account portion of your policy than any other insurance type does. A form of whole life insurance, it has elements of both life insurance and a securities contract. Because the policy owner assumes investment risks, variable universal products are regulated as securities under the Federal Securities Laws and must be sold with a prospectus.

Pros: Variable universal life enables you to make withdrawals or to borrow from the policy during your lifetime, and it offers separate accounts in which to invest. It combines the flexibility of universal with the ability to invest in mutual funds of the variable policy; universal variable can be the ideal tool for tax reduction and retirement wealth accumulation over a long time horizon.

Cons: It requires the policyholder to devote time to managing the policy's accounts. The policy's success is dependent on the investments you make. Premiums must be high enough to cover your insurance and your accounts.

Equity-Indexed Universal Life Insurance

A recent trend in the industry is to offer a universal life (UL) policy whose return is tied to the S&P 500. Because it is a universal life policy, the investor is given a 0% to 3% guarantee each year. On the upside, the investor may realize much higher returns (presently capped at a maximum of 10% to 12%).

Pros: The greater upside potential than standard UL or whole life products with guarantees that you don't get in a variable universal life product.

Cons: The upside return is capped and some companies only give you 50% to 75% of the S&P as your upside. This is referred to as a participation ratio.

◆

CHAPTER THIRTY-SEVEN

DISABILITY INSURANCE: INADEQUATE COVERAGE CAN BE MORE COSTLY THAN DEATH, DIVORCE, OR A LAWSUIT

Wealth Protection planning means designing a plan for the best possible future while protecting against the worst possible events. No one ever plans on becoming disabled, although *half* of us will experience a long-term disability at least once in our lives. In fact, the odds hold with the authors—Chris missed months of work about seven years ago when he injured his back playing basketball. It happened to one of us—it happens to half of the population. The odds are it will happen to you or your spouse. This chapter explains why you need disability insurance and what you should look for in a disability policy.

Though disability insurance may seem dull, compared to some of the more "exotic" topics in this book, this chapter may be the most crucial because it deals with protecting your earning potential—typically your family's single greatest asset. Unless you are near retirement, if you were to stop working, your family would suffer a significant financial strain. This is the reality that motivates you to buy life insurance as protection against a premature death. Purchasing life insurance is "common sense."

Although many of our clients are, initially, underinsured, they usually have *some* protection against a premature death. However, most professionals, entrepreneurs, business owners, and executives often overlook a more dangerous threat to their long-term financial stability—disability. The risk that the average individual will suffer a disability is great. The "probability of at least one long-term disability (90 days or longer) occurring before age 65 is 50 percent for someone age 35, 44 percent for someone age 45, and 26 percent for someone age 55."

In our opinion, disability can be more financially devastating to a family than premature death. In both cases, the breadwinner will be unable to provide any income for the family. If you die, you—the deceased earner—are no longer an expense to your family. However, if you are disabled, you still need to be fed, clothed, and cared for by medical professionals or family members. In many cases, the medical care alone can cost hundreds of dollars per day. Thus, with a disability, income is reduced or eliminated *and* expenses increase. This can be a devastating turn of events, which often leads to creditor problems and even bankruptcy.

If you are older, near retirement, and have saved a large enough sum of money to fund a comfortable retirement immediately, then you probably don't need disability income protection. Of course, you may have some long-term-care concerns (see Chapter 38). But if you are under age 50, or if you are older than age 50 and have several pre-college-age children, proper disability insurance is a necessity. The key issue is determining the type of disability income policy that is "right" for you.

EMPLOYER PROVIDED COVERAGE

If you work for a corporation, your employer may provide long-term disability coverage, usually paid for by you. The premiums are probably discounted compared to what you would pay for a private policy. We advise you to carefully review any employer-offered policy and supplement with a private policy if you need one. Often, employer-provided group policies are inadequate because they limit either the term of the coverage or the amount of benefits paid. For instance, benefits may last only a few years, or benefit payments may represent only a small part of your annual compensation.

POLICY CHECKUP

Here are some suggestions on what to look for when comparing your present disability policies. Be sure to ask these questions:

- How long does the disability coverage last?
- How much is the benefit? (Different plans may cap the benefits at $5,000 per month.)
- What percentage of my income is covered? (Generally, you cannot receive more than 60 percent to 80 percent of your after-tax income, and the benefit is capped at $7,500 or $10,000, depending on your age.)
- Who pays the premiums? (*Tip:* If you pay the premiums yourself, and not as a deductible expense through your business or practice, your benefits will be tax free. You may be seduced by the income tax deduction of the premiums, but the extra tax burden today is much easier to swallow than the tax burden will be if you suffer a disability and have a significantly reduced income *and* increased expenses.)
- Is the policy portable, or convertible, to an individual policy if I leave the group? If so, do I maintain the reduced group rate?
- If my business/company/group distributes all earnings from the corporation at year-end in the way of bonuses to all owners/partners (typical of C-corporations as a way to avoid double taxation), are these amounts covered by the group policy? (If not, and if bonuses or commissions make up a substantial part of your income, you'll probably need a supplemental policy.)
- What is the definition of *disability* in the group policy—own-occupation, any occupation, or income-replacement? (See page 217 for a discussion of these three terms.)

HOW DO I GET THE BEST COVERAGE FOR MY MONEY?

Once you have given yourself a checkup and decided that you need a new, or supplemental, policy, you'll need to know what to look for to give you the best coverage available at a reasonable rate. When you're considering a disability policy, review these issues:

WHAT IS THE BENEFIT AMOUNT?

Most policies are capped at 60 percent of income. Some states and insurance companies have monthly maximums as well. Ask yourself how much money your family would need if you were to become disabled. Generally, look for policies that offer a maximum of at least $7,500 or $10,000 monthly.

WHAT IS THE WAITING PERIOD?

The waiting period is the period of time that you must be disabled before the insurance company will pay you disability benefits. The longer the waiting period before benefits start, the lower your premium will be. Essentially, the waiting period serves a deductible relative to time; you cover your expenses for the waiting period, then the insurance company steps in from that point forward. This is not unlike the deductible you have on your car, except that auto insurance deductibles are in the form of amounts paid ($100, $250, $500, etc.), not relative to a period of time. If you have adequate sick leave, short-term disability, and an emergency fund and if you can support yourself for a while, choose a policy with a longer waiting period. Though waiting periods can be as long as 730 days (or as short as 30 days), a 90-day waiting period is the most common and may give you the best coverage for your money.

HOW LONG WILL COVERAGE LAST?

Many policies cover you for only two to five years, which is an inadequate period. But a policy that provides lifetime benefits, at costly premiums, is generally not worth it. A good idea is to get a benefit period that lasts until you turn 65, at which point Social Security payments may begin.

WHAT IS THE DEFINITION OF DISABILITY?

The definition of *disability* in a policy is significant. The main categories are Own-occupation, Any-occupation, and Loss of Income. The Own-occupation policies are the most comprehensive and, of course, the most expensive. Two key elements to look for in the definition of disability in your policy are (1) whether you are forced to go back to work in another occupation and (2) whether you will receive a partial benefit or your full benefit if you go back to work in a lower-paying occupation if you cannot perform the duties of your original occupation after the disability.

In other words, suppose you were a pilot earning $250,000 per year before you lost vision in one eye and started receiving $10,000 per month in disability income. If you become a flight instructor making $100,000 per year, will your disability policy pay you $10,000 per month (true own-occupation), $6,000 (loss of income—pro rata), or $0 (any occupation)?

DOES THE POLICY OFFER PARTIAL BENEFITS?

If you are only able to work part-time hours instead of your previous full-time hours, will you receive benefits? Unless your policy states that you are entitled to partial benefits, you won't receive anything unless you are totally unable to work. Find out whether Extended Partial Benefits are paid if you go back to work and suffer a reduction in income because you cannot keep up the same rigorous schedule you had before you were disabled. (This is an important benefit for many of us who often work ridiculous hours early in their career and most likely will work less after any disability.) Partial benefits may be available as a rider in some policies. This add-on rider should be seriously considered because only 3 percent of all disabilities are *total* disabilities.

Is the Policy Noncancellable or Guaranteed Renewable?

The difference between these two terms is very important. If a policy is "noncancellable," you will pay a fixed premium throughout the contract term. Your premium will not go up for the term of the contract. If it is "guaranteed renewable," it means you cannot be cancelled, but your premiums can increase. As long as noncancellable is in the description of the policy, you are in good shape.

How Financially Stable Is the Insurance Company?

Before buying a policy, check the financial stability of your insurer. If your insurer goes bankrupt, you may have to shop for a policy later in life, when the premiums will be more expensive. Standard & Poor's top rating for financial stability is AAA. A. M. Best Co. uses A++ as its top rating for financial strength. Duff and Phelps rates companies on their ability to pay claims and uses AAA as its highest rating. Moody's uses Aa1 to rate Excellent companies. (Table 37.1 shows all of the ratings.) There are no guarantees in life, but buying a policy from a highly rated company is the safest bet you can make, and we would not recommend gambling on your disability insurance to save a few dollars. See Table 37.2, which shows the various options available on disability policies.

Other issues include:

- Increased coverage.
- Cost-of-living increases.
- Waiver-of-premium.
- Return-of-premium waiver.
- Unisex pricing.
- HIV rider.
- Multilife pricing discounts.
- Protection of future pension contributions.

TABLE 37.1 LIST OF POSSIBLE RATINGS FOR INSURANCE COMPANIES

A. M. BEST[1]	STANDARD & POOR'S[2]	MOODY'S[3]	FITCH[4]	WEISS[5]
1. A++ Superior	AAA Extremely strong	Aaa Exceptional	AAA Exceptionally strong	A+ Excellent
2. A+ Superior	AA+ Very strong	Aa1 Excellent	AA+ Very strong	A Excellent
3. A Excellent	AA Very strong	Aa2 Excellent	AA Very strong	A- Excellent
4. A- Excellent	AA- Very strong	Aa3 Excellent	AA- Very strong	B+ Good
5. B++ Very Good	A+ Strong	A1 Good	A+ Strong	B Good
6. B+ Good	A Strong	A2 Good	A strong	B- Good
7. B Fair	A- Strong	A3 Good	A- Strong	C+ Fair
8. B- Fair	BBB+ Good	Baa1 Adequate	BBB+ Good	C Fair

(continued)

TABLE 37.1 (CONTINUED)

A. M. BEST[1]	STANDARD & POOR'S[2]	MOODY'S[3]	FITCH[4]	WEISS[5]
9. C++ Marginal	BBB Good	Baa2 Adequate	BBB Good	C– Fair
10. C+ Marginal	BBB– Good	Baa3 Adequate	BBB– Good	D+ weak
11. C weak	BB+ Marginal	Ba1 Questionable	BB+ Moderately weak	D weak
12. C– weak	BB Marginal	Ba2 Questionable	BB Moderately weak	D– weak
13. D Poor	BB– Marginal	Ba3 Questionable	BB– Moderately weak	E+ Very weak
14. E Under State Supervision	B+ Weak	B1 Poor	B+ Weak	E Very weak
15. F In Liquidation	B Weak	B2 Poor	B Weak	E– Very weak
16.	B– Weak	B3 Poor	B– Weak	F Failed

#			
17.	CCC+ Very weak	Caa1 Very poor	CCC+ Very weak
18.	CCC Very weak	Caa2 Very poor	CCC Very weak
19.	CCC– Very weak	Caa3 Very poor	CCC– Very weak
20.	CC Extremely weak	Ca Extremely poor	CC Very weak
21.		C Lowest	C Very weak
22.			DDD Insolvent
23.			DD Insolvent
24.			D Insolvent

[1] www.ambest.com
[2] www.standardandpoors.com/ratings
[3] www.moodys.com
[4] www.fitchibca.com
[5] www.weissratings.com

TABLE 37.2   DISABILITY INCOME POLICY OPTIONS

POLICY OPTION	DESCRIPTION OF OPTION	FOR THE TYPICAL INDIVIDUAL
Benefit period	Period of time the insurance company is obligated to pay the monthly disability benefits. Common periods are: 5 years, until age 65, and lifetime.	Lifetime is generally too expensive. Until age 65 is ideal. Five years is too short.
Waiting period	Period of time from the commencement of the disability to payment of monthly benefits. Common waiting periods run from 30 days to one year.	90 days.
Extended partial benefit	Pays a partial benefit when the insured is not totally disabled. Partial benefits are a percentage based on the amount of income loss.	Highly recommended, but the individual should make sure he or she is not required to take a job in another occupation if he or she is qualified.
Portability/ Transferability	If the insured leaves the group, he or she can continue the existing policy with the reduced rate.	Most desirable is a group or a multilife policy that offers this benefit.
HIV waiver	Pays a monthly benefit (up to 2 years) to a healthcare professional who has tested positive for HIV, even if he or she is still working.	Worth considering; for high-risk people, recommended.

TABLE 37.2 (CONTINUED)

Multilife discounts	Different discounts can apply if several people apply at the same time for disability.	Cheaper is always better.
Disability trust (pension) option	Pays up to $2,500 to a trust, representing the insured's lost pension contributions, if he or she is disabled.	Not recommended for older people with large retirement plans. Good idea for younger workers who can afford it.
Cost of living	Total disability and residual benefits each year are increased by a specified percentage or by the Consumer Price Index (CPI); does not increase benefits prior to the commencement of a disability claim.	May not be cheap, but could be very valuable if an individual is disabled for a long period of time.
Future insurability options	The right to purchase additional amounts of monthly benefits at regular intervals without the insurance company inquiring about the individual's health.	Very useful for young people who expect future increases in income.

LAST WORD

A disability is more likely to occur than premature death, a lawsuit, and bankruptcy combined. That's why disability insurance is the only way to protect your future income. When combined with other asset protection, tax, and estate planning, the proper disability coverage will help you sleep much more soundly.

◆

CHAPTER THIRTY-EIGHT

LONG-TERM CARE: PROTECT YOURSELVES, YOUR CHILDREN, AND YOUR PARENTS

You are probably reading this chapter because either you or your parents are at least 50 years old. Or you may be reading this chapter because you don't want your in-laws or parents to move in with you for the rest of their lives. Perhaps you are reading this chapter because you aren't sure if your children will be able (not to mention willing) to take care of you if and when you need assistance in your later years. As you now know, the key to Wealth Protection planning is integrating the different components of your plan. You don't want to save money only to have it all go to taxes when you die or to an undeserving creditor as a result of a lawsuit. Similarly, you don't want to save for retirement or to accumulate a nice inheritance for your children and grandchildren only to have rising medical bills wipe it all out. This chapter covers one of the most underutilized yet essential tools in a Wealth Protection plan—long-term-care insurance.

WHAT IS LONG-TERM-CARE INSURANCE?

Long-term-care insurance (LTCI) covers health insurance costs for those people who cannot take care of themselves. LTCI is designed to pay for all levels of nursing care in a nursing facility, care in an assisted-living facility, and optionally for care in a community-based setting (e.g., adult day care), or care provided in the home (e.g., skilled, custodial, or homemaker services).

WHY DO YOU NEED LONG-TERM-CARE INSURANCE?

More than half of all Americans will need some form of long-term care during their lifetime. This means that, next to life insurance, this is probably the single most likely insurance your family will need.

We already know that half of us will need long-term-care coverage at some point in time. This means that the odds are that one of your parents, one of your in-laws, and either you or your spouse will need long-term care. In the United States, the average stay in a nursing home is between two and three years. In some areas of the country, the cost of nursing home care or quality around-the-clock in-home care may be $200 to $300 per day. This means that the average two-to-three-year stay in those areas costs between $150,000 and $320,000—today. Additionally, the U.S. Health Care Administration reports that costs are increasing 5.8 percent per year and are expected to more than triple in the next 20 years. At these projections, the costs of the average two-to-three-year stay may be $500,000 to $1,000,000 by the time you or your spouse need long-term care. Will you, your parents, and your in-laws have hundreds of thousands of "extra" dollars in your retirement and estate plans to cover this highly possible expense?

As you are probably aware, advancements in medicine have helped to increase the average life expectancy. With this increased life expectancy, there is a greater chance that each person may suffer a debilitating illness that may entail significant long-term-care needs. With the trends of increasing life expectancies and increasing costs to medical expenses, the cost of long-term care can easily wipe out retirement savings and eliminate any inheritance you would have otherwise left your children or grandchildren.

Forty-two percent of people over age 65 will enter a nursing home and need LTCI. The average stay is 2.5 years.

Won't the government cover these long-term-care costs?

No, not the way you would like them to. Did you know that in California an individual does not qualify for LTC coverage until his or her net worth is less than $2,500? Furthermore, once that individual begins receiving LTC benefits, the state takes all but $30 per week of income from the patient. You would have to spend every last dollar of your savings before you would get any help. Though you may have more than enough saved to pay for these types of expenses, your potential health problem could wipe out all your assets, which you hoped would be an inheritance for your children or grandchildren. Incidentally, we see many of our successful clients buying LTCI on their parents because they know they will have to take care of their parents, if the need arises. It can be a major financial and emotional problem to be getting ready to retire and have one of your parents or in-laws get sick and need $75,000 to $150,000 per year of medical expenses.

Why don't most people have LTCI?

Most people don't want to bear the risk of self-insuring their long-term-care costs, yet many have not purchased LTCI. We see clients insure their lives, homes, cars, and income but not events like long-term illness and disability. Some people believe "It's not going to happen to me," and others refuse to consider paying LTCI premiums for the next 20 to 40 years with only a chance that they will ever use the insurance.

WHAT SHOULD YOU LOOK FOR IN AN LTCI POLICY?

Traditional LTCI policies feature benefits, options, and riders that vary in availability and scope among carriers. They don't have cash value, nor do they have a death benefit. Once eligible for benefits (unable to perform two of six activities of daily living—eating, bathing, dressing, toileting, transferring, continence), this type of policy pays a daily reimbursement for approved expenses up to the maximum daily benefit chosen by the insured. Upper and lower limits vary among carriers but are generally in the $20 to $300 per day range. Benefits can be received for life or for a period of time determined by a total-insurance-dollar value of the policy, referred to as a pool of benefits. "Facility only" or "facility and in-home care" policies are available. Elimination periods (deductibles) apply and can range from 0 to 90 days. Other features, options, and riders that vary among carriers are inflation protection; bed reservations; alternative plan of care; restoration of benefits; personal care advisor; respite care; joint policy discounts; premium waiver; rate classes; nonforfeiture benefits; indemnity benefits; caregiver indemnity benefits; and 10-year paid-up, 20-year paid-up, and nonlevel payment options. For more information on these options and riders, contact a licensed long-term-care insurance agent.

If you're unwilling to buy traditional LTCI because you feel you will be paying premiums forever and never need the policy, look for a carrier that offers paid-up policies and/or nonforfeiture riders. Paid-up policies will require yearly premiums for a specified number of years, usually 10 years or 20 years. After this time, you stop making premium payments, but you own the policy for life. Nonforfeiture riders allow the policy owner to name a beneficiary; and, upon death, all premiums that have been paid are then paid out to the named beneficiary, even if benefits have been received. However, the policy must be in force at the time of death for the beneficiary to receive the paid premiums.

An alternate way of addressing long-term-care needs is to purchase a universal life insurance policy with an attached rider that can accelerate all or a portion of the death benefit to be used for approved long-term-care costs should the need arise. Benefits are received in much the same way as with a traditional long-term-care policy. You make a single premium payment and purchase a paid-up policy. In most cases, an existing cash value policy can be exchanged with no tax consequence (consult your tax professional regarding your particular situation). The larger the single premium paid, the larger the death benefit that can be converted to daily benefit maximums for approved long-term-care costs divided over a two- or four-year or a lifetime period at a decreasing daily maximum amount. The policy can be purchased providing benefits for an individual or a couple.

The most important feature of a good LTCI policy is a financially sound insurance carrier. Don't purchase the cheapest LTCI policy that you can find. LTCI carriers must have the financial strength to sustain their claims-paying ability well into the future when the millions of baby boomers will begin needing LTCI benefits. In a nutshell, don't be penny-wise and pound-foolish.

Chapter 12 in Part III, Tax Planning, covers a tax-deductible treatment of LTCI policies.

◆

CHAPTER THIRTY-NINE

HOW TO BUY INSURANCE EVEN IF YOU'RE UNINSURABLE

Throughout this book, we have said that life insurance should be a central tool in your Wealth Protection plan because it can serve as a tax reducer, a portfolio diversifier, an asset protector, a death protector, and even a pension rescuer. Nevertheless, many of you may be concerned that you will not be able to take advantage of life insurance because you are uninsurable. Perhaps you believe you are too ill or too old to realize a cost-effective return. However, there are still several ways in which you can participate in the optimizing effects of life insurance to protect and to create wealth.

ARE YOU REALLY UNINSURABLE?

Whether you are concerned about yourself or a family member, such as a parent or grandparent, the first option you have is to verify whether you are truly uninsurable. Different insurance companies use different standards; and it is possible that even if you were turned down by one company, another will accept you. Also, as medical knowledge increases, conditions that previously disqualified you from insurance coverage might now be treatable so coverage can be issued. Finally, your condition may have improved or stabilized over time where, while you were once uninsurable, you are no longer considered in that category. For example, many insurance companies will insure cancer survivors if they have been "healthy" for five years. For these reasons, it is important that your insurance advisor be familiar with the underwriting practices of several insurance companies. It also helps if he or she knows some of the underwriters personally and if he or she does a considerable amount of business with that company. These factors do matter!

USE A "SURROGATE INSURED"

For someone who is not insurable at all, we can use a "surrogate insured" to be the person covered under the policy. We most commonly use the spouse as the surrogate. This is quite routine in the insurance industry. However, even if neither you nor your spouse is a good candidate for insurance coverage, there are still options.

Look around at the members of your extended family for someone more suitable to be insured. Perhaps your children have an uncle or an aunt, a godparent or a cousin who is in better health or younger than you are who can serve as the surrogate. In all likelihood, some member of your extended family would be a good candidate.

When you have selected that person who represents the best return on the insurance investment, arrange for that person to be examined. As long as that person has signed a completed life insurance application, the tests and analysis are paid for by the insurance company. Once this is done, you create a trust naming your children as trustees and gift the money to the trust on their behalf. There typically will be no gift taxes due, only the use of a portion of the lifetime exemption amount. The trust buys the insurance policy on the surrogate. The policy earns the appropriate rate, depending on the surrogate's age and health, and names the trust as its beneficiary.

The insurance proceeds ultimately come to your children, free of gift and estate taxes, upon the death of the surrogate. If the surrogate happens to die before you do, the policy proceeds will "wait" in the trust to pay the estate taxes due upon your death.

For example, assume that you have an estate valued at $5 million and that both you and your spouse are uninsurable. Your brother and his wife, who are around age 60, are insurable; so you select them to be your surrogates.

The estate taxes on your $5 million (if you have a properly structured and fully funded living trust) will be approximately $1.5 million, an amount that, without proper planning, your children will lose forever. At their average age of 60, you can purchase a $1.5 million, last-to-die insurance policy on the aunt and uncle for a single premium of $150,000 to $250,000 (depending on their health). To be more precise, you actually transfer the $150,000 to the trust, paying $0 gift taxes but using part of your exemption. The trust buys the insurance policy, which ultimately nets your children $1.5 million, completely replacing the amount that will be paid in estate taxes. The total cost of the plan was $150,000 for the policy and, at most, $0 in gift taxes. *This accomplishes exactly what you would want to achieve if you were insurable, with no extra cost.*

It is important to note that not all insurance companies accept the surrogate method and that the proposal must be presented properly to the ones that do.

FOREIGN INSURANCE COMPANIES THAT INSURE THE UNINSURABLE

In Chapters 31 and 32, you learned about the growth of offshore planning. Nowhere is this field more stable and mainstream than in the area of insurance. Many of the top 20 reinsurance companies in the world are domiciled in offshore havens such as Bermuda, the Cayman Islands, and Switzerland. The best-known insurance marketplace in the world is found in London—the Lloyd's of London insurance syndicate.

Given this, and our own contacts with top insurance companies offshore, we often offer the option to our uninsurable clients to have their insurance placed through a large international carrier. The reason this works is that many of these companies are much more liberal in their underwriting than U.S.–based companies are. In addition, their cost structure is much more streamlined than their U.S. counterparts; so the expenses and the commissions are typically substantially lower than those of U.S. products.

It is not surprising that many of our top clients also use offshore cash value life insurance as an excellent asset-protected and tax-deferred retirement vehicle. In fact, as long as the policy qualifies for U.S. tax treatment as a life insurance policy (and of that we as advisors make certain), then all of the benefits of U.S. cash value life insurance can be enjoyed through an offshore policy, but with fewer costs.

Even the investments of the policy, if it is a variable policy, can be managed with a U.S.–based advisor. Let's see how this strategy works.

CASE STUDY: LEONARD USES FOREIGN INSURANCE

Leonard, age 82, has a major estate tax problem. A widower, he has about $8 million in an estate, which will all be subject to estate tax when he dies because he has already used up his estate tax exemption amount. He wanted to use an irrevocable life insurance trust (ILIT) and life insurance to cover the estate tax bill of nearly $4 million, but he was deemed uninsurable by all U.S. insurance companies.

We found a well-established insurance company based in Bermuda that would write a policy on Leonard, so long as the policy was a variable universal life (VUL) product. Because the product would qualify for all IRS tests for life insurance (guideline premium, diversification, cash corridor, etc.), it would be treated by the IRS like any U.S.–based life insurance policy.

Leonard established and funded an ILIT to purchase the policy. Some gift taxes were due, as he gifted nearly $2 million into the trust. The trust purchased the VUL with a $4 million death benefit. As with any VUL, some of the funds went for expenses and the cost of the insurance with most of the funds going into an investment account.

Leonard was concerned that the bulk of the funds would be invested offshore, so we arranged for the variable account of the policy (with the lion's share of the funds) to be invested in New York with a major Wall Street firm. Furthermore, because the policy is a variable policy, this account is a segregated asset of the policy, not an asset of the insurance company. Thus, under both Bermuda law and U.S. law, the creditors of the insurance company can never claim those assets. No matter what happens with the finances of the Bermuda insurance company, Leonard's policy will not be at risk. This is exactly the same treatment that a variable policy of a U.S.–based insurance company would enjoy.

When Leonard dies, his family will get $4 million, free of both income and estate taxes. His estate taxes will be paid, and he was able to arrange this for a lower cost than if he had used a U.S. company. Of course, he did not even have that option here because of his poor health. Moreover, through this policy, most of his funds remained in the United States and were not subject to the financial risks of the offshore company.

Note: There were complex strategies employed to reduce the gift taxes. These are outside the scope of this chapter.

LAST WORD

Do not be discouraged if you or a family member has been deemed "uninsurable." There are a number of options to get insurance even when one is "uninsurable."

◆

CHAPTER FORTY

"Free" Insurance: Using Other People's Money to Pay for Your Estate Planning

B anks make money by borrowing money from people through deposits, certificates of deposit (CDs), checking and savings accounts, and so on. The banks then lend money to people to buy homes or cars or to start businesses. Because they may pay you only 3 percent or 4 percent for the money they borrowed and they lend money at rates of 7 percent to 9 percent, they are making money . . . on other people's money! This system has been used around the world for centuries.

This chapter will show you how to benefit from the same strategy banks have used for years. All you need is a home, some real estate, a business, accounts receivable, a brokerage account, or a letter of credit from a bank, and you can do your estate planning with someone else's money.

There is no such thing as *free* insurance. What we are talking about is borrowing someone else's money to pay for your insurance. You have heard that "it takes money to make money." We are going to show you how to use someone else's money to fund your estate plan.

How does this work?

Ideally, you want to borrow money at a favorable, and possibly tax-deductible, rate. Then, with the loan proceeds, you purchase a life insurance policy. Of course, the loan you take out has interest payments (which may be tax deductible). You might pay the interest payments, or you might let them accrue. You also have to eventually pay back the loan principal. With insurance, you have dividends, cash accumulation, and a death benefit. If the cash accumulation in the insurance policy (which is always tax deferred or tax free) is large enough to pay off the loan, you use tax-free loans from the policy to pay off the loan. Then, any remaining death benefit in the insurance policy is yours!

An alternative method, after securing the loan and purchasing the insurance policy, is to use the dividends to pay the interest on the loan. If you borrowed $100,000 to buy a $500,000 life insurance policy and the dividends are large enough to pay the interest payments, you can agree to pay off the $100,000 loan with a portion of the death benefit from the insurance. In this case, your family still has $400,000 left. That's $400,000 that cost you $0 out of pocket.

Is this possible?

In 2001, we had one client secure an interest-only home equity loan as low as 2.9 percent. We had another client receive a loan on his brokerage account for as little as 1.6 percent (in a unique international loan program). We had many clients take out home equity loans at rates of 6 percent to 7.5 percent. If you assume a 30 percent-to-40 percent income tax bracket, these clients received tax deductions that reduced their after-tax loan rates to 3.5 percent to 5.25 percent. At the same time, a AAA-rated insurance company credited 6.5 percent (tax free) to its universal life policies and over 7.2 percent to its whole life policies. You can use the difference to pay down the loan principal, too. This will leave the entire death benefit to your family.

Is it worth the effort?

"Financial insurance" is a growing trend with many multimillionaire families and businesses because these clients don't want to write checks for tens or hundreds of thousands of dollars for life insurance premiums out of their own pockets. They like the idea of using someone else's money. They may have a lot of wealth, but not a lot of available money to pay premiums, especially if the money is tied up in a business or other investment. While you may not be in this situation, financial insurance may still make sense. In the right circumstances, you could literally be providing your heirs a "free" death benefit.

PART VII

RETIREMENT PLANNING

CHAPTER FORTY-ONE

WE DON'T KNOW WHERE WE'RE GOING, BUT WE ALL WANT TO GET THERE

Most clients really aren't sure what they will do when they retire, and many don't know where they will do it. However, other than having the money to pay the bills, the most important reason most people give for working is to help them reach their lifelong goal—an enjoyable retirement.

We have analyzed thousands of clients' financial situations in our practices. We can tell you that there is great variation in ages of retirement and in amounts of money available in retirement for clients within the same professions or income brackets. You don't have to be lucky to retire early with plenty of money. Rather, you have to plan intelligently, diversify in your methods of saving, and avoid big mistakes along the way.

There are many different ways to save for retirement and even more pitfalls to avoid on the yellow brick road to your retirement Oz.

The purpose of this part is to explain what tools can be used to help you maximize the amount available to you in retirement and to explain how to withdraw retirement funds to make sure you don't unnecessarily pay too much in taxes or expose yourself to unnecessary investment risk.

As you will see throughout the book, many of the tools and strategies have multiple uses and offer more than one benefit. For that reason, it is imperative that you work with professionals who have multidisciplinary expertise and who can help you piece together your retirement, tax, asset protection, investing, and insurance planning without unnecessary overlap, overkill, or overpaying! Keep this in mind as you read this and other parts of your customized Wealth Protection plan (which resulted from your answers to the risk factor analysis—RFA—in Part 2).

CHAPTER FORTY-TWO

DEFINED-CONTRIBUTION PLANS: THE TRUTH ABOUT YOUR 401(K), PENSION, AND IRAS

O f the two types of retirement plans, most of us are more familiar with the defined-contribution plans than we are with the defined-benefit plans, covered in Chapters 43 and 44. Defined-contribution plans allow us to put away certain amounts (on a tax-deductible basis), which are determined by our annual salaries and by the type of plan created by our employer. These plans generally allow us some control over the direction of the investments within the plans.

WHY HAVEN'T I HEARD THE TERM *DEFINED CONTRIBUTION*?

There is no defined-contribution plan that goes by that name. We know the defined-contribution plans by other names: 401(k) plans, 403(b) plans, individual retirement accounts (IRAs), simplified employee pension (SEP)-IRAs, Keoghs, profit-sharing plans (PSPs), and money purchase plans (MPPs) are all types of defined-contribution plans. They are all designed for different situations and offer different annual funding amounts. The recent law change allows for a scheduled increase to many of the retirement plans. Please talk to an expert in this area before making any contributions because the amounts will be changing. As of 2002:

- A 401(k) is restricted to $11,000 ($15,000 by 2006)
- IRAs are restricted to $3,000 (growing to $5,000 in 2008)
- PSPs and MPPs are restricted to 25 percent of your income or $40,000, whichever is less.

In addition to funding limits, there are also restrictions on who can create each type of plan and what investments can be purchased within each plan.

As you can imagine, you cannot get something for nothing. If your employer creates the plan (and pays for it), your maximum contribution amount is rather low (401[k]—$11,000). If you are self-employed and create your own plan, the cost of a PSP or an MPP is higher, but those plans would offer you greater contribution amounts. If you are an employer, you have to provide something for your employees so you can get a larger benefit for yourself. This may mean creating a larger contribution plan, which is typically more costly to create and administer.

OTHER BENEFITS

Along with the tax deductions, there are other benefits that you get from certain plans. As described in Part V on asset protection, retirement plans are generally excellent asset protection tools, especially ERISA-qualified plans (ERISA means Employee Retirement Income Security Act), which are shielded under federal law. Even non-ERISA-qualified plans and IRAs can be protected under your state's law. (For more on this, see Part V.)

If your defined-contribution plan is subject to a *vesting* period, you do not technically "own" the contributions your employer makes for you until you stay at your place of employment for a specified period of years—usually two to seven years. This usually helps employers retain employees a little longer because employees don't want to leave if they will lose money from the unvested portions of their retirement plans. Of course, if you stay long enough to vest (earn your employer's contributions made on your behalf), you will have a much larger retirement account balance. If you have a retirement plan where you work, make sure you understand the vesting schedule before you even consider leaving. Leaving could be more costly than you think.

POTENTIAL PITFALLS

If you are an employee, setting up a SEP-IRA for yourself or participating in your employer's 401(k) plan is fairly simple. But if you are an employer, properly administering a retirement plan for yourself and employees is fraught with potential problems. The combination of rules of the Internal Revenue Service (IRS), ERISA, and the Department of Labor makes keeping the plan out of trouble a harrowing matter for employers. Discrimination, top-heavy, and over-funding issues abound. As an employer, you can be subject to fines if your plan does not comply with all of these complicated regulations. If you are in this position, you must consult a professional who has a great deal of experience in retirement plan administration. A growing trend is to use a professional employer organization (PEO—see Chapter 68) to shift the burden and liability. It is truly one area where you don't want to skimp on fees only to end up with poor quality knowledge and experience.

CHOOSING THE RIGHT PLAN FOR YOU

If you are an employer, before you choose a retirement plan for yourself and your employees, make sure you contact a specialist with a great deal of experience in this area. You also should make sure you understand all the nuances of defined-contribution plans, defined-benefit plans (covered in Chapters 43 and 44), and all other deferred compensation arrangements (some described later in this part and many more at www.mywealthprotection.com). The benefits can be extraordinary, but the pitfalls are not to be taken lightly.

CHAPTER FORTY-THREE

DEFINED-BENEFIT PLANS: CATCH UP IN YOUR RETIREMENT PLANNING

Defined-benefit plans are very different from defined-contribution plans. Some actuaries might say they are actually "opposites." In a defined-contribution plan, the amount you can contribute is restricted. In a defined-benefit plan, it is the benefit that you can realize in retirement that is the restricted value. An actuary calculates the monthly retirement benefit to which you are entitled, based on your present salary and your desired retirement age. Then, the actuary calculates the anticipated rate of return on the investments to be purchased in the plan. This rate of return is determined by the types of investment vehicles that are purchased inside each plan (stocks and bonds for standard defined-benefit plans and the guaranteed returns of the annuities and insurance in a 412[i] plan, which is covered in the next chapter). With those assumptions, the actuary will determine the contribution that you can make each year.

Rule of thumb: defined-benefit plans are very appealing if you:

- Are at least 50 years old (though they also work for individuals over 40 who wish to retire early).
- Want to contribute more than the defined-contribution limits allow.
- Have less in your retirement plan accounts than you should at this time.

Why would an age 50+ client have relatively low balances in his or her retirement plans? There are many reasons, from starting a career later in life to not regularly contributing to a defined-contribution plan throughout their careers, to losing a significant amount of retirement funds in a divorce, to having a financial hardship that required him or her to liquidate retirement funds for an emergency earlier in life, or even to having experienced very poor investment results inside the retirement plans.

CASE STUDY: CLAYTON GETS A LATE START

After pursuing a professional surfing career for decades, Clayton went back to business school, received his M.B.A., and then began a lucrative consulting career. After working for a Big-Five firm for two or three years, he started his own firm. At this point, he was 50 years old and had no retirement savings. We helped him create a defined-benefit plan for his corporation, and our calculations showed that, based on his age of 50 and his salary of $175,000, he would be able to put away $69,000 per year (on a tax-deductible basis). This saved Clayton over $30,000 in income taxes and helped him begin recouping the time he lost in saving for his retirement. He also implemented other strategies that are described later in this part.

If you are a good candidate for a defined-benefit plan, the reason for your present shortfall in retirement savings is not important. What is important is that the government allows you to "catch up" by contributing larger amounts per year on a tax-deductible basis with a defined-benefit plan.

ARE YOU A GOOD CANDIDATE FOR A DEFINED-BENEFIT PLAN?

Unfortunately, there are many factors that determine the amount you can contribute to a defined-benefit plan, and many of these change every year. Contact us to get an estimate. To give you an accurate proposal, most plan administrators will need to see a complete employee census (Appendix 6) that shows the names, dates of birth, sex, marital status, salary, years of service, and hours per week for every employee who has worked for the corporation for a given year. There are both sample and blank employee census forms at www.mywealth protection.com for your viewing or downloading.

CHAPTER FORTY-FOUR

THE PERFECT RETIREMENT PLAN IF YOU ARE OVER AGE 50: THE 412(I) PLAN

I f you were directed to this chapter by the RFA, it is because you make over $150,000 per year and are over the age of 50. For clients like you, the best retirement plan option may be a fully insured defined-benefit plan, or 412(i) plan—especially if you have not yet much put away into retirement plans. The 412(i) plan takes its name from the Internal Revenue Code section that governs its rules—section 412(i).

As you learned in Chapter 42, a basic 401(k) offers an employer very little in the way of annual deductions, and there are "antidiscrimination" rules that threaten your deductions if employees don't participate. A money purchase plan may offer you deductions of up to 25 percent of compensation or $40,000 (whichever is less), as long as you contribute the same percentage of each employee's compensation to his or her account.

BEST CANDIDATES FOR A DEFINED-BENEFIT PLAN

Generally, a defined-benefit plan (explored in the previous chapter) allows for much bigger deductions for individuals who fit into any of the following categories:

- Those who are getting a late start in saving for retirement (in qualified retirement plans only. If you have $10,000,000 of nonplan assets, you can still participate).

- Those who may have lost their plan assets in a divorce or may have been forced to prematurely withdraw plan assets as a result of a financial hardship.

- Those who have lost significant amounts of their retirement plan assets as a result of poor decisions, fraud, or terrible market conditions.

For example, a 55-year-old who makes more than $200,000 per year and who is just starting to make contributions to a newly formed defined-benefit plan may make up to $100,000 of tax-deductible contributions per year.

THE BASICS OF
DEFINED-BENEFIT PLANS

Defined-contribution plans, like 401(k) and profit-sharing plans, restrict your contributions but do not put a cap on the potential growth of the plan assets. Of course, every person will have a different amount available in his or her plan at retirement as a result of the investment results inside the plan. Furthermore, there is no guarantee on how much will be available for retirement unless the investments inside the plan are all in guaranteed, fixed investments.

In a defined-benefit plan, the amount with which you will retire (at a predetermined age) is set, based on your salary and year of retirement, as well as on IRS-approved and actuarially reviewed assumptions. Of course, if the plan accounts for 8 percent growth in your investments and you get 6 percent, there will be much less available in retirement. To make up for this risk, the government allows you to alter the amount each year, based on the returns on the investments in the previous year. There is also a possibility that your investments may exceed the assumed rate of return. If that happens, you will not be allowed to make as much in annual deductible contributions in future years.

Because of the annual costs of the actuarial review, defined-benefit plans are more costly than the defined-contribution plan alternatives. However, if you are over the age of 50 and have little in retirement plan savings, the tax deductions will more than offset the additional cost of $500 to $1,000 per year. Furthermore, you will be able to save more for your retirement.

A VARIATION ON THE THEME— HOW TO DEDUCT OVER $100,000 PER YEAR

A 412(i) plan is a type of defined-benefit plan. This plan works almost exactly the same way as the typical defined-benefit plan. However, there is one major twist—the benefit in retirement is guaranteed. If you construct a 412(i) plan to give you a monthly benefit of $10,000 in retirement, it is guaranteed to be at least that high.

The 412(i) plan purchases annuities from insurance companies that may offer guarantees of 2 percent or 3 percent. With a 2 percent or 3 percent return guaranteed, the IRS allows you to use the 2 percent or 3 percent return in your calculation of future value of the plan. Because the regular defined-benefit plans assume a nonguaranteed return of 6 percent to 8 percent when determining the amount of tax-deductible contributions the owner can make and the 412(i) plans use a much lower return, 2 percent to 3 percent, in the assumptions, the 412(i) plans allow for significantly more in tax-deductible contributions annually. For example, it is possible for the same 50-year-old physician mentioned before to make tax-deductible contributions of over $150,000 into a 412(i) plan annually.

WHY WOULD I WANT LOWER RETURNS?

You are not getting lower returns. You are just guaranteed a lower amount—with the upside potential of greater returns. The annuities in the 412(i) plan may still give you 6 percent to 8 percent or more per year. In fact, the 412(i) plan's investments will likely give you much more than the 2 percent to 3 percent. However, we only have to use the guaranteed amount in our actuarial calculation. This is what allows some 60- to 65-year-olds to make $300,000 in tax-deductible contributions per year into a 412(i) plan.

You are saving significant income taxes in your prime earning years, you are getting a guaranteed return on your investment, you have the upside of the market, and you do *not* have to have any employees to start a 412(i) plan. If you work for yourself, work in a small business with few or no employees, or implement one of the asset protection strategies mentioned earlier and create your own corporation, you can create the retirement plan that best fits your individual needs.

PITFALLS OF DEFINED-BENEFIT PLANS

As with all retirement plans, the 412(i) can be a double-edged tax sword. You can save quite a bit of money, if you qualify. However, if you die with a substantial estate and have money in any retirement plan, there may be a significant (up to 83 percent) tax on those retirement plan assets when you pass away. This is covered in Chapters 57 and 58 later. If you presently have or intend to have significant retirement plan assets, please read those chapters as well.

LAST WORD

For those of you who have fallen behind in your retirement savings for one reason or another, want to achieve significant tax savings, and like the idea of *guaranteed* retirement benefits with further upside potential, the 412(i) plan can be invaluable in helping you achieve your goals.

CHAPTER FORTY-FIVE

VARIABLE ANNUITIES: ASSET PROTECTION, TAX DEFERRAL, AND CAPITAL PRESERVATION FOR YOUR RETIREMENT PLAN

The questions most clients ask about retirement planning are:

1. How can I reduce my taxes?
2. How can I protect my retirement funds from lawsuits?

The recent volatility in the stock market and the uncertainty of our political landscape have led to a third pressing concern:

3. How do I protect my investments from depreciation?

We have devoted entire parts of this book to asset protection and investing and have mentioned variable annuities in both of those parts. For a complete understanding of all the benefits that are afforded variable annuities, you should read Chapters 21 and 28 as well. In this chapter, we will discuss how variable annuities can be an integral part of your retirement plan. Of course, you should read the remainder of this part so you understand all of your retirement planning alternatives. In addition, there is no substitute for meeting with a retirement specialist to determine the best mix of strategies and vehicles for meeting your retirement, asset protection, investing, tax, and estate planning needs.

WHAT IS A VARIABLE ANNUITY?

A variable annuity is a personal retirement vehicle that brings together the features of investments and insurance. Money is invested in various investment options of your choosing, with potential growth treated on a tax-deferred basis. At retirement, the money in a variable annuity can be converted into income that is guaranteed to last for life (that guaranteed income depends on the claims-paying ability of the issuer of the annuity, so you should research the insurance company issuing the annuity).

Variable means that the return on your investment depends on the composition and the performance of the investment portfolios you choose. These investment options, including stock- and bond-based alternatives, give your assets the potential to grow more quickly than traditional fixed annuities, but they also provide for greater downside risk.

WILL HAVING A VARIABLE ANNUITY AFFECT MY PENSION CONTRIBUTIONS?

No. The typical variable annuity sets virtually no limit on the amount or the frequency of your contributions (unless, of course, you are using a variable annuity to fund a qualified plan).

As you learned in the previous chapters of this part, you may be limited to only $10,000 to $40,000 of tax-deductible contributions to a retirement plan. If you are earning much more than you need to live, you may be adding $10,000 to $100,000 per year to your brokerage account, which you fund after paying taxes. This brokerage account offers no tax deferral and no asset protection. The variable annuity may be the ideal tool for deferring taxes to a later date—when you may be in a much lower income tax bracket—and for protecting your investments from lawsuits.

ADDITIONAL BENEFITS OF
VARIABLE ANNUITIES

1. *Asset protection.* Variable annuities are protected in some states. To see a list of which states protect variable annuities from lawsuits, visit www.mywealthprotection.com.

2. *Principal protection.* Generally, the insurance company issuing the annuity "insures" your heirs against lost capital at the time of your death. For example, if you put $500,000 into an annuity and the account is worth only $400,000 when you die, your heirs will receive the full $500,000, less any withdrawals taken. There are ways to increase the insured amount each year. These were covered in Chapter 21 in Part IV.

3. *Additional benefits.* Variable annuities offer dollar cost averaging (Chapter 21), interest sweeps, automatic portfolio rebalancing, annual ratchet protection, and other options that are covered in greater detail in Chapter 21 and in a chart on page 118.

LAST WORD

In most cases, individuals in high tax brackets with a great deal of investment income or individuals who live in states where variable annuities are protected from lawsuits receive the most benefit from variable annuities. Most others find more benefit from using life insurance as a retirement tool, which is described in the next chapter.

CHAPTER FORTY-SIX

◆

LIFE INSURANCE AS A RETIREMENT TOOL

A s you learned in Part VI on insurance planning, we consider life insurance to be the cornerstone of Wealth Protection planning. That is because it can play so many roles in a plan, from death protection for a family to income tax reduction on investments, asset protection, and pension tax reduction. These roles are covered in Chapters 22, 28, 36, and 58. Here we discuss using life insurance as a retirement vehicle.

Life insurance is the *only* effective tax-deferred savings vehicle available to those who want to retire before they turn 59½.

Retirement plans and variable annuities both allow for tax-deferred growth. However, those benefits come at a price—you can't get to the funds before age 59½ without paying a 10 percent penalty on top of the income taxes. That could mean taxes of up to 60 percent in some states! Furthermore, when you die, the funds are completely income taxable before your spouse can get to them (with the same penalties applying before she turns 59½), and the funds may be taxed at rates up to 80 percent before your children get access to any of the principal (covered in Chapter 57 on IRD).

The only retirement tool that allows for tax-deferred growth, tax-free withdrawals before age 59½, and completely tax-free money for your heirs and that protects your family from your premature death is life insurance. One thing you should realize after reading this book is that the key to inexpensive and effective Wealth Protection planning is *flexibility*. In other words, you want to implement tools and strategies that can help you in multiple situations. This way, you don't have to redo your plan every time one little part of your life changes. There are going to be many changes between now and the time you pass away, and a flexible plan that includes flexible tools and strategies (especially life insurance) can change with you and help you to meet your new goals and objectives.

Most people are very skeptical about life insurance because they may have had some unscrupulous life insurance agent sell them some terrible policy years ago. Life insurance is just like every other product or service. There are good and bad products and good and bad people who offer them. Just because some doctor hurt his patients, or even killed one in a hospital, doesn't mean that all doctors or hospitals are bad.

WHAT ARE THE BEST TYPES OF INSURANCE TO USE FOR RETIREMENT PLANNING?

Variable universal life, equity-indexed universal life, or whole life policies are primarily used as a supplemental retirement plan, to compliment other retirement and investment programs, for investment diversification, or as protection against a premature death with the thought of using the cash values if they are needed in retirement.

WHY USE AN INSURANCE POLICY AT ALL?

- The money invested inside the policy grows tax deferred.
- The money inside is available to you, by way of loans, without penalty or taxes before age 59½, unlike most other tax-deferred plans.
- There is usually no limit to the amount you can have and therefore no limit on the amount you can invest. There are some limits, but most people seldom reach them. You do have to qualify healthwise and financially in order to get it, since it is life insurance.

- All money in this type of policy goes to your heirs outside of probate court and totally income tax free!

- This is the *only* investment other than a Roth IRA that can possibly provide *tax-free* (that's right—tax-free, not just tax-deferred) growth on your money. It could become one of your primary investments for long-term retirement money.

WHY USE A VARIABLE POLICY?

- All of the aforementioned benefits, plus . . .

- More investment choices. Some variable policies offer over 40 mutual funds, whereas 401(k)s generally offer only 4 to 11 funds.

WHY USE A WHOLE LIFE POLICY?

- All of the aforementioned benefits of insurance policies, plus . . .

- Whole life policies have guaranteed death benefits and guaranteed annual returns. This makes for a perfect complement to the other investments you have that will vary based on the stock market. Remember, don't put all your eggs (or risk) in one basket.

CASE STUDY: JIM AND JANINE WANT TO RETIRE EARLY

Jim, 34, and Janine, 32, made the maximum contributions to their 401(k) plans every year and had put some money into variable annuities over the past few years. However, they knew that they would never be able to retire in their early to middle 50s with the projected amounts in their retirement plans—especially because the withdrawals from the 401(k) and variable annuities would be taxed and hit with an additional 10 percent penalty before age $59^1/2$. They were diligent at saving, putting an extra $1,000 per month away for their retirement (in addition to saving for vacations and home repairs on their lakeside home outside Minneapolis). They wondered where they should invest the $1,000 per month.

We explained that the average return of the stock market (Standard & Poor's 500) was 11 percent per year over the past 70 years and that the average tax on mutual funds is 32 percent (not counting state taxes). They said: "So we should expect the average after-tax returns to be closer to 7 percent." We told them that we had a better idea. Because (1) they have a $250,000 mortgage on their homes, (2) they want to start having children very soon, and (3) they have no life insurance yet, we told them we might be able to kill three or four birds with one stone.

We explained that a AAA-rated insurance company was presently crediting 7.5 percent (not guaranteed) on its whole life policies (all tax-deferred growth). In addition, if they put $500 per month away on each of their lives (into two separate policies), they would have $533,000 of coverage on Jim and $722,000 of coverage on Janine (who made more money). These amounts (which increase every year) would more than cover the mortgage on the home and a portion of the living expenses and college costs of their unborn children, should either Jim or Janine die prematurely.

Perhaps more importantly, they were very excited that this investment would help them create a more diversified portfolio (because all of their retirement plan assets were invested in mutual funds) and allow them tax-free withdrawals in their fifties—unlike their 401(k) funds, which would require them to pay an additional tax penalty of 10 percent if funds were withdrawn before age $59^1/2$. When Janine turns 55 in 23 years, they will have over $500,000 total in cash value saved and available for tax-free withdrawals. This should help support their retirement until they turn $59^1/2$ and can access their 401(k) and variable annuity funds. They will also have close to $1,700,000 in combined life insurance that they may wish to use to help them meet their estate planning goals (if that becomes a concern by then). In summary, they have much more flexibility.

LAST WORD

Any retirement plan that doesn't include some type of cash value insurance policy is probably subjecting the owner to unnecessary investment and tax risk and is probably costing the family a great deal of planning flexibility that will have to be handled through increased estate planning costs. Consult a professional to see how you can avoid unnecessary risk and provide the most flexibility to your plan by using life insurance in your retirement plan.

CHAPTER FORTY-SEVEN

DON'T RUN OUT OF MONEY (OR PAY TOO MUCH IN TAXES) IN RETIREMENT: LIFE ANNUITIES

In the past few chapters, we have helped you look at ways to save for retirement. This and the following chapter focus on how to *spend* your retirement savings. We aren't going to try to sell you ocean-front property in Phoenix or direct you a web site where you can buy discounted prune juice or MedicAlert bracelets so if you fall, you *can* get back up.

We are going to help you identify which assets must be spent down first and which assets should be left untouched for as long as possible. We will also show you a way to make sure that you don't run out of money in retirement. The reason this chapter is so important is that you don't know the exact day when you will die. Because you don't know when that day will come, you will either die with money left-over for your heirs, or you will run out of money in retirement. If you die with money leftover, we assume you would rather leave it to your heirs than to the federal government (this is where this chapter over-laps with Part VIII on estate planning). We also assume that you don't want to have to rely on your children, your children's spouses, or your grandchildren to support you.

How can I take the stock market and interest rate risk out of the retirement picture?

Retirement is a time for you to worry less, not more. You have already worked for 30 or more years, raised children, dealt with weddings (and maybe divorces), and handled many other life events. The last thing you want to do in retirement is worry about how you're going to support yourself and still leave something for your children, grandchildren, or favorite charity. Our strategy with our clients is to eliminate the risk, "guarantee" the clients an adequate income in retirement, and, if there is anything left, leave as much as possible to the heirs and/or charities. In our best-case scenario, we can do all of this while reducing, if not eliminating, the income and estate taxes in the process.

The life annuity (not to be confused with the variable annuity) is designed by the actuaries to pay interest and principal back to you over your lifetime. The amount the insurance company pays you is "fixed" and will not decrease if the stock market crashes or if interest rates fall. And if you outlive your life expectancy, the insurance company continues to pay you and/or your spouse for as long as you are alive. This is a good way to remove the investment risk of your retirement plan assets and to lock in a fixed income in retirement.

How much income can I expect from a life annuity?

Table 47.1 shows some numbers for clients of ours (two individuals, one couple) at varying ages. Of course, these numbers are only examples and may differ based on a variety of economic and medical factors. However, once a life annuity is purchased, the monthly or annual income amount cannot change.

TABLE 47.1   ANNUITY COST AND ANNUITY
             INCOME

CLIENT	COST OF LIFE ANNUITY	MONTHLY INCOME FOR LIFE
Mr. B—age 82	$500,000	$6,659
Mrs. G—age 71	$1,000,000	$8,028
Dr. and Mrs. C—ages 67 and 68	$1,500,000	$10,100*

*Pays this amount as long as either Dr. or Mrs. C is alive.

HOW DO I USE A LIFE ANNUITY AND STILL LEAVE SOMETHING FOR MY CHILDREN OR GRANDCHILDREN?

In most cases, the life annuity pays you more than you need to cover your cost of living. We recommend you gift the "excess" to an irrevocable life insurance trust (see Chapter 55) and buy life insurance to replace the value of the pension assets. Because pension assets are often only worth 20 percent to your heirs after income and estate taxes (see Chapter 57), this solution almost always gives more to the heirs, reduces income taxes paid on withdrawals, *and* provides a fixed income stream in retirement. If you're not sure how this solution would work in your situation, please feel free to call us, and we'll run an illustration for you.

IS THERE A WAY TO GET TAX-FREE INCOME WITH A LIFE ANNUITY?

Yes. If you purchase a life annuity with non–retirement plan assets, you will receive a significant tax benefit. Each life annuity of this type has what is called an "exclusion ratio," which is the amount of the monthly or annual payment that is *not* income taxable. The older you are, the greater the tax-free percentage of the life annuity payment. For an 80-year-old retiree, 70 percent of the annuity payment may be tax free. For this reason, many retirees like to purchase life annuities, rather than planning to live off the interest of their retirement savings and subject themselves to the risk of outliving the retirement funds. Of course, if you decide against utilizing the life annuity and take your chances with the stock market, it is possible that you could end up with a sizable retirement plan balance at the time of your death. You may think this will just benefit your children or grandchildren. If so, you are gravely mistaken. Many of your retirement plans will be subject to taxes of 80 percent when you die. Avoiding this hidden tax trap is the next concern we would like to address.

LAST WORD

Retirement should be a time for you to worry less, not more. Unfortunately, there are many concerns our generation must consider that our parents and grandparents didn't. If any of these concerns in this or the next two chapters hits home for you, take a step in the right direction and consult a professional.

◆

CHAPTER FORTY-EIGHT

AVOIDING OUTRAGEOUS TAXES ON RETIREMENT PLAN WITHDRAWALS

I n Chapter 15, we discussed the problem of income in respect of a decedent (IRD). This was that dreaded 80 percent tax on your pensions of which you were not made aware before you started your retirement plan. You were simply told to "Save, save, save" and you will make it to a beautiful place called Oz . . . we mean retirement. This chapter is designed to help you avoid this tax problem. If you have any money left in your retirement plan and you don't want to leave only 20 cents on the dollar to your heirs when you pass away, this may be the single most important chapter in the book for you!

Because all of your contributions to retirement plans are income tax deductible, all of your withdrawals from your plans will be fully taxable at ordinary income tax rates (as high as 50 percent in some states). Because of this tax, many clients are advised by their short-sighted advisors to "spend down other assets in retirement" and to continue "deferring taxation on the pension assets" as a way of avoiding unnecessary taxes.

A *Wall Street Journal* article on April 15, 1999, explained why this strategy is a "tax trap" for many of us whose savings or investments mean we will not need a significant portion of our qualified plan to live on during retirement. Anyone worth more than $2 million should know that 83 percent of retirement plan assets can be eaten up by the combination of income and estate taxes due on IRD. Because losing 83 percent of your plan assets is the worst possible tax trap, we don't want to be penny-wise and pound-foolish and avoid 50 percent taxation now just to leave an 80 percent tax bill for our heirs later.

CREATING TAX-FREE INCOME AND AN ESTATE TAX–FREE INHERITANCE

There are many different investment options within self-directed retirement plans. In some instances, these assets may have values, for tax purposes, that are 70 percent less than their cost. What this means is that these investments can be removed from a retirement plan with 70 percent of the income taxes avoided. If properly structured, these investments can avoid 70 percent of the income taxes, provide a stream of tax-free income payments during your retirement, and leave more to your heirs while avoiding the 80 percent tax on IRD. An example follows.

CASE STUDY: DR. GEORGE REDUCES UNNECESSARY TAXES ON HIS RETIREMENT PLAN

Dr. George is a 51-year-old cardiologist in Chicago. He has a retirement plan worth approximately $1,500,000 and has investments in excess of $2,400,000 (half in real estate and half in stocks and bonds). He intends to retire in nine years. He expected to have to pay nearly 50 percent in income taxes on all withdrawals (plus 10 percent in penalties if he takes money before age 59$^{1}/_{2}$). However, he was surprised to hear that over $1,060,000 of his $1,500,000 pension will go to taxes when he dies, in addition to the $750,000 of estate taxes that will be due on the non–retirement plan assets. He was eager to learn how he could reduce his income tax liability and find a way to leave more than 30 percent of his plan assets and 50 percent of his total estate to his heirs.

At our urging, Dr. George implemented the capital transformation strategy (CTS) at an investment of $600,000 from his retirement plan assets. He will then retire, as anticipated, in nine years and begin spending down his remaining pension assets to support his retirement. This should support him for nine years. Then, from his CTS investment, he will receive $120,000 per year tax-free for 27 years, or until age 96. In addition, because of the insurance component of this strategy, he will leave over $1.5 million to his wife and kids, income and estate tax free, when he passes away. This solution turned $600,000 of 50 percent taxable money into over $3,200,000 of tax-free retirement income. This solution also allowed him to avoid the 80 percent estate tax and left a $1,500,000 inheritance (from his pension) to his kids. Because he also implemented a living trust, a family limited liability company, and an annual gifting program, 100 percent of his $2,400,000 investments and their appreciation went to heirs tax free as well. He successfully avoided all estate taxes and received over $3,000,000 in tax-free retirement income.

LAST WORD

The details of this transaction are too complex to discuss completely here. However, if you have significant retirement plan assets and if you want to reduce the income taxes on your withdrawals and eliminate the 80 percent tax on the assets when you die, please go to www.mywealthprotection.com and download the materials on the "Capital Transformation Strategy." The frequently asked questions and executive summary may prove very helpful in educating you on one of several strategies that may help you.

CHAPTER FORTY-NINE

DON'T LET MEDICAL CONDITIONS RUIN YOUR RETIREMENT: TAKE ADVANTAGE OF LONG-TERM-CARE INSURANCE

U nfortunately, we can't offer you tricks from Ponce de Leon. We have not found the fountain of youth . . . yet. However, we can offer you the idea of using long-term-care insurance (LTCI) to protect your retirements (and your and your children's inheritances) from the outrageous costs of medical care not covered by Social Security, Medicare, or Medicaid.

Most baby boomers—the so-called "sandwich generation"—are saddled with the problem of having to take care of their children, themselves, and their parents. If you are in this generation, the biggest financial disaster that can impact your retirement is that you, your spouse, your parents, or your in-laws suffer significant health problems. In some states, the government will not pay for in-home or nursing home care until you have spent down all but $2,500 of your entire net worth. In addition, once the government begins paying for your care, it may take all but $30 per month of income from you, the person receiving the medical benefits. This would certainly destroy your retirement and any inheritances that might exist before the illness arose.

The cost of long-term care for one person can be hundreds of dollars per day. For this reason, many clients don't purchase long-term-care insurance just on themselves and their spouses, but they also buy long-term-care insurance on their parents and in-laws. There are many different insurance bells and whistles to consider, and payment options can be single-payment, 10-payment, 20-payment, and life-pay programs. To determine which type of policy is right for your family, read Chapter 38 on LTCI.

PART VIII

ESTATE PLANNING

CHAPTER FIFTY

MAKING SURE FAMILY ASSETS AREN'T LOST TO DISINHERITANCE, COURTS, OR THE IRS

I t should be apparent from your responses to the risk factor analysis (RFA) that you may need to consider certain estate planning tools as part of your Wealth Protection plan. Perhaps you have neglected to implement wills, living trusts, or other basic estate planning documents. Or you may hold property in joint ownership or have life insurance policies owned in your own name. Regardless of the specific reason, this part will help you understand how the estate planning portion of your Wealth Protection plan can be redesigned to better meet your family's needs.

It is very likely that many of you haven't done much estate planning, even though this planning deals with two of life's certainties: death and taxes. Unfortunately, millions of unnecessary taxes will be paid by families like yours until you realize that estate planning is crucial to an overall Wealth Protection plan.

If you think that estate taxes are no longer relevant because of the 2001 "repeal," then you should read the first chapter of this part, which shows the hidden taxes lurking in the so-called repeal.

Also, it isn't just taxes that you want to avoid in Wealth Protection estate planning. It's also the unintentional disinheritance of family members. Each year, millions of people title property in joint ownership without realizing that this ownership form might trump wills, leaving the property to the joint owner, rather than to those whom they named in their wills. This "disinheritance risk" may be in your estate plan right now.

The costs and delays of probate are also an important threat to avoid in estate planning. Remember the story of Chris's family back in the Introduction? When Chris's stepfather died, his estate was stuck in the probate process for over a year, while Chris's family desperately needed the inheritance to pay bills. This threat eventually caused Chris's mother to file for bankruptcy.

In this part, you will read about all of the tools you can use to reduce and even to eliminate estate taxes; avoid disinheritance risk; avoid probate; and deal with "problem assets," such as pensions, individual retirement accounts (IRAs), and family businesses.

CHAPTER FIFTY-ONE

THE TRUTH ABOUT THE ESTATE TAX "REPEAL"

Before discussing specific solutions, it is worth stressing that estate planning is more important now than ever before. Many of you may incorrectly assume that the estate tax has been repealed and, therefore, that estate planning is no longer important.

Although Congress repealed the estate tax as part of the 2001 Tax Relief Act, there is much uncertainty about future estate taxes. There is a strong likelihood that estates will be taxed heavily for the foreseeable future. Let's see how that will happen.

THERE IS NO ESTATE TAX REPEAL: ONLY A GRADUAL REDUCTION OF THE ESTATE TAX BITE

The full tax repeal, if it even occurs at all, will not take place until 2010. Before that time, the law reduces the estate tax on the estates of those who die during the intervening transitional period. It does this in two ways:

1. A provision that benefits all estates steadily increases the individual exemption amount so that it will be $1.0 million in 2002 and 2003; $1.5 million in 2004 and 2005; $2.0 million in 2006, 2007, and 2008; and $3.5 million in 2009, the final year before repeal. Married

couples, with proper planning, are able to take advantage of two exemptions in their estates. Thus, in 2002, a couple with a $2.0 million estate will no longer be subject to the estate tax.

2. There is a reduction in the top estate and gift tax rates, both 55 percent as of 2001. This change will help only wealthier taxpayers because these top rates affect only estates of more than $2.5 million. Effective January 1, 2002, the top rates of 53 percent and 55 percent are eliminated and replaced with a rate of 50 percent on taxable estates in excess of $2.5 million. The top rate is then further reduced by 1 percent a year until 2007, when it will be 45 percent; and it remains at that level until the tax is repealed at the end of 2009.

In these ways, the 2001 act has some effect on trimming the estate tax immediately, although this is far from a repeal.

WILL THERE BE ANY SO-CALLED REPEAL AT ALL?

Remember the fairy tale about Cinderella? If she did not return to her home by the time the clock struck midnight, her fine clothes would turn back to rags and her carriage would again be a pumpkin. Similarly, the estate tax repeal becomes fully effective January 1, 2010. However, unless the entire estate tax repeal is reapproved by Congress prior to 2011, then the clock strikes for the repeal as well, and the current law will be automatically reinstated. No one knows whether the repeal will be reapproved 10 years from now. Certainly you should not bank your family's estate plan on it.

It is important to understand that, in the absence of a reapproval of the repeal, the estate tax is not simply reinstated at the lower tax rates and larger exemption amounts enjoyed in 2009. Rather, the exemption amount is returned to the level allowed by the law we have today in 2002 (a relatively minor $1 million per person exemption), and the marginal tax rates are again raised (to a top rate of 50 percent). In this way, if not reapproved in 10 years, all of the estate tax reduction gained over the 10-year period will be lost.

Even more likely, according to many experts, is that the repeal will itself be repealed before 2009. When Congress passed this legislation, the budget office was projecting huge multitrillion-dollar surpluses in the federal government. This was back in the spring of 2001, before the economy continued to falter, before the destruction of September 11, 2001, and before the prolonged military battle with terrorism at home and abroad. At the time of this writing, much, if not all, of these surpluses have been eroded. No longer can the federal government afford to give away predicted future surpluses. In fact, it may have to take back some of the funds it has already given away.

Experts predict that the estate tax arena will be the first one targeted in this way, as the 2001 repeal helped only the richest 1 percent of taxpayers—a small enough minority that politicians won't be overly concerned about a public relations nightmare. Certainly, an unrepeal of the estate tax would be easier to pass than a further reduction of Social Security benefits (which most people over age 65 utilize).

EVEN IF THE ESTATE TAX REPEAL MAKES IT THROUGH, THE GIFT TAX REMAINS

To the surprise of many experts, the 2001 act did not repeal the gift tax. Even after the potential estate tax repeal, the gift tax will continue to be imposed on gifts in excess of the lifetime gift exemption, which will increase to $1.0 million in 2002, with no further increases slated.

The gift tax rates will also be reduced to a maximum rate of 35 percent by 2010, equal to the top income tax rate for individuals. (The top income tax rate today is 38.6 percent.) There is good reason for this linking of the top gift tax and income tax rates. Congress decided to retain the gift tax to discourage taxpayers from making tax-free gifts of income-producing property to family members in lower income tax brackets. Such transfers would be an easy way to reduce the overall income tax burden on the family. Although it will still be possible to make such transfers after the potential estate tax repeal, the reduced gift tax will act as a "toll charge" for taxpayers engaging in this type of planning.

STATE ESTATE TAXES MAY APPEAR

Under current law, an estate is entitled to a dollar-for-dollar federal estate tax credit (subject to a cap) for any state death taxes paid by the estate. Further, under this scheme, individual states share heavily in the tax revenue collected by the Internal Revenue Service (IRS). Thus, the states have no need to impose their own estate tax. This scheme was repealed by the act, effective for those dying after 2004, and replaced with a state death tax deduction.

While this repeal will have no immediate effect on most estates (because most state death taxes apply only if they qualify for the federal credit), it may encourage a new type of estate tax imposed directly by the states. States stand to lose billions of dollars annually by this change in the law, and their tax revenues need to be replaced by something. Many experts agree that individual state estate taxes are likely to appear to make up for this dramatic loss of tax revenue.

ANY REPEAL MEANS A LOSS OF BASIS STEP-UP AT DEATH

The quid pro quo for repeal of the estate tax was the loss of step-up in income tax basis at death. Currently, most property owned by a decedent for estate tax purposes receives a tax basis equal to its value at the date of death. Under the act, after December 31, 2009, property acquired from a decedent will retain the decedent's tax basis. This is known as "carryover" basis. When the recipient of the property eventually sells it, he or she will be compelled to compute the gain using the decedent's basis. In most cases, the decedent's basis will be less than the date-of-death value, resulting in an increased capital gains tax.

The legislation contains two major exceptions to carryover basis: (1) for estates less than $1.3 million and (2) for property up to $3 million passing to surviving spouses. Nonetheless, for larger estates, the additional capital gains taxes will take a large bite out of any potential estate tax savings. Furthermore, there will certainly be an increase in administrative difficulty and an increased cost in determining the cost basis of assets purchased 20, 30, 50, or more years ago by now-deceased relatives.

THE REPEAL LEAVES IRD ALONE

In addition to the estate tax, income tax must be paid on certain assets left in a decedent's estate at death. This tax is levied on what is called income with respect to a decedent (IRD). Because federal and state income taxes—including those characterized as IRD taxes—can be as high as 45 percent to 49 percent in many states, and estate taxes can range from 45 percent to 50 percent during the transitional period, the combined tax rate can escalate to 75 percent or more on IRD. What is the most common item of IRD subject to this high tax burden? Amounts left in pensions, profit-sharing plans, and IRAs.

Although there was much rhetoric in the 2000 presidential campaign about reducing the death tax on a family's assets, the 2001 act does nothing to eliminate, or even reduce, taxes on IRD. Thus, it remains an important part of Wealth Protection planning. For that reason, we have dedicated an entire chapter to the problem of IRD and another chapter to strategies for avoiding this outrageous tax problem (Chapters 57 and 58).

CHAPTER FIFTY-TWO

WILLS AND LIVING TRUSTS: THE BUILDING BLOCKS OF EVERY ESTATE PLAN

Did you know that you already have a will, even if you have never written one or had an attorney draft one? That's because if you die without any will, you get the universal will that your state government has written for all of its citizens. While this may seem like a practical concept, it is not, because there is no guarantee that the government will split up your estate in exactly the way you would want your property to be divided.

The precise rules vary among the 50 states; but typically, the laws (called the *intestacy laws*) are very rigid and formulaic. Usually, all your nearest relatives get a piece of your property, but not friends or charities. Furthermore, no one gets more than the state-allotted share. Often, this ends up hurting the surviving spouse. In this all-too-common scenario, the decedent's grown children may get some of the money meant for the surviving spouse, even if this means the surviving spouse then has too little to live on. In some states, the surviving spouse may get less than one-third of the decedent's property.

Moreover, the absence of a will often leads to expensive and lengthy court battles by family members contesting the division of assets. Sometimes family members produce questionable wills in court, trying to establish a rightful claim to a portion of the estate. Once again, this can be avoided by having a valid will in place.

Finally, if both parents of minor children die without a will, the courts will decide who becomes the legal guardian for your children. What parent would want to have a judge decide who will care for their children? You can avoid this tragedy by creating a valid will sooner rather than later. (For a detailed description of one state's intestacy laws, see Appendix 3.)

WHY YOU NEED A WILL *AND* A LIVING TRUST: TO SAVE TIME AND MONEY AND TO KEEP YOUR ESTATE PRIVATE

While having a will is certainly better than not having one at all, it is not enough. You also need a living trust. If you only have a will, then your entire estate will be stuck in the probate process, which is usually time-consuming, public, and costly. However, if you combine a living trust with a short will—called a "pour-over will" because it pours most of the assets into the living trust—then the vast majority of your estate will avoid probate completely. Before we examine how a living trust works, we will first explain why probate must be avoided.

THE PITFALLS OF PROBATE

- *Time:* Probate often takes between a year and two years to complete in many states. During that time, your beneficiaries must wait for their inheritance.
- *Money:* Probate can cost between 3 percent and 8 percent of your probate estate: the value of all your property passing under the will. This cost includes fees to the courts, the lawyers, appraisers, and your executor (the person in charge of handling your affairs during this process), among others. In some states, these probate fees are paid on your gross estate—not taking into account any mortgages on your assets! In these states, if you die owning $1 million worth of assets, assets that have mortgages of $800,000, your estate will pay probate fees on the $1 million, or around $50,000—money that could have gone to your beneficiaries rather than to courts and lawyers.

- *Privacy:* Probate is a public process in all states. Anyone interested in your estate can find out who inherits under your will, how much he or she inherits, the beneficiaries' addresses, and more. You may not be famous and worry about the newspapers exploiting this information, but think of your beneficiaries, your surviving family members. They certainly will not appreciate the many financial advisors calling them with "hot tips" on investments. Salespeople often find beneficiaries by examining probate records. They know who they are and how much "found money" they have to invest.
- *Control:* In probate, the courts control the timing and the final say-so on whether your will—and your wishes expressed in the will—are followed. Your family must follow the court orders and pay for the process as well. This can be extremely frustrating.

We are continually astonished by how many families endure the time and the expense of probate, when it is completely avoidable. Remember reading our introduction—Chris's stepfather was an attorney, and he only had a will!

HOW A LIVING TRUST SOLVES THE PROBLEM

A living trust, also called a "family trust" or a "loving trust," is a legal document that creates a trust to which you transfer assets during your life. As you learned in Chapter 30, a living trust is a revocable trust, meaning you can change it at any time. During your life, the assets transferred to the trust are managed and controlled by you—just as if you owned them in your own name. When you die, these trust assets pass to whomever you designated in the trust, automatically, outside of the probate process. Other benefits of the living trust include:

- Avoiding the unintentional disinheriting risked by joint tenancy (happens in many second marriages).
- Preventing court control of assets if you become incapacitated.
- Protecting dependents with special needs.

- Reducing or eliminating estate taxes (see the next chapter for more on this).

How to transfer assets to a living trust

When you transfer your assets to your living trust while you are alive, you maintain 100 percent control over these assets—just as if you still owned them in your own name. For your car, stocks, bonds, bank accounts, home, or any other asset, the process of transferring an asset to your living trust is the same. If the asset has a registration or a deed, change the name on such a document. If the asset is jewelry or artwork that has no official ownership record, use an assignment document to officially transfer ownership to your living trust.

These ownership changes will transfer the name of the registration or deed to "John Doe Revocable Living Trust" or "John Doe, Trustee of John Doe Revocable Living Trust," rather than "John Doe" as it now reads. As sole trustee of the trust, you have unlimited power to buy, sell, mortgage, invest, and so on, just as you did before. Furthermore, because the trust is revocable, you can always change beneficiaries, remove or add assets, or even cancel your trust entirely.

And remember, the transfer of assets to the living trust (called "funding the trust") is a necessary activity. Although it has no income tax ramifications at all (you are still treated as the owner for income tax purposes), it is crucial to gain the probate-saving benefits afforded to you at the time of your death.

You may name yourself or someone else as trustee

You need not name yourself as the trustee of your living trust, although most people do. You could name an adult child, another relative, a close friend, or even a corporate trustee, like a local bank or trust company. However, if you do not like the way the outside trustee is handling the trust, you always have the power to remove him or her. This power remains with you, the Grantor (creator) of the trust.

WHEN YOU DIE, YOUR SUCCESSOR TRUSTEE WILL TAKE OVER

If you are the trustee while you are alive, you will name, in your living trust, someone (or something like a corporate trustee) as the successor trustee. That person or entity will take over trustee duties when you die. If you have a third-person trustee or a co-trustee while you are alive, that person will complete trustee duties after you have died.

Trustee duties involve collecting income or benefits due your estate, paying your remaining debts, making sure the proper tax returns are filed, and distributing your assets according to the trust instructions. This person or entity acts like an executor for a will. However, unlike a will, actions under a living trust's directions are not subject to court interference.

YOU DECIDE WHEN YOUR BENEFICIARIES RECEIVE THEIR INHERITANCES

Another significant advantage of a living trust over a will can be that you, rather than the courts, decide when and how your beneficiaries get their inheritance. Because the court is not involved, the successor trustee can distribute assets right after he/she/it concludes your final affairs. This can take as little time as weeks or even days.

If you choose, assets need not be distributed right away. Instead, you may direct that they stay in your trust, managed by your individual or corporate trustee, until your beneficiaries reach the age(s) at which you want them to inherit.

THE SUCCESSOR TRUSTEE MUST FOLLOW YOUR TRUST INSTRUCTIONS

Your successor trustee (as well as your primary trustee, if it is not you) is a *fiduciary*—legal term meaning that he/she/it has a legal duty to follow the living trust instructions and to act in a reasonably prudent manner. The trustee must treat the living trust as a binding legal contract and must use "best efforts" to live up to the obligations of the contract. If your successor trustee mismanages the trust by ignoring the instructions in your living trust, he/she/it could be legally liable.

LAST WORD

As you have seen, wills and living trusts are a must for any Wealth Protection plan. They are truly the estate planning "building blocks." If you do not have such documents in place yet, you should remedy this problem as soon as possible.

⬥

CHAPTER FIFTY-THREE

THE A-B LIVING TRUST: HOW TO SAVE OVER $400,000 IN ESTATE TAXES FOR UNDER $3,000

Many married couples in the United States have a tragic financial blunder hidden in their estate plans. Numerous couples plan to provide for the surviving spouse by having the first-to-die spouse leave everything to the surviving spouse. Most Americans, in fact, don't know any other way to leave money to support the survivor. This mistake may cause your family to pay hundreds of thousands of dollars in estate taxes unnecessarily. To understand why, you must learn about the two fundamental rules of the estate tax system: (1) the unified estate tax credit and (2) the unlimited marital deduction.

THE UNIFIED ESTATE TAX CREDIT

The unified estate tax credit (UTC) translates into a dollar amount that can be left by a decedent estate tax free (commonly called the "estate tax exemption"). As explained in Chapter 50, after the 2001 changes, this exemption is $1 million in 2002 and 2003 and will rise to $3.5 million in 2009. Thus, in 2002, an individual can leave $1 million of property at his or her death to anyone, without any estate taxes being imposed.

We often explain the UTC as a "get-out-of-estate-taxes-free" card, like in the game Monopoly. Everyone gets one of these cards, to use either during his or her life or at the time of death. However, the card is nontransferable; and if it is not used at death, it is lost forever.

THE UNLIMITED MARITAL DEDUCTION

The unlimited marital deduction (UMD) states that a decedent can leave an unlimited amount to a surviving spouse without any estate tax—provided both spouses are U.S. citizens. (If you are interested in learning about the special estate tax rules applying to non–U.S. citizens, please visit our website www.mywealthprotection.com.)

Unfortunately, when thinking about their estate plan, too many married couples look at the UMD as their solution. They simply leave everything to their spouse, using the UMD to avoid all estate taxes. This does effectively eliminate all estate taxes at the first death, but it is a "penny-wise" and "pound-foolish" mistake. That's because the first spouse to die did not use his or her UTC, or "get-out-of-estate-taxes-free" card. Because it wasn't used, it is gone forever.

Although this seems innocuous when the first spouse dies, when the second spouse dies, the IRS gets you back. At that point, the surviving spouse's estate can only make use of one $1,000,000 exemption. That means everything over $1,000,000 will be subject to estate taxes—which begin at 37 percent and quickly rise to 50 percent. Look at this case.

CASE STUDY: TINA AND MIKE

Tina and Mike own a home worth $300,000; life insurance policies with combined death benefits of $900,000; another $200,000 in a retirement plan; a business worth $300,000; and general investments totaling $300,000. They might not think of themselves as millionaires, but to the federal estate tax authorities they are.

(continued)

If Mike dies and leaves everything to Tina, there will be no federal estate tax because of the UMD. Assume now that Tina has in-
herited the entire $2 million estate and lives off the earnings for the
rest of her life.

When Tina dies (let's assume in 2003), her will leaves the entire
estate to her children. In 2003, the children are not taxed on the first
$1 million worth of property they inherit from their mother because
of the UTC. The children do, however, pay federal estate taxes on
the amount in excess of $1 million, or in our example $1 million. The
tax rate starts at 37 percent growing to 50 percent, meaning the
children will be paying over $400,000 in federal estate taxes.

The terrible fact about this case is that the entire $400,000 of taxes
could have easily been avoided by using an A-B living trust. Tina still
would have been able to live on the earnings of what Mike left her
during her last years.

HOW AN A-B LIVING TRUST USES BOTH GET-OUT-OF-ESTATE-TAXES-FREE CARDS

Using an A-B living trust, at the death of the first spouse, the property is divided into two "buckets," bucket "A" (or Trust A) and bucket
"B" (or Trust B). Most people transfer assets that are the equivalent
of the UTC amount into bucket "B," which ultimately goes to the
heirs. The balance of the property will be transferred to "Trust A,"
which will be the trust for the surviving spouse. During her or his
lifetime, the surviving spouse will be full legal owner of Trust A and
can do virtually anything with the assets of the trust. This portion is
completely revocable during the lifetime of the surviving spouse.

The concept of Trust B is different. The surviving spouse does not
technically own Trust B. But he or she can draw income/interest from
the trust; use the property (for example, live in the home); use the
principal for support, maintenance, health, and lifestyle maintenance; and use either 5 percent of the principal or $5,000 a year for
any reason whatsoever.

After the death of the second (the surviving) spouse, Trust B directly goes to the heirs without any estate taxes, provided the assets transferred at the first death are equivalent to the UTC amount. All growth and principal goes to the heirs both income and estate tax free.

Trust A, which belonged to the surviving spouse, will now be distributed to the named beneficiaries. First, all the debts or liabilities, if any, will be paid off. Then depending on the year of the death, the wealth that is equivalent to the UTC amount will be transferred estate tax free to the beneficiaries. If the value of Trust A exceeds the UTC amount, then that portion of the estate will be subject to estate taxes. After paying the federal and state estate taxes, the estate will be transferred to the heirs.

CASE STUDY: TINA AND MIKE REVISITED

Let's now assume that during their lives Tina and Mike set up a joint A-B living trust and funded it properly. When Mike dies, the trust creates Trust B and funds it with the UTC amount in 2002—$1 million. During the rest of her life, Tina can access the principal of Trust B for support, welfare, health, and lifestyle maintenance. She can live in the home as well. The remainder of the property—$1,000,000— funds Trust A, which Tina can access and spend for whatever reason she wants.

When Tina dies in 2003, Trust B pays out directly to the beneficiaries of that trust—their kids. Because Trust B qualified for Mike's UTC when it was funded, there is no estate tax due on what is left in the trust, whether it has grown past $1 million or been spent down to less than $1 million.

Any property left in Trust A will qualify for Tina's UTC. Thus, when Tina dies, if there is less than $1 million in this trust (and that is likely because she has been living on the interest and a portion of the principal of the $1,000,000), there will be no estate tax on this portion either. In this way, the A-B living trust would save Mike and Tina's family over $400,000 in estate taxes.

LAST WORD

Any married couple whose total assets might put them above the estate tax exemption amount by the time they pass away (in 10, 20, or 40 years) should use A-B trusts. Without such a trust, one spouse is throwing out the get-out-of-estate-taxes-free card for no good reason.

CHAPTER FIFTY-FOUR

Avoiding Joint Ownership and the Disinheritance Risk

Why joint ownership is so dangerous

Joint ownership is the most popular form of ownership in the United States for stocks, bonds, real estate, and bank accounts. As we explained in Chapter 26 in Part V on asset protection, when one joint owner dies, property owned in joint ownership automatically passes to the surviving joint owner(s). In this way, jointly owned property passes outside of a will and avoids the expense of probate. Because it avoids probate, many financial and legal advisors recommend joint ownership. However, these advisors may not tell you that there are ways that you can be burned by owning assets in joint ownership.

As you have seen, using joint ownership is almost always a big mistake. In Chapter 26, you learned how joint ownership subjects you to lawsuit and creditor risks. Now you will learn how joint ownership can frustrate your true estate plan.

Joint ownership can ruin your estate plan

Joint ownership threatens to ruin your estate plan because, in many instances, any property you own jointly will pass automatically by the right of survivorship to the surviving joint owner(s). This automatic transfer takes effect, in the eyes of the law, the very instant you die, before any will or living trust can dispose of your property. In this way, your will or living trust will have no effect on jointly held property. If you designated certain beneficiaries in a will or a trust to receive your share of jointly held property, they will be "disinherited" because the surviving joint owner(s) will take the property. This avoidable tragedy occurs every day in this country because people don't realize the dangers of joint ownership. Consider these true cases.

CASE STUDIES: JOINT OWNERSHIP

- William, a man in his late sixties, marries for the second time. Shortly after the wedding, he puts all of his significant property—his main home, his winter vacation condominium, and his stock portfolio—into joint ownership with his new wife. In his state, joint ownership had an inherent right of survivorship. Within six months, William dies. The home, the condo, and the stocks all go to William's new wife. His three children and eight grandchildren inherit virtually nothing, even though William had made ample provisions for them in his will.
- In the same state, Susan's will left her property equally to her son and daughter. Because her son lives near her and pays Susan's bills, Susan puts her house, her safe deposit box, and her bank account in joint ownership with him. When she dies, Susan's son will get all of the money in the bank account and the safe deposit box, as well as the house, regardless of the will provisions. Unless the son is extremely generous, the daughter will get close to nothing.
- Assume a situation similar to Susan's, but add to it the fact that the son has serious creditor problems. Overdue on $15,000 in

credit card bills and a defaulted loan, the son's creditors can come after the bank account, the safe deposit box contents, and likely the house the instant the mother dies. The only real beneficiaries of the mother's estate may be banks and finance companies.

- Cecilia, a single mother in her thirties, is trying to build a college fund for her eight-year-old daughter, Debbie. Cecilia has invested some of her excess income to buy old residential, multifamily homes, which she and her partner then fix up and rent to tenants. Although her relationship with her partner has been strained at times, Cecilia thinks nothing of taking title to the investment properties in joint ownership with her partner, never realizing that if she dies before they resell the properties, her partner will take them all, leaving nothing for Debbie.

Why do well-intentioned people get stuck in these predicaments? They may not know any better, and their advisors may not be giving them smart advice. Sometimes, owners may not even realize what type of ownership they have chosen. In other cases, people consciously decide to use joint ownership because they know it will avoid probate. But this is never a reason to use joint ownership.

LAST WORD

Assets titled in joint ownership and assets titled in a living trust both avoid probate. Thus, if your goal is to avoid probate, use a living trust rather than joint ownership. You will get many more benefits without any of joint ownership's pitfalls.

CHAPTER FIFTY-FIVE

KEEP THE VALUE OF YOUR LIFE INSURANCE BY USING AN IRREVOCABLE LIVING TRUST

M any sophisticated Wealth Protection estate plans include life insurance. Clients can leverage today's wealth to create a very large estate (or to cover the estate taxes on an estate) in the future. Just as important, however, there's a natural logic to using life insurance in estate planning: An estate plan takes effect when you die, and that's when life insurance policies pay off. The IRS, unfortunately, doesn't always recognize simple logic, and the unwary could face a huge tax *trap*. If you were sent here by the RFA, you may be one of these unwary taxpayers.

The problem isn't income tax because life insurance proceeds generally avoid income taxes. Instead, the proceeds from the life insurance may be subject to federal estate taxes, where, as you've seen, the rates are much higher (up to 50 percent) than income tax rates. Of all the money the IRS collects in estate tax, more comes from improperly owned life insurance than from stocks, bonds, closely held businesses, and real estate!

CASE STUDY: THROWING AWAY LIFE INSURANCE

Let's assume you leave an estate of $1 million, plus a $200,000 life insurance policy. That brings your total (taxable) estate to $1.2 million. If you die in 2002 or 2003, an estate tax will be owed on the amount over $1 million—the estate tax exemption amount. The estate tax rate is 41 percent for estates worth between $1 million and $1.2 million. Therefore, your heirs owe an extra $82,000 in estate tax. In other words, you've paid for $200,000 worth of life insurance, but your family only ends up with $118,000. You paid for that extra $82,000 needlessly!

If you own your life insurance policies in a way that keeps them out of your taxable estate, those policies will maintain their value and be worth close to twice as much to your heirs. In the aforementioned example, the policy will be worth $200,000 to your family—not $118,000—and the insurance won't cost you one cent more!

REMOVING THE INSURANCE FROM YOUR ESTATE

You now see how important it is to keep life insurance policies out of your taxable estate. The following are two popular "strategies" for doing so. Both have distinct drawbacks and pitfalls.

HAVING THE SPOUSE OWN THE POLICY OR BE ITS BENEFICIARY

One popular method of sheltering life insurance proceeds from estate tax is to name your spouse as owner or beneficiary of the policy. This works temporarily, but not in the long term. As you learned in Chapter 53 on A-B trusts, the IRS is happy to have you pass everything to the surviving spouse so that you throw away one get-out-of-estate-taxes-free card (unified tax credit) without using it. That's because when the surviving spouse dies, the IRS gets a piece of everything above only one exemption amount, rather than only the amount above two combined exemptions.

A second pitfall of this approach is that you lose all control of the proceeds when you die. They will pass to your surviving spouse outright. If he or she spends them down foolishly, gets remarried and divorced, is sued, and so forth, then your planning just benefited someone other than your family members. There are ways you can control the funds even after you're dead and keep them in the family for generations by using a special life insurance trust, which dictates exactly how the funds can be used.

HAVING THE CHILDREN OWN THE POLICY

An alternate approach is to have your children own your life insurance policy, and they will receive the proceeds at your death. They can apply for the policy, pay the premiums (with money you may gift to them), and receive the proceeds at your death. If the policy and the proceeds are outside your estate, no estate tax will be due.

There are some drawbacks with this strategy, however, including:

- If the proceeds are paid to children, your surviving spouse may run short of funds to pay bills and to support himself or herself. This can be a very big problem in the situation of second or third marriages if the children don't agree to support a stepparent.

- If the policy is a cash-value policy (typical in estate planning situations because the policy is permanent), your kids may be tempted to borrow against the policy, thus reducing the death benefits payable.

- If there's a divorce, the policy may be considered a marital asset of your children, and some of the cash value could end up going to an ex-son-in-law or ex-daughter-in-law.

- If a creditor has a claim against your grown child, the policy may be seized as part of his or her assets. For example, the child may be a shareholder in a failed business, who has made personal guarantees on the company's notes.

- If your children are still minors, the policy would have to be owned by a custodian or a guardian.
- If you have more than one child, co-ownership of a valuable insurance policy may prove awkward or a point of contention.

THE SUPERIOR STRATEGY: USE AN IRREVOCABLE LIFE INSURANCE TRUST

You can avoid all these pitfalls by creating an irrevocable life insurance trust (ILIT) to be the owner and the beneficiary of your life insurance policies. If the ILIT owns the policy, it's out of your taxable estate. Moreover, a properly structured ILIT can keep the proceeds from children and their disgruntled spouses or creditors. The funds can then be used to cover estate taxes, to provide an income stream, to pay off debts and mortgages or notes, and to keep other valuable and needed assets intact for the family.

In many cases, the ILIT will use the insurance proceeds to buy illiquid assets, such as shares of a closely held business, real estate, or other assets from your estate, to keep them in the family. These types of purchases are considered a tax-neutral exchange, so no tax will be due on the asset itself. Alternatively, the trust can lend money to your estate, with the loan secured by the estate's assets. This is sometimes done to use the money to pay the estate taxes that are due on the other assets. Because estate taxes are due within nine months from the date of death, this ability to have liquid cash available is crucial to avoid selling assets in a quick sale, where the family may not get the best price. This is what happened to Chris's mother when his stepfather passed away. The real estate market was depressed, and interest rates were high. Because we can't predetermine when we will die, we want to make sure we avoid all unnecessary problems.

Either through a purchase or a loan from the ILIT, the estate will receive cash that can be used in a variety of ways. Later, the trustee can distribute the assets to the trust beneficiaries, likely any surviving spouse and children. This can be done in a lump sum; or, if desirable, the assets can be maintained in trust for their later benefit and use. If kept in trust, these funds can be structured so that credi-tors of the surviving spouse, children, and even grandchildren will have no access to the funds. This includes potential lawsuits, bank-ruptcy, and potential divorces. In this way, the ILIT can be an asset-protecting Wealth Protection tool for many generations.

If the trust is structured for the long term, it often makes sense to have its assets grow in a tax-efficient manner. This can easily be accomplished by having the trust purchase a variable annuity (see Chapter 45 on variable annuities in Part VII on retirement). The bot-tom line is that by using an ILIT, all the insurance proceeds are avail-able to help pay estate taxes and to provide cash for whatever need might arise. Your family keeps control over the assets. No distress sale is necessary to raise money to meet the estate tax obligations.

REQUIREMENTS FOR YOUR ILIT

Your ILIT, for maximum protection, must follow these three guide-lines:

1. *Make the proper transfers.* You must fully fund the ILIT with the insurance policy in order to gain the protective value of the ILIT. Contact your insurance carrier, and change the ownership of the policy to the trust. Make the ILIT the beneficiary of the policy as well. The trust beneficiaries (spouse, child, etc.) will eventually receive the proceeds as you instructed in the trust document.

If the policy is owned by you individually before transferring it to the ILIT, the policy will be "brought back" into your taxable estate if you die within three years of the transfer. This is the IRS's "three-year-look-back" rule. Because of this rule, it is preferable that you set up the trust to purchase the insurance policy from the beginning, as the three-year-look-back rule does not apply in that instance.

2. *The trust must pay the premiums.* One indication of ownership is who pays the policy premiums. If you continue to pay the policy premiums while the trust is the owner of the policy, the courts may disregard the ownership of the policy and consider you the owner. This allows your creditors to "step into your shoes" and to take the policy proceeds away from your family members. This would also mean that the policy would be in your estate for estate tax purposes.

For these reasons, the trust must pay premiums out of trust funds. You will have to gift funds to the trust to pay the premiums. This can be done on a one-time or an annual basis. You should be advised by a competent professional to minimize or to eliminate any gift tax consequences of these gifts.

3. *You cannot be trustee.* If you are the insured life, you must *not* be the ILIT trustee. You may name your spouse, an adult child, or another trusted individual as trustee. Corporate trustees are often preferred because of their familiarity with ILITs and because of their reliability in following trust instructions and paying premiums promptly.

How to use an ILIT and keep an income stream during your lifetime

Quite often a client will ask us if there is a way to use an ILIT to own life insurance and still have access to the policy's cash values during retirement. In order to accomplish this, you have to keep in mind the guidelines just explained, particularly guideline 3.

Essentially, the only people who could access the cash values during your life would be the ILIT beneficiaries. However, if the policy insures your life, then you cannot be the trustee—or the beneficiary—of the ILIT. Thus, you personally could not have access to the cash values. However, if the policy insures only your life, then your spouse could have access to the cash values if she were a trust beneficiary. Further, if the policy was on your joint lives (often called a "survivorship" or "second-to-die" policy), then the children or grandchildren could access the cash values, to the extent they were trust beneficiaries.

Last word

We consider an ILIT to be one of the three building blocks of an estate plan, along with a will and a living trust (A-B or not). If you have life insurance you are using for estate planning, strongly consider an ILIT.

CHAPTER FIFTY-SIX

FLPs AND LLCs: TRIPLE-PLAY TOOLS FOR ESTATE PLANNING

B y now, you may be familiar with family limited partnerships (FLPs) and limited liability companies (LLCs). Depending on your RFA analysis, you may have already read about FLPs and LLCs in Part V, Asset Protection, as these are two essential building blocks of any asset protection plan. You also may have read about these tools in Part III, Tax Planning, as both entities allow for powerful income tax leveraging between family members. If, because of your RFA analysis, you were not previously directed to either of the chapters on FLPs or LLCs, please do so now. Turn back and read Chapters 11 and 29. They will give you important background on both types of entities, which you need to better understand this chapter. Also, you'll learn how similar the two tools are, including why we can refer to them with one term: the FLP/LLC.

In this chapter, you will learn how FLPs and LLCs—in addition to being excellent asset protectors and income tax reducers—are superior estate planning tools as well. In fact, the FLP/LLC has three major benefits when it comes to estate planning: They (1) avoid probate and continue to operate; (2) allow you to gift property while retaining control of it; and (3) lower estate taxes.

FLP/LLC ASSETS AVOID PROBATE AND CONTINUE TO OPERATE

Assets owned by your FLP/LLC do not go through probate. Only your interest in the FLP/LLC will. However, if you structure your LLC so your intended beneficiaries eventually own most of the FLP/LLC shares when you die, these beneficiaries will control the FLP/LLC and its assets when you die. Your beneficiaries can effectively control the FLP/LLC assets or business while the probate process for distributing your remaining membership interests continues. As probate can last several years, this continued control can be crucial for operating a business or a real estate investment.

FLPs/LLCs ALLOW YOU TO GET PROPERTY OUT OF YOUR ESTATE WITHOUT GIVING UP CONTROL

Because your estate pays taxes only on property you own at death, a common tax-saving strategy is to gift your property away during your lifetime. The property goes to the people you intend to inherit your assets at the time of your death, and the government gets a smaller share. The main objection you might have to this type of planning is that you will have to give up control of the property while you are still alive. That's where the FLP/LLC comes in.

If the FLP/LLC owns the asset(s) and if you are made the FLP general partner or LLC managing member, you get the best of both worlds. You can gift FLP/LLC interests to intended beneficiaries and remove the value of those interests from your estate. Yet, you still control the FLP/LLC and all of its assets while you are alive. Let's see how this works.

CASE STUDY: ROBERT'S MUTUAL FUNDS

Robert Jones, a 63-year-old retired corporate executive, owned just over $1 million in mutual funds. He set up an FLP to own the mutual funds, naming himself as the sole general partner. At the outset, he owned 2 percent of the FLP as general partner and 93 percent as limited partner, gifting 1 percent to each of his five grandchildren. This 1 percent was worth approximately $11,000, so the gift to each grandchild was tax free.

Robert can continue to gift each grandchild $11,000 in FLP interests each year, completely tax free. If Robert lives to age 75, he will give $660,000 worth of FLP interests to his grandchildren ($132,000 each) tax free. This equates to 60 percent of the FLP.

This $660,000 will no longer be in his estate, and it will not be subject to estate tax. (Furthermore, any growth of the FLP and of the value of that 60 percent will also be out of the estate).

Because Robert's other assets put him in the 50 percent estate tax bracket, his tax savings using the FLP will be 50 percent of $660,000, or $330,000. Because he is the FLP's sole general partner, Robert controls the mutual funds while he is alive and can distribute the income to himself or sell some of the funds to cover his expenses. In this way, Robert maintains control of his assets for his lifetime, pays less estate tax, and also provides more for his grandchildren.

FLPs/LLCs LOWER ESTATE TAXES ON ASSETS THEY HOLD

You may not want to gift all of your FLP/LLC interests during your lifetime or may start such a gifting program too late to "give away" much of your wealth. In either case, you will die owning FLP/LLC interests, which are then subject to the estate tax. The issue then becomes the value that the IRS will use to tax your remaining FLP/

LLC interests. It will not be "your percentage ownership in the FLP/LLC" multiplied by "the fair market value of the FLP/LLC assets." This is because of powerful tax rules applying to FLPs and LLCs regarding valuation discounting.

VALUATION DISCOUNTING USING FLPs/LLCs

An important estate tax benefit of the FLP/LLC is that FLP/LLC interests enjoy discounted values by the IRS. The IRS recognizes that owning a percentage ownership of an FLP/LLC that owns an asset is worth less than owning the asset outright. If you own a $20 bill and hold it at death, then the IRS would assign an estate taxable value of that bill of $20. However, if you died owning a 20 percent interest in an LLC with four other family members, and the LLC owned $100, the IRS would allow a valuation of your 20 percent interest at a number well below $20! Here's why:

1. The IRS would first allow a *lack-of-marketability* discount to that interest, recognizing that your LLC interest is not really marketable, so its value should be reduced for tax purposes. There is likely not much of a market for your 20 percent LLC interest when the other LLC members are all family members. Who would want to own part of an LLC worth $100 when the other owners are members of one family? What would an outsider pay for such an interest?

2. Because you own less than 50 percent of the LLC, the IRS will also apply the *minority-ownership* discount to your interest. Again, the IRS recognizes that there is very little market for interests in an LLC that others control.

Both of the aforementioned tax valuation discounts can be maximized by the proper drafting of the FLP/LLC agreement. Any provisions that restrict the transferability of any FLP/LLC interests will weigh toward a higher lack-of-marketability discount. Likewise, clauses that limit the control of minority interest holders will substantiate greater minority-ownership discounts. In this way, with proper drafting, FLPs and LLCs can often enjoy valuation discounts of 25 percent to 40 percent or more. This can translate into an estate tax savings of millions of dollars in larger estates.

CASE STUDY: ROBERT JONES'S MUTUAL FUNDS REVISITED

Assume that when Robert dies, he still owns 40 percent of his mutual funds FLP interests, having gifted 60 percent to his grandchildren during his lifetime. This 40 percent partnership interest, as part of his estate, is subject to estate taxes. Assume also that the FLP mutual funds value is $2 million when Robert dies. His 40 percent interest in the FLP is then economically worth 40 percent of $2 million, or $800,000.

For estate tax valuation, however, the IRS may agree that Robert's FLP interest is worth only around $500,000. The IRS will allow both the lack-of-marketability discount and the minority-ownership discount. The lack-of-marketability discount exists because Robert's five grandchildren own the other FLP interests, so nonfamily members would not be interested in buying his interests. Also, under the FLP agreement, the FLP interests are not freely transferable. The minority-ownership discount may be applied because Robert owns only 40 percent of the FLP when he dies.

These valuation discounts translate into an estate tax savings of about $150,000 (50 percent of $300,000). And, Robert lost no control over his funds during his life.

LAST WORD

The FLP and LLC are tremendous Wealth Protection tools that allow you to control your assets during your lifetime and reduce estate taxes. They should be seriously considered as part of any comprehensive Wealth Protection plan.

CHAPTER FIFTY-SEVEN

◆

WHY YOUR PENSION, 401(K), OR IRA MAY BE AN 80 PERCENT TAX TRAP

Most financial professionals say you should contribute as much as you can to your retirement plans (pensions, profit-sharing plans, IRAs, 401[k]s, etc.). The conventional wisdom is that these plans are a huge tax win for you, because you get an income tax deduction and tax-deferred growth.

Unfortunately, for many clients, especially highly compensated individuals, following this "conventional wisdom" could have a catastrophic effect on your family's financial well-being. Retirement plans can be tax traps for three reasons: (1) it is likely that the client will ultimately pay income taxes on these retirement contributions at the same or higher rates than he or she would have paid during his or her "working years," (2) the client may not need most (or all) of the funds in retirement, and (3) most damaging, any funds left in these plans at death will be decimated by taxes. Quite literally, these plans act as "traps," capturing huge sums of money that are eaten up at tax rates of 70 percent to 90 percent.

If you may accumulate more in your pension, profit-sharing plan, IRA, or other retirement plan than you will use (because you have other assets or an inheritance or die early), this chapter is a crucial one for your overall estate planning. If you have been directed to this chapter by the RFA, then this problem may be a real possibility for you.

You may pay tax at the same— or higher—tax rates

A common misconception among working people today is that when they retire, they will be in a lower income tax bracket. Though this may be true for some, there are myriad reasons why this may not be true for you. One is simply that you may become accustomed to a certain quality of life that you don't wish to "scale back" when you retire. You didn't work hard in your career and as a parent so you could be put out to pasture and live on tomato soup and grilled cheese sandwiches. In fact, many retirees will increase their expenses and do the things they didn't have time to do when they were working 50, 60, or 70 hours per week. The most notable thing to do in retirement is travel. Nonetheless, even if you do scale back your quality of life, you still may have to pay *more* in living and entertainment expenses because of inflation.

Just 15 years ago, you could go to the movies for $3 to $5 and you could see the Red Sox play at Fenway Park for $17. Now, you pay up to $12 to see a movie, and the same Red Sox tickets are $55 . . . each!

Not only might your lifestyle, which you can control, increase your expenses (and taxes) in retirement, but your plan itself might also contribute to increased taxes. The IRS has what are called minimum required distributions (MRD) on retirement plan assets. This means you *must* start taking money out of your retirement plans at age 70½, whether you need the money or not. Of course, if you take the money out of the plan, you must pay income taxes on those withdrawals.

When you invest your funds inside the retirement plan, those assets grow on a tax-deferred basis. This means you get greater accumulation than you would in a taxable account. When you consider this tax deferral along with the stock market returns you may realize (despite current market conditions, the 70-year average is still 11.5 percent per year), it should not be surprising when plan balances grow to significant amounts. The larger the plan accumulation, the higher the MRDs. This can affect your tax bracket in retirement significantly.

Lastly, you may have other income-producing assets like rental real estate; another business; limited partnerships; and dividend-paying stocks, bonds, and money market accounts. Each of these income-producing assets adds to your income . . . and may put you in a higher income tax bracket.

With the amount of invested assets inside and outside of retirement plans and with the continued long-term growth of the securities markets, many Americans will enjoy retirement incomes that put them in the same tax bracket as the one they are in now.

For example, we have a client named Frank, a 50-year-old physician with $500,000 in his profit-sharing plan. By the time he is in his late sixties and begins his planned retirement, assuming annual growth of 9 percent to 10 percent, the plan funds will grow to $3 million. If Frank then withdraws only the interest from the plan from then on—not considering using any principal or other sources of income (like Social Security)—Frank and his wife will likely still be in the top tax bracket and will stay there for the rest of their lives.

What this means is that, for many highly compensated taxpayers, the value of the tax deduction and deferral are not as great as "conventional wisdom" would espouse. Clients like this have no tax arbitrage—they simply get the deduction at one tax rate and then pay the tax at the same rate. In fact, the plan may actually cause "reverse arbitrage" because distributions from the plan will be taxed as ordinary income (likely 38.6 percent for wealthier clients), while gains outside of a plan will be subject to capital gains rate, capped at 20 percent. A *Wall Street Journal* columnist reviewed this comparison a few years ago (April 15, 1999), concluding that for many taxpayers, qualified plans were a "fool's game."

You may not need the funds in retirement

The amounts contributed to retirement plans are relatively small for highly compensated taxpayers. If plan contributions are capped at $40,000 or less (in most cases), what happens to the rest of the after-tax earnings, which can be a significant amount? Over a career, they end up in non–retirement plan brokerage accounts, ownership interests in closely held businesses, rental real estate, precious metals, or any number of other investments.

The compounded interest on your investments in the securities and real estate markets may accrue for 10 to 30 years. These nonplan investments can create significant income in retirement, so much so that the retirement plan assets are hardly even needed. Though this is a "problem" we should all hope to have, it is a problem nevertheless and needs to be addressed.

We see this problem with many of our clients, including, by way of example (see Table 57.1), Charlie, a 58-year-old software executive. He contributed $20,000 to his pension for each of the past 25 years. Meanwhile, he and his wife, Margie, have also amassed $1.2 million in other investment accounts. By the time he retires, planning to do so at age 65, he should have enough in his brokerage accounts for a very comfortable retirement.

As you can see from the table, Charlie, who earned about $275,000 per year over the first 25 years of his career, did not even maximize his pension contributions over that time ($30,000 per year

TABLE 57.1   CHARLIE AND MARGIE WON'T NEED PENSION FUNDS TO RETIRE

Clients	Charlie and Margie
Ages	Charlie, 58; Margie, 57
Average pension contribution	$20,000 for 25 years
Nonpension investing	$20,000 for 20 years
Present pension balance	$2.2 million
Outside investments	$1.2 million
Planned retirement age	65
Forecasted pension balance, age 65	$4.4 million (10% annual return)
Forecasted outside investments, age 65	$2.3 million (8% posttax return)
Posttax earnings on outside investments, age 65	$184,000 per year ($15,000+ per month)
Posttax amount needed for retirement	$10,000 per month

was allowed). Instead, he chose to control some of his investments himself (about $20,000 per year) in a separate investment account. By the time he retires at age 65, Charlie will clearly have enough to fund his retirement (he and Margie need about $10,000 per month posttax), just from his non–pension plan investments.

To be extremely conservative, let's advise that Charlie and Margie keep another $1.4 million of the pension funds secured for emergencies. At age 65, that will still leave $3 million in the pension, which will continue to grow. Charlie and Margie think that this $3 million, plus most of the growth, will benefit their children and grandchildren, as they designated in their will and trust. As you'll see in the next section, they are really benefiting the IRS and state tax agencies—over 80 percent of the funds will end up eaten by taxes if they don't change their plan!

ANY FUNDS LEFT WILL BE DECIMATED BY TAXES

What happens to the assets left in the retirement plan if they are not used by the taxpayer and spouse during their lifetimes? Most of these funds will end up with state and federal tax agencies. Did you think that, after paying taxes during your entire working life, your "tax-qualified" plan would be taxed at rates between 70 percent and 90 percent? Most clients, when hearing these facts, are shocked and appalled, and they want to learn how to do something about it. The first thing you must learn is what "IRD" means.

BASICS OF INCOME IN RESPECT OF A DECEDENT

As you would have learned if you were directed to Chapter 15 by the RFA, IRD means "income in respect of a decedent" (a deceased person). This is income that would have been taxable to the decedent had the decedent lived long enough to receive it. Whoever receives these items of IRD must report them in gross income and pay any resulting income taxes in the year in which the items are actually received, typically, the year of death.

The IRD tax is an income tax that is assessed in addition to any federal estate (death) taxes and state estate/inheritance taxes. Because federal and state income taxes (including those characterized as IRD) can reach up to 45 percent in many states and estate tax is assessed between 37 percent and 50 percent (we'll assume 50 percent here), you can see how quickly the combined tax rate escalates. Although the rules provide for a partial income tax credit for estate taxes paid, the total tax on assets characterized as IRD assets can be over 80 percent in some cases.

What types of assets qualify for the dreaded IRD treatment? Income earned by a decedent but not yet paid, like bonuses or commissions, qualify as IRD. Once they are paid to the estate, they'll be hit with income taxes and estate taxes under the IRD rules. The most important asset hit by IRD? Retirement plans, such as pensions, 401(k)s, and IRAs (to the extent contributions were originally tax deductible).

CASE STUDY: HOW IRD EATS UP A RETIREMENT PLAN

Jim is a single professor whose nonplan assets exceeded the estate tax exemption in place when he died in 2001. His IRA was fully taxable—it was funded entirely with tax-deductible contributions. (The same illustration could be made for a married couple; but the estate tax wouldn't be due until the second spouse dies if he or she were the plan beneficiary, due to the unlimited marital deduction.)

Jim's fully taxable estate of $1 million was held in the IRA, so Jim's estate (or heirs) first paid $550,000 in estate taxes upon Jim's death and then paid another $262,242 in state and federal income taxes (i.e., 45 percent of the amount remaining after a deduction for federal estate taxes paid). Thus, only $187,758 was left out of the IRA for Jim's beneficiaries—less than 20 percent! Over 80 percent of the funds—built over a lifetime of working and paying income taxes—was taken by the IRD tax system. Table 57.2 shows how that happened.

Table 57.2 Jim's IRA: IRD Eats Up More Than 80 Percent!

Value of IRA—IRD item		$1,000,000
Federal portion of estate tax (75.7% of 55%)	$416,350	
State portion of estate tax (24.3% of 55%)	$133,650	
Total estate taxes		$550,000
Balance in estate		$450,000
Income in respect to a decedent		$1,000,000
IRD deduction (on federal portion of estate tax)	$416,350	
Taxable IRD		$583,650
Income tax (45%) on taxable IRD	$262,242	
Total taxes ($550,000 + 262,242)		$812,242 (81.2%)
Amount for beneficiaries		$187,758

What if Jim liquidated the IRA on a Tuesday, paid the income taxes, and died the next day, at which time his estate would pay the death taxes? The taxes are not the same. Look at Table 57.3

Table 57.3 If Jim Liquidated the IRA Today, Less Tax Would Be Due

Value of IRA—Income item	$1,000,000
Federal and state income taxes (45%)	−$450,000
Balance in estate	$550,000
Estate tax (55%)	−$302,500
Total taxes	$752,500 (75.25%)
Amount for beneficiaries	$247,500
Difference ($247,500 - $187,758)	$59,742

(continued)

In this scenario, Jim paid the income taxes on the $1,000,000 liquidation himself. Then he died, and his estate paid the estate taxes the next day (under 2001 rules). Although these transactions were only one day apart, his heirs were better off because there was no IRD. This quirk exists because the federal tax rules do not allow an income tax credit for the state portion of estate taxes paid, only for the federal portion of estate taxes paid. Here, this means Jim's estate got credit only for the $416,350 that eventually ends up with the federal government, not the $133,650 that ends up with the state government. In this way, by leaving the funds in the IRA, Jim's heirs had to pay income taxes on $133,650 that they never even received. In essence, they are paying the income taxes for their state government. In this illustration, the heirs benefited by only an extra $60,000 by early liquidation. There are strategies that are better than liquidation and that can save 70 percent or more of the IRD taxes, as you will see in the next chapter.

◆

CHAPTER FIFTY-EIGHT

AVOIDING THE 80 PERCENT RETIREMENT PLAN TAX TRAP

In Chapter 57, you learned how pensions, 401(k)s, IRAs, and other retirement plans can be 80 percent tax traps. This is a huge threat for millions of Americans who have no idea what is facing them and their families when they die with funds left in such plans. Nevertheless, *you* now know the harsh reality. So what can you do about it? The answer to that question depends on where you are in your retirement plan funding.

IF YOU ARE EARLY IN YOUR CAREER, MONITOR PARTICIPATION IN QUALIFIED PLANS

For many Americans, it still makes sense to maximize participation in qualified retirement plans when they are working. In fact, this may be 100 percent true for your Wealth Protection plan at this point. It really depends on an accurate financial analysis of what your plan balance is and what you project you will need to spend in retirement. If, after such a financial analysis, it looks like you now have more in your retirement plans than you will need in retirement, then you should consider ending participation as soon as possible. Ideally, you want to amass just enough in retirement plans to cover retirement expenses and a "safety buffer." Beyond this, you are simply accumulating 80 cents for the government for every 20 cents you will leave your family.

What if you have already built up a large balance in a pension or an IRA and now realize that you won't need some or all of the funds in retirement? Unless you want 80 percent or more of these funds to go to state and federal taxes, you must do something . . . and the sooner, the better.

Essentially, you have three options (given in ascending order of tax-saving usefulness) to attempt to reduce the heavy tax burden on qualified plans: (1) stretch IRAs, (2) the liquidate-and-leverage strategy, and (3) the capital transformation strategy. We will examine each separately.

OPTION 1: STRETCH IRAS

Recently, stretch IRAs have been discussed as a viable tax-reduction option. Stretch IRAs lengthen the time over which distributions must be taken from retirement plans or rollover IRAs. They also allow you to leave the IRA to your heirs, who can then stretch out the distributions over their lifetimes and pay income taxes as they receive the funds. The common belief underlying this strategy is that tax-deferred growth is always a great idea. However, when you crunch the numbers you will realize that the stretch IRA is generally a bad idea for anyone who will have an estate tax liability and it may be only of minor benefit to everyone else.

There are at least two reasons why stretch IRAs are not beneficial: (1) stretch IRAs completely ignore the estate tax problem, and (2) they may create additional unnecessary taxes for your heirs. Let's consider both problems briefly.

STRETCH IRAS IGNORE THE ESTATE TAX PROBLEM

If you think your estate will be worth more than $1 million when you die, you will probably have an estate tax problem. The stretch IRA gives your heirs the benefit of deferring their withdrawals and deferring their income tax liabilities. The IRS doesn't care that the children or grandchildren have not received the money. The value of the IRA is included in the estate, and your heirs still owe the estate tax (which can be 37 percent to 50 percent). Look at this case.

CASE STUDY: JEFF LEAVES A BUSINESS AND A STRETCH IRA

Jeff listened to his advisor, who told him to create a stretch IRA so he would avoid the 80 percent IRD problem at death. When Jeff passed away, his three children received his family restaurant and a stretch IRA worth $800,000. The total estate tax bill was $700,000. His children didn't want to sell the restaurant, so they took the $700,000 out of the stretch IRA to pay the estate tax bill. The kids should be happy because they now have the business and an additional $100,000, right?

Wrong. The kids now owe income taxes on the $700,000 withdrawal (income taxes are never waived or avoided with a stretch IRA). Their average state and federal income tax rates were 40 percent. Therefore, they owed $280,000 in income taxes because of their $700,000 withdrawal. They used the last $100,000 from the IRA and took out a $180,000 loan against the business to pay the $280,000 tax bill. Then, they owed income taxes on the $100,000 withdrawal (another $40,000 to the IRS), and they owed another $15,000 of interest on the loan. This put them in the hole another $55,000. Eventually, they had to sell the business to pay off their debts. Jeff's estate plan failed because he received bad advice.

STRETCH IRAS WILL COST YOUR HEIRS *MORE* TAXES

The stretch IRA may generate more taxes to your heirs for three reasons:

1. Your heirs may be in the same or higher tax bracket than you are by the time you die. If you die in your seventies, eighties, or nineties, your heirs will be in their prime earning years (forties, fifties, and

sixties) and will likely have enough income to put them in a higher bracket. You may be deferring 27 percent taxable income in lieu of 38.6 percent taxable income later.

2. All withdrawals will be taxed as ordinary income (27 percent to 38.6 percent) when withdrawn from the plan by you or your heirs. The long-term capital gains rate (20 percent) doesn't apply to appreciated investments. If you had taken the funds from the plan and paid the taxes earlier, you would have had the opportunity to invest in long-term investments, and you or your heirs could possibly realize 20 percent tax on your gains—or no taxes on the gain, if you received the step-up in basis at your death!

3. You have no flexibility for intergenerational planning. You can only invest in securities inside a stretch IRA. You cannot buy life insurance. If you left the stretch IRA to your children and they didn't need it and wanted to leave it for their children, they would have to let the income-taxable IRA appreciate. It would continue to be income and estate taxable (again) until their children receive the money. If you had paid the taxes and left the children after-tax dollars, the children could have invested in tax-free life insurance or a tax-free 529 plan (Chapter 14) for your grandchildren. You wouldn't be handcuffing them with the stretch IRA.

In our opinion, the stretch IRA can be both shortsighted and penny-wise and pound-foolish. Of course, if you and your spouse are completely uninsurable, if your IRA is your only asset, and if your estate definitely will not be worth over $1,000,000 when you pass away, then the stretch IRA may make sense. If you don't meet all of those conditions, you should seriously consider one of the next two options.

OPTION 2: LIQUIDATE AND LEVERAGE

The liquidate-and-leverage (L&L) strategy is much superior to the stretch IRA. In fact, you can think of this strategy as allowing you to leverage your IRA, 401(k), or pension five to twenty-five times!

Assume that you and your spouse are 60 years old and have $1 million in your qualified plan. Because you have accumulated significant assets outside of your plan, you are sure that you won't need

$600,000 of the funds, or the interest on those funds, in retirement. Let's assume that other assets will use all but $400,000 of your estate tax exemption amount. In that case, more than 80 cents of every dollar in your plan will go to the government if you don't take action.

ONE L&L METHOD: ONE TIME GIFT

The L&L strategy will ensure that your heirs get not only the full $600,000, but also an additional $2.7 million. Best of all, they will receive the $3.5 million tax free! The L&L steps are:

1. Take $600,000 out of the plan and pay the $240,000 in income taxes (assuming a tax rate of 40 percent). As we learned from Jim's case, this liquidation eliminates IRD and saves at least 6 percent of the $600,000, or $36,000.

2. Use a portion of your estate tax exemption amount, and gift the after-tax amount of $360,000 to a properly drafted irrevocable life insurance trust (ILIT—see Chapter 55 for further explanation).

3. The ILIT then purchases a second-to-die life insurance policy on you and your spouse. Depending on your age, health, net worth, and other factors, that policy might be worth $1.5 to $3.5 million.

4. When you die, the insurance company pays up to $3.5 million, income tax free, to the ILIT. Then, all $3.5 million will be available to your heirs estate tax free as well.

If you consider that the $600,000 in your plan would have been worth less than $800,000 to your children and grandchildren (if you lived to age 80 and the funds grew at 8 percent), the L&L strategy left your heirs more than four times the original amount—over $2.7 million more to your heirs after taxes!

8% growth for 20 years =   4.66
4.66 × $600,000   = $2,786,000
After 72 percent tax, your heirs receive approximately $783,000.

ALTERNATIVE L&L METHOD: GUARANTEED INCOME/ANNUAL GIFTS

Many people don't like paying for insurance in one lump sum. Others already have life insurance policies that require annual premiums.

Still others aren't sure how much of their retirement plans they need. They only know how much they need each month to pay their bills. For these people, the guaranteed income/annual gifts method of L&L is ideal. Consider this example.

CASE STUDY: MARION'S GUARANTEED INCOME ALLOWS GIFTING

Marion is 78 years old and has $800,000 in retirement plan assets. By purchasing a life annuity with the $800,000, she receives a guaranteed monthly income of $8,600. After taxes, she still has $5,400 per month. Because she has some income from her municipal bonds (which are outside her retirement plan) and from Social Security, she only needs $2,000 of the retirement plan income to pay for her bills and for the college funds she created for her grandchildren. This leaves Marion with $3,400 per month of "excess income." She gifts this $3,400 per month to an ILIT, which pays for a $1 million life insurance policy that is guaranteed to Marion's 115th birthday!

By using these steps, Marion took $800,000 of potentially 80 percent taxable money and turned it into guaranteed supplemental income and a $1 million inheritance for her son and grandchildren.

OPTION 3: THE CAPITAL TRANSFORMATION STRATEGY

Of the three options, the capital transformation strategy (CTS) is by far the superior tax-saving strategy because it reduces the income taxes on the funds in the strategy by up to 70 percent *and* uses the leverage of the life insurance *and* uses income and estate tax–free proceeds to cover all estate taxes. However, it is also the most complex. For this reason, we are going to spare you the technical details and give you a brief overview of what the CTS accomplishes and why it is so powerful (for the technical explanation and details, go to www.mywealthprotection.com). Then, we will give you two examples (one for retirement income and estate planning and the other solely for estate maximization) to illustrate how powerful the CTS can be. The CTS steps are:

1. *Buy life insurance with pretax dollars.* The IRS and the Employee Retirement Income Security Act (ERISA) allow for certain types of retirement plans to purchase life insurance within the plan with pretax dollars. Typically, we use profit-sharing or money-purchase plans because the rules are most generous for these type of plans. As of 2002, all IRAs can be converted to profit-sharing or money-purchase plans.

2. *Remove the policy from the plan with reduced taxes.* In Chapter 56, you learned how to use family limited partnerships and limited liability companies to discount the value of assets when transferring them from your estate. With a similar goal in mind, we purchase specific insurance policies that are valued after a certain time period, by the IRS and by ERISA, at 50 percent to 75 percent less than what you paid for them. This allows us to remove them from the plan at a fraction of the cost.

3. *Take advantage of the benefits and the flexibility of life insurance.* In Chapter 36, you learned the benefits of life insurance policies: tax-free accumulations, tax-free withdrawals, tax-free death benefits, and the ability to gift or to sell a policy to a family member. Once the policy has been properly removed from the plan, you have all of these benefits available to you. Some of our clients use the CTS to increase after-tax retirement income. Some use the CTS to remove highly taxable assets from an 80 percent tax trap (the retirement plan) and move them into an income and estate tax–free environment (an ILIT—Chapter 55) in an attempt to create a sizable estate.

CASE STUDY: INCOME FOR MR. SMITH AND BENEFITS, TOO

Mr. Smith is 51 years old and has $1.2 million in his profit-sharing plan. He also has $2.5 million of other assets—mostly real estate. He

(continued)

plans to retire in 10 years and estimates he will need $12,000 per month, after taxes, to support his quality of living. He is worried that more than half of his estate and almost three-quarters of his retirement plan will go to taxes at his death.

Mr. Smith used $600,000 from his profit-sharing plan to fund the CTS over three years. He continued to make tax-deductible contributions until he retired nine years later—a year ahead of schedule. In the third year, he purchased the policy from his plan for approximately $180,000 (he would later be able to use this $180,000 as withdrawals from his plan). He used the remaining profit-sharing-plan assets and the subsequent contributions to support his retirement for 17 years. Then, from years 18 through 36, he took annual tax-free loans of $180,000 per year from the insurance policy. That accounted for over $3.2 million of tax-free income from a $600,000 taxable asset. As an additional benefit, there was a $1.8 million death benefit for his wife and kids.

If you think Mr. Smith could do just as well by investing on his own and deferring the tax, consider this: To get the same retirement benefit for him and his wife and the same inheritance for his children, he would need to achieve these goals:

- He would need his investments to grow by 10 percent every year (the CTS assumes 6.2 percent). If he only sees 9 percent returns, he runs out of money in year 35 and leaves no inheritance whatsoever.

- He or his wife would have to live to be at least 97 years old. Because his life expectancy is 81 and hers is 84, the odds of living to 97 are probably around 1 percent to 5 percent.

- He would have to live in a state with no state income tax (forget California and New York).

What are the odds that the investor will average at least a 10 percent return each year for over 45 years and that he and his wife will both live to age 97? Would you bet on these odds? That is what he is doing if he simply continues to invest in the retirement plan as he always has. This shows the risk of "business as usual" planning!

CASE STUDY: JOE AND SUSAN WANT TO HELP THEIR KIDS

Joe and Susan are ages 57 and 52, respectively. They have been very successful in their investment banking and consulting practices. They feel they are fortunate that they don't need their retirement plans, valued at $600,000 to support their retirement. They want to leave these funds to their children, but they are afraid of the 80 percent tax trap.

Susan attended a seminar and learned of the capital transformation strategy. In their case, they could use $600,000 in the CTS over a number of years. When they remove the policy from their retirement plan, they would have an income tax liability of $100,000, which they will pay from their brokerage account. In the end, they will leave over $7.5 million tax free to their children. Considering that retirement plan assets are taxed at 80 percent, they would have had to turn their $600,000 into over $37.5 million just to break even with the CTS. Again, what are the odds of a couple being able to grow $600,000 to over $37 million over their life expectancy? Would that be a wise gamble?

LAST WORD

Often, Wealth Protection planning is as much about avoiding pitfalls as it is about implementing the "right" strategy. This chapter is a good example of that. In our opinion, the stretch IRA is almost as big a tax trap as the IRD problem. You or your heirs will still be taxed at rates up to 80 percent.

The liquidate-and-leverage strategy is a very solid alternative. Just make sure you use an advisor who understands estate planning, tax planning, life annuities, and life insurance. It is also important to work with a firm that has relationships with many different insurance companies because rates really do differ substantially between companies.

The CTS is the most powerful strategy for handling this tax trap. However, because it is so complex, you must find an advisor who is adept with all of the tax, ERISA, and Department of Labor rules and who is also an expert in insurance policies. Only this type of advisor can deftly implement such a strategy. If your estate is worth over $2 million, this is probably the most important issue for you to address in your planning.

CHAPTER FIFTY-NINE

GETTING LIFE INSURANCE FOR HALF THE COST

In the previous three chapters, you have seen the important role life insurance can play in a Wealth Protection estate plan. You have seen how it can be the ideal funding source to pay estate taxes because it can provide tremendous leverage over a client's lifetime. You have also seen the tremendous tax benefits of insurance—it can pay out to heirs income and estate–tax free, if structured properly. In addition, you have seen how insurance can be used to diminish the terrible consequences of someone dying with money in qualified retirement plans, such as 401(k)s or IRAs. Given all this, you should now be very interested in making life insurance part of your Wealth Protection plan.

You can reduce the cost of life insurance by up to 50 percent without losing any of the benefit by making the purchase of the life insurance tax deductible. As you learned from Part III on income tax planning, if an asset can be bought with pretax (tax-deductible) dollars, then its cost is reduced by your tax rate. Thus, if your marginal income tax rate is 50 percent (state and federal), deducting your life insurance would truly make it half as expensive.

In Part III, you also learned that welfare benefit plans (WBPs) allow business owners to provide life insurance for their employees, including the owners themselves, on a tax-deductible basis. Go back to Chapter 10 to review that planning option.

Important Note: At the time this book went to press there were a number of fundamental changes to the potential tax treatment of WBPs. Be sure to consult a licensed tax professional when examining a WBP as a planning option.

CHAPTER SIXTY

LONG-TERM-CARE INSURANCE FOR ESTATE PLANNING: PROTECT YOUR ESTATE FROM RISING MEDICAL COSTS

You ou probably have read about the soaring costs of medical procedures and nursing home care. You may also be familiar with the folly of relying on the government to provide for your medical coverage and your comfortable retirement. In this chapter we'll discuss how long-term-care insurance (LTCI) plays a very important role in the estate planning segment of your Wealth Protection plan.

Long-term-care is a type of health insurance that pays for a variety of health costs that may or may not be covered by Social Security, Medicare, or your state medical plan. The details of LTCI and our recommendations on what to look for in an LTCI contract are covered in Chapter 38. Part III on tax planning has a small chapter that discusses the retirement and income tax benefits of LTCI planning (Chapter 12). The purpose of this chapter is to explain where LTCI fits in your estate plan. The three chapters on LTCI should all be read so you'll have a full understanding of how LTCI will help you and your family.

If you met with your advisors recently to discuss your estate plan, you probably didn't think about having to pay $100 to $300 per day for nursing home or in-home care. Also, you probably didn't factor in the medical expense inflation rates of 5 percent to 10 percent per year that could make a very mediocre $200 per day nursing home in year 2000 dollars cost over $1,000 per day in 2020. If you need long-term care for just one year, you could use up $365,000 of funds that you had hoped would go to your children or grandchildren.

Do you need LTCI?

Recent estimates show that 50 percent of Americans will need long-term-care coverage for an average of two to three years. A large percentage of people will need coverage for *many* years. The longer people live, as a result of medical advances, the greater the likelihood that they will eventually need some significant medical assistance on a long-term basis.

The average cost of this benefit is $35,000 to $100,000 per year, and medical costs are increasing at a rate of 5.8 percent. Estimates are that the costs of long-term-care coverage will triple in the next 20 years!

Eventually you will have to pay for long-term-care coverage. The question is whether it is paid for in advance or from your intended inheritance or retirement funds.

It's apparent that you could deplete your assets very quickly. Ignoring long-term-care planning could be a potentially devastating mistake.

If you intend to leave an inheritance, then you may wish to purchase long-term-care insurance now, while you have the money. You can purchase an LTCI policy in one year, over 10 years, over 20 years, or make payments every year for the rest of your life. You also have options to have all of your premiums go to your heirs at death, even if you collect on the policy during your life. In fact, there are policies on the market today that combine a universal life insurance guaranteed death benefit for your heirs with a guaranteed daily benefit for long-term-care costs. This can be an ideal tool to achieve two family Wealth Protection goals.

Last word

By purchasing LTCI, you are making sure that soaring medical costs don't take away the head start you wanted to leave your children or grandchildren or destroy the legacy you wanted to leave behind. It can be an important part of any Wealth Protection estate plan.

◆

CHAPTER SIXTY-ONE

CHARITABLE ESTATE PLANNING: HOW TO GET MORE TO YOUR FAMILY AND BENEFIT A CHARITY

To give away money is an easy matter and in any man's power, but to decide to whom to give it, and how large and when, and for what purpose and how, is neither in every man's power nor an easy matter.

—Aristotle

In Chapter 13, we introduced the topic of charitable giving. There, you learned the basic tax rules that make charitable giving so attractive for family Wealth Protection purposes. In that chapter, we also explained the basics of the two leading tools used to make charitable gifts: charitable remainder trusts (CRTs) and charitable lead trusts (CLTs). Because charitable planning is such a grand topic, we can only give you a small hint of the types of planning we implement for our clients.

We think it best to be succinct and show the power of charitable planning through one case study.

CASE STUDY: STEVE AND MARTHA USE A CRT

Steve, age 56, is a software developer for one of the biggest suppliers of sophisticated computer equipment for the Internet. He and his wife, Martha, age 48, have two girls, both finishing graduate school. As a result of prudent investing, good luck, and a successful public offering of his employer's stock, Steve is considering early retirement so he can travel and enjoy his hobbies of flying and sailing.

Besides his significant retirement plan account, Steve has $3 million in zero-basis stock in his employer's company and is in line with qualified stock options to acquire an additional $5 million over the next three years. Faced with planning for the disposition of an estate of $10 million (almost all of it in an undiversified portfolio), Steve and Martha decided that they'd like part of their Wealth Protection plan to be paying $0 in estate taxes, if that were possible. In short, they're willing to give to charity those assets that would otherwise default to the IRS in the form of estate and capital gains taxes.

As a part of this strategy, they will also make gifts of stock to their two daughters and other family heirs over the next few years, through family limited partnerships (FLPs explained in Chapter 56).

We developed a plan for Steve and Martha through which we hope they will be able to eliminate all unnecessary estate taxes by freezing estate growth and squeezing the value of the assets. Additionally, our plan will provide an excellent retirement income stream through the use of a CRT. The stock that Steve owns is publicly traded, so its value is readily ascertained and is easily transferred to the family CRT. This CRT will take the highly appreciated stock and sell it without being taxed on its sale. It will then reposition the proceeds into a more balanced portfolio of equities designed for both growth and security.

The CRT will buy and hold stocks and mutual fund shares so that most of the portfolio will continue to appreciate while Steve and Martha, as income beneficiaries, receive quarterly payments of 5 percent of the trust's value every year. They've made the decision that leaving each daughter with a $5 million inheritance is part of their

(continued)

Table 61.1 Steve and Martha: Selling the Stock Outright Versus Utilizing a CRT with Wealth Replacement

	Sell	CRT
Net fair market value (FMV)	$3,000,000	$3,000,000
Taxable gain on sale	$3,000,000	
Capital gains tax (20%) at federal level	$600,000	
Net amount invested	$2,400,000	$3,000,000
Annual return of reinvested portfolio	10%	10%
Reinvested for 10% annual growth produces annual retirement income	$240,000	
Trust payout of corpus (averaged with 10% returns over trust term of 40 years)		$433,190
Annual average after-tax cash flow at 39% tax	$146,400	$264,246
Projected joint life expectancy (in years)	40	40
Taxes saved with $579,600 deduction at 39% tax rate		$226,044
Single pay life insurance premium ($3 million death benefit)		$226,044
Death benefit to heirs' estate tax free		$3,000,000
Tax savings and cash flow over 40 years	$5,856,000	$10,795,884
Total increase in cash flow		$4,939,884
Amount left at death	$2,400,000	$21,000,000
Estate taxes	$1,200,000	$0
Left to heirs	$1,200,000	$3,000,000
Left to charity	$0	$21,000,000

family's financial goals; so with some stock and life insurance held in an irrevocable life insurance trust (see Chapter 55), the two girls will be well protected for the future.

Everything else in their estate will be either spent during retirement or left to their charitable trust when they pass away. After examining the numbers, Steve and Martha felt that it made sense to reexert control over their social capital and follow through with their plan. Because Steve felt a need to sell in order to diversify his unbalanced portfolio, the only comparison to be made was between (1) selling—paying tax—reinvesting the net proceeds and (2) contributing the stock—reinvesting inside the CRT. We have made such a comparison in the "sell" and "CRT" columns of Table 61.1.

You can see that the benefit to their family of the CRT is significant. Steve and Martha will enjoy almost $118,000 in additional annual retirement income in the CRT scenario ($264,246 after taxes versus $146,400 after taxes). Over their joint life expectancy, this difference will amount to over $5 million!

Furthermore, because of the use of life insurance in a "wealth replacement trust," their children will get more out of that asset than in the "sell" scenario ($3 million of insurance proceeds income and estate tax–free versus $2.4 million asset netting $1.2 million to the family after estate taxes).

In this way, by combining a CRT with a wealth replacement trust for their heirs, Steve and Martha were able to enjoy a greater retirement income than they had anticipated, leave a substantial legacy to their children, and pay nothing in estate taxes. And, on top of it all, they were able to leave over $21 million to charity. This is quite an accomplishment.

Note: The benefits of every charitable strategy depend on interest rates, discount factors, the tax rate, the size of your estate, and the type of charity. Consult an expert in this area before implementing any plan.

LAST WORD

You don't have to be very wealthy to use charitable planning to save on estate taxes.

PART IX

BUSINESS PLANNING

CHAPTER SIXTY-TWO

TURNING YOUR COMPANY INTO A FINANCIAL POWERHOUSE

Many of you own your own business now or hope to sometime in your career. In many ways, owning one's own business is part of the American dream. As business owners ourselves, we appreciate this. We know what it takes to start and to continue a successful business. It certainly can be one of the most rewarding professional experiences in one's career.

However, it is also a risky pursuit, both financially and legally. Unfortunately, 90 percent of closely held businesses do not make it beyond five years. Fewer still make it to the second generation. Almost one million Americans file for bankruptcy protection each year.

The purpose of this part is not to discourage people from starting new ventures or expanding successful businesses, but rather the opposite—to give business owners and entrepreneurs the knowledge they need to maximize the legal protections and the financial and tax benefits from their business.

Along with the joys of self-determination and the freedom of being one's own boss, most business owners start their business with the idea that they would be able to take significant financial rewards out of the business once it became successful. Unfortunately, many business owners to whom we have spoken feel that they are not taking enough benefit out of their business. Either the taxes take too much of their profits, or they don't know how best to structure benefit plans to legitimately reserve the great majority of the rewards for themselves.

If you are interested in getting more financially out of your business—beyond the typical cookie-cutter planning—this part will help you. You should bear in mind that this area of planning is the most fact-sensitive part of our practice. In other words, there are few tools or strategies that work well for all businesses; and often, the same tools may be used differently in distinct cases. For more information on these areas of planning, we encourage you to contact advisors who specialize in advanced strategies.

You will learn about a few very important and underutilized tools available to owners of closely held businesses and professional practices. You'll learn about buy-sell agreements, welfare benefit plans (WBPs), professional employer organizations (PEOs), closely held insurance companies (CICs), and more.

These tools can help you improve not only your financial stake in the business, but also the financial health and viability of the business itself.

CHAPTER SIXTY-THREE

WELFARE BENEFIT PLANS: ASSET PROTECTION, TAX REDUCTION, AND ESTATE PLANNING ALL IN ONE

As an owner or a partner of a business, you may be able to take advantage of a tool that can significantly reduce your taxable income, protect your assets, and provide a tremendous estate for your family. This tool is called a welfare benefit plan (WBP).

As a successful business owner, you may be tired of hearing from your pension plan provider that the maximum amount of money you can contribute and deduct each year is $35,000 to $40,000. Perhaps you are also frustrated that you are not a good candidate for a 412(i) plan, which would allow greater deductions (see Chapter 44). If so, would you like to have the option of deducting up to $100,000 a year or more? Would you like to provide financial security for your family without paying estate or income taxes, while at the same time protecting your assets from creditors? If your answers to these questions are YES, then the WBP may be for you.

BRIEF HISTORY OF WELFARE BENEFIT PLANS

Prior to the Deficit Reduction Act of 1984 (DEFRA), Voluntary Employee Beneficiary Associations (VEBAs), and WBPs were used to defer compensation on a tax-deductible basis for later payouts to highly compensated employees or to owners of closely held corporations. In DEFRA, Congress responded to the perceived abuses of VEBAs and WBPs by sharply reducing allowable deductions and imposing new nondiscrimination rules. However, contributions to WBPs were not limited if the plan was part of a multiple-employer benefit plan that qualified under section 419A(f)(6) of the Internal Revenue Code (IRC). In response to the allowance of WBPs under 419A(f)(6), various companies created large trusts to meet all criteria under 419A(f)(6), thus allowing small employers to use the WBP as a viable option for benefits planning and income tax reduction.

HOW A WELFARE BENEFIT PLAN WORKS

A company implements a WBP for the benefit of its owners and employees. Then, on an annual basis, the company makes tax-deductible deposits payable to the multiple-employer benefit plan (a trust), which administers the WBP on behalf of many employers. The trust company invests the deposits with investment-grade insurance companies (i.e., the trust buys life insurance). If any of the employees or owners pass away during the life of the plan, his or her heirs will receive a considerable benefit, income and estate tax free. If all of the participants have not passed away by the time the company ends its participation in the WBP, all is not lost. The contributions have been growing in the life insurance policy on a tax-deferred basis. If the company stops operating and must terminate the plan, there can be a lump sum payout (after taxes are paid) to the participants. However, the tax treatment of the WBP may have changed since this book went to press. (See the note at the end of this chapter.) A case study is the easiest way to explain how a WBP works.

CASE STUDY: JOHN'S MEDICAL PRACTICE

Let us assume that John, a dermatologist, is the only physician in his practice and has three employees: Mary, Matthew, and Mark. John decides to create a WBP for his practice and employees.

Sample Death-Benefit-Only Proposal: John's Practice

Planned annual contribution	$100,000
Annual tax saving at 40% federal tax rate	40,000
Net annual cost (after federal tax)	60,000
Years of contribution	25
Total contributions (value on an after-tax basis)	$1,500,000

Projected benefits: Assume owner's salary is $500,000. Plan provides a preretirement death benefit of six times salary and optional plan termination at age 65.

Once the plan is in place and the policies within the plan are funded, if any covered employee dies, the insurance proceeds will pay out to their beneficiaries. This provides a valuable estate planning benefit to the covered business owner, as well as to employees.

If the business terminates the WBP (because the business is closing or for another reason) and a policy for any covered employee has accumulated cash value, then that employee has a right to the policy. The employee will pay tax on the accumulated cash value and then can enjoy that asset in retirement. (Based on the tax treatment of WBPs at the time this was written.)

Remember, however, that the WBP is *not* a retirement plan and should be established with the intent of providing welfare benefits (i.e., life insurance coverage) for employees of a business.

Also, in this case, Matthew passed away as a result of leukemia while he was still an employee of the practice. His family received a tax-free death benefit of $180,000 that helped his wife pay off their mortgage and pay the bills for a few years while she went back to school. This was a benefit Matthew's wife didn't know she would receive, but she was very grateful for it!

KEY BENEFITS OF WBPS

There are several reasons why a successful business owner would want to start a WBP.

- *Reduction of income taxes.* Either you can choose to pay 40 percent of your income to the federal government every year, or, through a WBP, you can purchase life insurance that is worth significantly more than 60 cents on the dollar the day you buy the life insurance.

- *Tax-deferred growth of contributions to the WBP.* Not only is the expense of funding the WBP tax deductible, but the money inside the plan is also allowed to grow tax deferred. (Based on traditional tax treatment of WBPs. See note at the end of this chapter.)

- *Asset protection.* Unlike funds owned in your own name, assets held by the trust under the WBP are fully asset-protected against your creditors and the creditors of the business.

- *Death protection for the family.* The WBP provides an enormous benefit to your family—death protection in the event that you die prematurely before terminating the WBP. If, instead of Matthew, John had passed away before he had retired or closed or sold his practice, his family would have received a significant death benefit. Furthermore, the WBP could be structured so that the proceeds are paid out income and estate tax free!

- *Elimination of the need for other life insurance.* Often, clients enjoy enough death protection from the life insurance held in the WBP that they no longer need their other life insurance. The other life insurance is 67 percent more expensive ($1.00 is 1.67 times 60 cents), because it is bought with posttax dollars, so clients often stop paying on that insurance, letting it lapse or reducing it to a paid-up policy. In John's case, prior to implementing the WBP, John had a term policy costing him $2,000 per year in premiums. He no longer needs that policy so he can cancel it and save another $3,332, pretax, per year.

- *Flexibility.* Unlike 401(k)/profit-sharing plans that have minimum mandatory contributions for your employees even if you do not contribute for yourself, the WBP only requires contributions to be paid on behalf of your employees when you make contributions for yourself. If you want to contribute $100,000 a year, you can; but if you do not have the money to contribute to the plan during any given year, you can choose not to contribute for anyone.

Also, unlike irrevocable life insurance trusts (which are commonly used to avoid estate taxes), in a WBP you have the option of changing the beneficiary of the life insurance policy. Thus, if one of your children turns out to be unworthy of the life insurance benefit (he joins a cult or becomes super-rich himself), you can change the beneficiary and exclude that child from receiving insurance proceeds.

Beware of aggressive WBP "consultants"

Although we believe WBPs are a viable option that should at least be considered by successful small businesses, there are several WBPs around the country that we would not recommend to clients. For intance, you shouldn't choose a WBP provider over the Internet. Rather, you need to find a consultant who knows how to review WBPs and will recommend one that is right for your business.

Last word

As a successful business owner, you should be looking for every avenue you can find to deduct excess revenue—revenue that you do not need to pay your bills. The key is to find deductible expenses that also provide you benefits that you desire. If you like the idea of tax-free money going to your heirs if you die prematurely, then the WBP is one of the few options available under the IRC that allow this. Be excited about what you have read here, but be cautious in your approach. If you use qualified experts, WBPs can certainly be an important part of your business Wealth Protection plan.

> *Important Note:* At the time this book went to press there were a number of fundamental changes to the potential tax treatment of WBPs. Be sure to consult a licensed tax professional when examining a WBP as a planning option.

WHY YOU SHOULD CONSIDER A CAPTIVE INSURANCE COMPANY

Of all the Wealth Protection planning tools we have encountered, the "captive" or closely held insurance company (CIC) can be the most powerful for a successful business. It has the capability of shielding millions of dollars of a client's assets from significant risks, potentially lowering the need for third-party commercial insurance. It also asset-protects the funds accumulated in the CIC from both business and personal creditors. Finally, it can produce powerful ancillary tax benefits as well.

The potential benefits of a CIC can only be achieved if the planning involved is justified by an economic and risk-management need and if the transactions involved are reasonable. It is crucial that one use an advisory team that specializes in this type of planning.

WHAT THE CIC IS

The CIC we are discussing here is a legitimate insurance company. It is registered with the IRS for domestic tax treatment, but typically it is based in an offshore jurisdiction, such as Bermuda or the British Virgin Islands. Most CICs are established in these countries because of their favorable insurance laws and local tax treatment, although the funds in the CICs can be maintained and managed in the United States.

In fact, the number of offshore CICs has grown to over 4,000, writing an estimated US$20 billion in premiums per year. This represents more than a third of the total commercial insurance market in the United States. While Fortune 500 companies have long used CICs to protect assets and to gain tax advantages, only in the last decade have individuals, small businesses, and professionals begun to take advantage of them as well.

The CIC may be used to insure all, or portions of, the client's or his or her business's significant risks. These may include risks like wrongful termination, sexual harassment, worker's compensation, business interruption, or even health insurance. A client who wants to participate in the risk of the business in a tax-favored way should consider the CIC as an option. Alternatively, or in addition, the CIC might be used to insure relatively low liability risks, like computer problems or weather-related damage to the office. Thus, the CIC can be structured to have as much or as little economic risk as the client chooses.

CASE STUDY: TOM AND DICK USE CICS

Tom and Dick each own manufacturing companies with about a hundred employees and similar revenues. Tom feels like he is paying too much for his health insurance. He creates a CIC that issues his company a policy that covers the smallest, most common health insurance claims, under $500. This significantly reduces his health insurance premium because he now has a higher deductible. Moreover, he gets a deduction for writing premiums to the CIC, which are available to pay claims as they arise.

For the past five years Tom has been able to actuarially justify over $500,000 in deductible premiums each year. Although a significant amount has been paid out on claims, there is well over $1 million in his CIC reserves, being managed by his money manager at a top Wall

(continued)

Street firm. Tom feels comfortable that the law firm and the insurance management firm have instituted a turnkey program for his company.

Dick establishes a CIC to insure lesser risks, including a litigation expense policy, which is available to pay for the company's legal fees but not to pay claimants. Again, the policy premiums are deductible to Dick's company. So far, the CIC has not had to pay any claims. Thus, all of the premiums are growing in reserves of the CIC, invested in a portfolio of U.S. mutual funds.

CIC AS A RISK MANAGEMENT TOOL

The CIC must always be established with a real insurance purpose, that is, as a facility for transferring risk and protecting assets. The transaction must make economic sense. Beyond this general rule, there is a great deal of flexibility in how you can benefit from the CIC.

You can use the CIC to *supplement your existing insurance policies*. Such "excess" protection gives you the security of knowing that you will not be wiped out by a lawsuit award in excess of traditional coverage limits. As wealthy individuals and businesses see more and more outstanding jury awards in areas as diverse as medical malpractice, sexual harassment, product liability, and breach of contract, this protection can be significant. Furthermore, the CIC may even allow you to reduce existing insurance because the CIC policy will step in to provide additional coverage, if needed.

Using your own CIC gives you flexibility in *using customized policies* that you would not get using large third-party insurers. For example, many physician clients would like a malpractice policy that would pay legal fees (and allow full choice of attorney) but that would not be available to pay creditors or claimants (what we call "Shallow Pockets" policies). This prevents the client from appearing as a "Deep Pocket" (a prime lawsuit target). Avoiding this appearance is a necessary asset protection strategy today.

The CIC has the flexibility to *add coverage for liabilities ignored by traditional general liability policies*, such as wrongful termination, harassment, or even Americans with Disabilities Act (ADA) violations. Given that the awards in these areas can be over $1 million per case, you would be well-advised to use the CIC for this alone.

Furthermore, entertainers and professional athletes can use these tools as well. Consider Mike's case.

CASE STUDY: MIKE, THE PROFESSIONAL ATHLETE, USES A CIC

Mike is a professional basketball player, earning over $8 million per year in salary and endorsements. As with any athlete, the risk of an injury interrupting or ending his career is significant. Mike would like to insure against this risk. Many of Mike's fellow players have been advised to get an insurance policy from a specialty lines carrier such as Lloyd's of London, but Mike gets better advice.

Mike is most concerned about a career-ending injury, not a relatively minor or even "average" injury. Mike decides to set up a CIC that writes policies on all types of injuries (knees, ankles, wrists, hands, etc.). A reasonable premium for Mike is about $1 million per year, given his age and preexisting conditions. Mike gets to deduct the full $1 million he pays to his CIC, which, in turn, reinsures the risk of most serious injury to Lloyd's for about $500,000 in premium. This way, Mike is covered for all injuries. He self-insures for minor injuries and gets the same coverage as his teammates for serious injuries. All of his dollars are treated in a tax-favored way and are asset-protected from his creditors.

This example demonstrates that you can sometimes purchase policies like the ones CICs can provide from traditional third-party insurers. However, these policies would not enjoy the powerful asset protection and tax advantages described later. The key question is: If you are going to use insurance to protect your assets, why give away the potential profits, asset protection benefits, and tax savings to the insurance company, when you could own the company yourself? Let's examine this more closely.

COMPARED WITH SELF-INSURING: ANNUAL DEDUCTIONS AND SUPERIOR ASSET PROTECTION

Because our society has become so litigious in recent years, many people have been "self-insuring" against potential losses like the ones previously named. These individuals have simply saved funds that will be used to pay any lawsuit expenses that arise. While this planning may prove wise, the client would be better off using a CIC to insure against such risk. That is because, as discussed in the next section, premiums paid to the CIC are fully tax deductible, whereas amounts saved to self-insure are not. The CIC, in other words, allows you to get a full deduction each year—protecting against the same risks you previously self-insured against without the benefit of a deduction.

Moreover, when you self-insure, the funds stay in your name, or the name of the business. Thus, they are available to any lawsuit claimants, creditors, divorce proceeding, bankruptcy trustees, and so on, who may attack your assets. Simply put, there is no asset protection tool shielding the self-insured funds.

Conversely, using the CIC, you have transferred such funds to an independently operating, fully licensed insurance company. Furthermore, this company is domiciled in an offshore jurisdiction—with all of the foreign hurdles to litigants described in other parts of this book (Chapters 31 and 32). Finally, the reserves in the CIC are shielded by the insurance company laws, which have powerful barriers protecting them from outside threats (the funds are there, you must remember, to pay potential claims in the future). Thus, the funds in the CIC are ideally asset-protected against any litigation against you.

CICs' ANCILLARY TAX BENEFITS

Although the primary reason for using the CIC must always be economically justified and risk-management oriented, the CIC does carry with it powerful ancillary tax benefits. In fact, the CIC allows you to build CIC reserves through tax-deductible contributions from your businesses. This is because premiums paid by you or your business to the insurance company are deductible as ordinary expenses under IRC section 162. These deductions for premiums can be over $1 million per year, far more than the set-up costs of the CIC.

Furthermore, if the CIC is maintained as a tax-exempt company, which is quite often the case, it opens up numerous tax planning opportunities as well. These entities can allow significant legitimate tax deferral and avoidance in extremely flexible ways.

No loss of control

When considering the merits of a CIC, you may be concerned about losing control of the funds paid to the CIC. While these concerns are certainly justified, the proper CIC structure allows for complete and discloseable control by you. There is no need for you to trust any other person or entity with the CIC assets. Furthermore, while the CIC is typically established outside the United States—to keep administrative costs low—the CIC funds can remain in the United States, in stocks, mutual funds, money management accounts, and so on.

Avoiding land mines

As previously mentioned, the CIC structure must be properly created and maintained. If not, all risk management, asset protection, and tax benefits can be lost.

For these reasons, using professionals who have expertise in establishing CICs is critical—especially the accountants, attorneys, and insurance managers involved. The CIC should not simply be a straw corporation, lacking the necessary parties to run an insurance operation, such as actuaries and underwriters. Using such experts and a real CIC structure may be more expensive than some of the cheaper alternatives being touted on the Internet or at fly-by-night seminars, but this is one area where doing it right is the only way to enjoy the CIC's benefits and to stay out of trouble with the IRS.

Can you afford a CIC?

Setting up a CIC requires particular expertise, as explained earlier. Thus, as might be expected, the professionals most experienced in these matters charge significant fees for both the creation and the maintenance of CICs. Set-up costs typically range around $50,000 to

$75,000, and annual maintenance costs are another $35,000 to $50,000, although CICs can often be established for a group of partners (where all funds are segregated for each client) for about $15,000 per partner. While these fees are significant (and often fully tax deductible), given the CIC's potential risk management, tax, and asset protection benefits, they are viable options for many high-income businesses where such tax-favored asset protection is extremely valuable.

CASE STUDY: DANNY'S CIC INSURES HIS BUSINESS

Danny is a successful Southern California restaurateur who was concerned about protecting his assets beyond insurance coverage and who wanted to build tax-favored wealth. He established a CIC for his business. A look at the benefit Danny enjoyed from his CIC in just the first year shows that CICs are ideal vehicles for many businesses.

Danny and His CIC: Effects on Business Bottom Line

	Previous Year	Now
Lawsuit protection	Traditional coverage	$1 million additional
Income (net)	$300,000	$300,000
CIC premium paid	$0	$100,000*
Personal income: stock transactions	$75,000	N/A
CIC income: stock transactions	N/A	$75,000
Taxable income	$375,000	$200,000
Federal and state income taxes**	$168,750	$90,000
Adjusted after-tax wealth***	$206,250	$285,000
Benefit to Danny's bottom line		**$78,750**

*Deductible premiums can be as high as $1.2 million per year.
**Assumes combined federal and state income taxes of 45 percent.
***Exclusive of transactions costs.

Danny's CIC: Growth of Reserves

	Previous Year	Year 1	Year 2	Year 10
Annual premium paid to CIC	N/A	$100,000	$100,000	$100,000
CIC income: return on prior reserves	N/A	$10,000[+]	$21,000	$159,374
CIC reserves	N/A	$110,000	$221,000	$1,753,117

[+]Assumes 10 percent return on investments.

LAST WORD

Because they have both significant and minor risks to insure against, CICs are ideal for many businesses that have high income tax liabilities and that can use significant tax deductions. They are especially beneficial for business owners who have royalties, patents, or sizable debt-free property or equipment. In short, CICs should be considered as an integral part of any successful business owner's Wealth Protection plan.

CHAPTER SIXTY-FIVE

BUY-SELL AGREEMENTS ARE ESSENTIAL

WHY THE BUY/SELL AGREEMENT IS SO CRUCIAL

As an owner of a private business, professional practice, or other venture, you may well work 24 hours a day, 7 days a week to get your business to the point where it can provide a measure of security for your family. We know because we have been there ourselves. Nonetheless, if you ignore one fundamental legal contract, all of your work may be in jeopardy. That contract—a key to your business Wealth Protection plan—is the buy/sell agreement. The buy/sell agreement is a necessity for any partner or shareholder in a private company.

Have you ever considered the following questions?

- What happens if and when any of my partners die? How will their families fare as owners of my company? Do I want them as new partners? How will I buy them out at that time?

- What happens to my share of the business if I decide I want out of the business or when I eventually retire?

- What happens if any of my partners become disabled or get into messy divorces? Will I have to take on their ex-spouses as partners?

- What happens to my family if I die or become disabled? How will I know they get a fair amount for their share of the business?

Let's look at a typical case where a buy/sell agreement has great utility.

CASE STUDY: WHEN A TWO-PERSON FIRM LOSES A PARTNER

Fred and Bob are owners of a box manufacturing company with $10 million in annual revenues. Fred has the sales expertise, and Bob runs the production side of the operation. Their overall profitability is due to their joint efforts. If Fred were to die prematurely, Bob would have to hire a new employee to fill Fred's position or promote someone to fill the position. It's unlikely that the replacement could duplicate Fred's results.

At the same time, Fred's widow would want to continue to take the same money out of the business that Fred had received. In fact, if Fred's widow is raising a young family or has children in college, she may have to force a sale of the business at distressed prices just to meet her needs. Maybe Fred's son is also in the business and has his own ideas on how things should be run. Perhaps Fred's spouse wants to see Fred's son take his father's place. It doesn't matter that he is incompetent.

You can see how several problems can arise. It may be impossible for Bob to continue a profitable business under such circumstances.

Only by planning ahead can you and your partners answer these questions in a way that all parties are satisfied and the business is maintained. The best tool for solving these dilemmas is the buy/sell agreement in its various forms.

BUY/SELL BASICS

There are various types of buy/sell agreements (buy/sells), but some basics regarding all buy/sells apply to any type of business—specifically, the benefit that various stakeholders can gain when a buy/sell is in place.

Buy/sells can be used for S- and C-corporations, for partnerships, for limited partnerships, for limited liability companies (LLCs), and for other forms of business as well. For these discussions, we will use the words *business owner* generically to mean any type of business owner (i.e., shareholder in a corporation, partner in a partnership, member in an LLC, and so on).

BENEFITS TO THE BUSINESS AND TO THE REMAINING OWNERS

From the standpoint of the business and the remaining partners, a properly planned buy/sell agreement will provide the orderly continuation of the ownership and control of the business in the event of the death, disability, divorce, or bankruptcy of any owner; or the desire of any owner to sell his or her ownership share.

The buy/sell can prevent unwanted outsiders from becoming owners and can eliminate the need for negotiation with surviving spouses and/or children. The agreement may also perform the role of a succession plan, providing for continuity or orderly succession of business management. In addition, the buy/sell is often used in conjunction with life and disability insurance policies to effectively provide liquidity for the business to purchase outstanding ownership interests.

This, in effect, guarantees that the remaining owners will continue to control the business, and will be able to participate in the future growth of the business, while also preventing a competitor from purchasing ownership interests from a retired, disabled, or deceased owner or from surviving family members. This guarantees continuity of management in the business, which makes the business more attractive to customers, creditors, and employees.

BENEFITS TO EACH OWNER

From the standpoint of a living business owner, the buy/sell can provide the individual partner with an opportunity to negotiate and obtain the fairest or best price for his or her share of the business. Furthermore, in the case of retirement or disability, the agreement can be a source of additional funds for each owner.

BENEFITS TO FAMILY MEMBERS

For a deceased owner's family, the existence of the buy/sell can assure the family or estate a liquid asset rather than an interest—often a minority interest at that—in a private business that is extremely difficult to sell. This can be very important because the family is now burdened with estate tax payments. Also, the agreement itself may provide an estate tax valuation of the family's business interest, saving them the headache and the expense of fighting the IRS on valuation.

In the event that an owner becomes disabled, the buy/sell guarantees that the disabled owner's family does not have to become involved in the business in order to protect the total family's interest. It frees the disabled owner and his family from the risk of future business losses and creates funds that may be used to pay medical bills and living costs of his or her own family, thus protecting the rest of the family's estate. This, in turn, creates peace of mind because the disabled owner can rest in comfort knowing that he or she has retrieved his or her investment in the business organization and does not have to continue to worry about its future.

FUNDING THE AGREEMENT

Where the agreement contemplates a buy/sell transaction at the time of an owner's death or disability, insurance policies are generally recommended to fund the transaction. There are many reasons for this, including:

- Insurance policies pay a predetermined amount, with proceeds available at exactly the time when they are needed as a funding source (no liquidity concerns).
- Proceeds will be available regardless of the financial state of the business at that point (so long as premiums have been paid).
- The business "leverages" the cost of premiums to create the proceeds, thus it costs the business less to buy insurance than to save money in a special buy-out fund.
- The economic risks of early death or premature disability of any owner are shifted to the insurer.
- Insurance proceeds are paid to the owner/owner's family income tax free.

If the payment contemplated under the agreement is not a lump-sum cash payment at closing, or is a periodic payment other than through a disability insurance policy, it is important to consider some type of security arrangement for the departing owner. These might include personal guarantees from remaining owners, mortgages or security interests in real estate, a bank standby letter of credit, or even collaterally assigned life insurance. The key here, of course, is what is negotiated up front between the various owners—ideally, before there is any notion of who may die, be disabled, retire, or divorce first. This way, each owner will be unprejudiced in determining what a fair buyout is.

THE NEED FOR A COORDINATED TEAM

Creating a buy/sell that fits a particular business requires expertise and experience, especially in dealing with different owners and in being able to negotiate and draft an agreement that meets the needs of all parties involved.

Too often business owners make one of two key mistakes when they decide who should oversee the creation of a buy/sell agreement: (1) choosing a lawyer friend to create the strategy and draft the document, rather than an expert in the area; and (2) not having a coordinated team to implement the plan.

Ideally, a coordinated buy/sell team involves an attorney experienced in creating these arrangements, a life or disability insurance professional who has worked on these issues before (especially with first-to-die life insurance), and a business appraisal firm, whose expertise may be needed continually in the future, for annual business valuations.

LAST WORD

As with any legal or insurance planning, the early bird is richly rewarded. Nowhere is this more true than in buy/sell planning. The reason is not so much economic as political. If this planning is done before an owner is close to disability, divorce, retirement, death, and so on, then all owners are in the same position relative to each other. That makes the negotiation of a standard deal for all owners a much easier and smoother process. Planning early for a buy/sell will truly benefit you, your family, and your business. Consider it an essential part of your Wealth Protection planning.

CHAPTER SIXTY-SIX

CORPORATIONS: THE STANDARD BUSINESS ENTITY

CORPORATION BASICS

1. A corporation is a legal entity owned by shareholders. The shareholders elect a board of directors who set policies for the corporation, allowing their selected officers (president, secretary, etc.) to run the corporation day to day.

2. There can be as few as one shareholder who owns the corporation and elects a board consisting of one director. In this way, one person can be a corporation's sole shareholder and sole director and can serve as every officer (president, vice president, secretary, and treasurer).

3. Corporations can be C- or S-corporations—the letter stands for a section of the tax code that controls that type corporation. C-corporations are taxed on income twice (first, the corporation is taxed, and then the shareholders are taxed), whereas S-corporations are not taxed—only the shareholders are taxed.

CHARACTERISTICS OF A CORPORATION

The most important aspects of a corporation for asset protection purposes are:

- *Created by state law.* Each state has a statute that sets the requirements for establishing and maintaining a corporation. Some state laws are more corporate-friendly than others.

- *Distinct legal entity, like another person.* A corporation is a separate legal entity, distinct from its shareholders. The law, in fact, treats the corporation as a separate person in many circumstances. For example, the corporation has constitutional rights, such as the right to due process under the Fifth and Fourteenth Amendments and the right to be free of unreasonable searches and seizures under the Fourth Amendment. Thus, if an asset is titled in a corporation, that corporation owns the asset, not the corporate shareholders.

- *Limited liability of shareholders.* Because a corporation is a legal entity distinct from its shareholders, its shareholders are not generally liable for the debts of the corporation. This is the key attribute in terms of asset protection. The shareholders can only lose their investment (what they paid for their shares) in the corporation if the corporation cannot pay its debts.

- *Unlimited existence.* Unless the corporation states otherwise in its Articles of Declaration, it lasts forever.

- *Centralized management.* Shareholders do not manage the corporation even though they are its owners. The board of directors, elected by the shareholders, sets the overriding corporate policy and approves major deals. The daily operations are run by the corporate officers, who are chosen by the board.

USING A CORPORATION TO PROTECT YOUR WEALTH FROM YOUR BUSINESS CREDITORS

Incorporating your business is an absolute must (your only other option should be a limited liability company [LLC]). Although it may not provide 100 percent protection from business creditors, incorporation is an important first step.

INCORPORATION PROTECTS YOU FROM TORT CLAIMS AND BUSINESS DEBTS

You can shield your personal wealth from many of the most popular forms of lawsuits by incorporating your business. These claims are based on negligence (e.g., slips and falls, car accidents) or arise out of the employer-employee relationship (e.g., being held responsible for the acts or omissions of your employees, employment discrimination). You are also protected from the corporation's debts, provided you did not personally guarantee the debt.

INCORPORATION PROTECTS YOU FROM CLAIMS OF YOUR CUSTOMERS

By incorporating, you can usually protect yourself from claims arising from the goods or services you provide to your clients or customers. These lawsuits are for product liability claims, negligence, breach of warranty, and even malpractice, which often bring outstanding jury awards.

INCORPORATION DOES NOT PROTECT YOU ON PERSONALLY GUARANTEED DEBTS

Often someone doing business with a corporation will require an officer (e.g., president, vice president) to sign a personal guarantee backing up the corporation's debt. For example, your landlord may ask you to guarantee your corporation's lease for the business premises. If the corporation breaches the lease and cannot make the payments, the landlord can sue you personally on the guarantee. In this way, any debt that you guarantee for your corporation overrides any corporate protection.

INCORPORATION DOES NOT PROTECT YOU WHEN YOU CAUSE THE HARM

If you personally caused the harm for which someone is suing, you are not protected by the corporate shield. For example, if you are driving the corporate car and cause a car accident, the victim can sue both the corporation and you personally, as you were personally negligent.

Special considerations for professionals

Many physicians, dentists, accountants, lawyers, architects, and other professionals use professional corporations (PCs) or professional associations (PAs) to structure their practices. Most of these professionals originally set up their entities for tax reasons, without regard to their corporation's asset protection attributes. Nevertheless, there are important asset protection characteristics of a professional corporation. The most important are:

- *Professional corporations cannot protect the professional from personal acts of negligence.* For example, if you as a consultant act negligently regarding a client, you cannot avoid personal liability in a tort action.
- *Professional corporations can protect the professional from the acts or omissions of subordinates and associates.* To take advantage of this type of protection, professionals often combine a PC with a partnership entity whereby the various professionals working together each set up a PC. These PCs then become the partners in the partnership. The professionals then protect themselves from the lawsuits caused by anyone but themselves, but they still get the benefit of working as a partnership.
- *Professional corporations can protect the professional from other types of claims that do not involve the act or omission of the professional* (car accidents by employees using the corporate car, slips and falls at the place of business, etc.).

Thus, the professional corporation can protect the professional from lawsuits arising from the behavior of others, but not from their own behavior.

Requirements for corporate protection

You will not enjoy the limited liability associated with corporations simply by setting up the corporation and paying the registration fees. Whether you are using a corporation to structure your business or practice or to work as a personal holding company, you must strictly adhere to "corporate formalities" to enjoy corporate asset protection. You must observe these procedural formalities:

- *Do not commingle cash or other assets.* You cannot commingle corporate funds with personal funds. Use separate bank accounts. If you loan money to the corporation or vice versa, make certain the loan is well documented. The same prohibition against commingling applies to other assets, like accounts receivable or inventory.

- *Always sign corporate documents with your corporate title.* Documents signed on behalf of the corporation should state your position in the corporation, for example, "President of XYZ Corp., John Doe" or "John Doe, as President of XYZ Corp." (not just "John Doe"). This is true for invoices, contracts, checks, orders, and so on.

- *Identify the corporation.* Have the word *Incorporated* or *Inc.* on all letters, signs, bills, checks, and so on. Creditors and others then know that the business is a corporation—this in itself will discourage lawsuits.

- *Keep adequate corporate records.* Maintain records of the articles of incorporation, the corporate bylaws, and minutes of board meetings, and pay the annual registration or franchise fees.

- *Keep the corporation sufficiently capitalized.* Check with a corporate attorney to determine the proper capitalization for your type of business with a given amount of debts. Certain states require predetermined minimal capitalization.

- *Maintain other indicators of a legitimate corporation.* This can be as simple as listing a phone under the corporate name, transacting business with noninterested third parties, and obtaining a business license under the corporate name. Set up the corporation with the formalities of a Fortune 500 corporation, on a tiny scale.

If you don't follow these formalities, then the court may not recognize the corporation as a legitimate stand-alone entity. Instead, the court will decide that the corporation is a sham entity and your alter ego. If the court makes this decision, it may then pierce the corporate veil, ignoring the protection the corporation gives to its shareholders. Rather than limit your liability to your investment for the corporate shares, the court will allow your personal wealth to be seized by the creditors of the corporation. When the corporate veil is pierced in this way, you are as vulnerable as when operating a proprietorship.

How strictly you must adhere to the required formalities is difficult to say. Certainly, if you are missing minutes of one director's meeting or failed to use "Inc." in certain letterheads, this alone will not be enough to lose corporate protection. However, there are cases in which an officer/shareholder lost corporate protection for certain contracts where she forgot to sign using her corporate title. The safest strategy is to learn and to adhere to the corporate rules as diligently as you can.

CHAPTER SIXTY-SEVEN

ADVANCED ASSET PROTECTION FOR YOUR BUSINESS: TURNING YOUR BUSINESS INTO A CREDITOR-PROOF FORTRESS

STRUCTURE YOUR BUSINESS FOR MAXIMUM WEALTH PROTECTION

No matter what type of business you own, you can transform it into a creditor-proof, lawsuit-proof financial fortress. The challenge is to determine how to implement types of entities described earlier in the book, primarily corporations and LLCs. You then have the *asset protection battle plan* for your business. The specific blueprint depends on the structure and nature of your business. Three structures are described here.

ONE COMPANY WITH MULTIPLE BUSINESS UNITS: USE A DISTINCT LEGAL ENTITY FOR EACH BUSINESS UNIT

What do these two businesses have in common: (1) a company that operates a restaurant and a catering service and (2) a lumber company that manufactures lumber products, sells its products at retail outlets, and performs construction consulting work? They both have multiple business units that operate separately from each other. It would be a terrible mistake to operate these different business units under one legal entity. Instead, each should operate under its own corporation, LLC, and so on. This way, a lawsuit or a creditor of one unit is isolated from the assets of the remaining units. Consider this case study.

CASE STUDY: WESTSIDE CONSULTING GROUP—BEFORE AND AFTER

The Westside Consulting Group rendered computer-consulting services to businesses and also operated a separate software sales division. Before consulting us on how best to structure their operations, the three-partner firm (with over 40 employees) operated both the consulting and the sales divisions under their general partnership. In so doing, these well-intentioned entrepreneurs walked a liability tightrope. Any slip-and-fall accident at their sales stores or product liability claim could threaten their $18 million per year consulting practice. Similarly, a lawsuit against their consulting practice could jeopardize their growing retail business. It was only a matter of time until one business threatened the other.

Fortunately, the owners implemented asset protection planning before serious damage occurred. After learning about their business organization and company goals, we developed their "financial fortress blueprint," which had two phases. In phase 1, the partners would reduce their personal liability arising from their consulting practice. Each partner established his own limited liability company, which then became the partner in the general partnership. In that way, the personal liability of any one partner was then limited to his own errors, not to the acts or omissions of the other partners. Also, the owners had all of the control and tax characteristics as before.

In phase 2, we separated the consulting practice from the store. An S-corporation was formed to operate the store, with each of the

(continued)

owners a one-third shareholder in the new *Westside Computronics, Inc.* Each owner's personal wealth was then protected from the liabilities of the store, including suits from employees. Furthermore, by incorporating the store, the owners effectively separated their business risks. Their store can no longer threaten their consulting practice, and vice versa. And because it is an S-corporation, the owners continue to enjoy pass-through tax status.

The owners had not originally structured their businesses this way because they had not been advised to do so and because they incorrectly assumed the structure would be extremely expensive to set up. In the end, the additional costs for the new fortresslike arrangement are less than $5,000 annually—less than 0.01 percent of their annual revenues. This is very cheap insurance!

FOR ONE BUSINESS UNIT WITH MULTIPLE LOCATIONS OR OUTLETS: USE A DISTINCT LEGAL ENTITY FOR EACH LOCATION OR OUTLET

What do these three companies have in common: (1) a dry-cleaning business with 16 locations throughout the state; (2) a chiropractic practice with four clinics around the city; and (3) a taxicab company with 100 cabs? They each operate one type of business in multiple outlets. That's right—even the taxicab company has multiple locations because the business is conducted in different taxicabs. Don't put all your eggs in one basket. Create a separate protective basket for each business location. If one location fails, it is isolated to the one location, and the rest of your business continues unscathed.

CASE STUDY: METROPOLIS CHIROPRACTIC OFFICES

Metropolis Chiropractic Offices is partially owned by Clark, the chiropractor who set up his first office over 15 years ago in a wealthy suburb. It was initially established as a professional corporation and continued to operate as such. Throughout the first 10 years, Clark's practice grew, as did his good reputation of strong yet sensitive hands, and the opportunity arose to expand his practice to additional locations.

Over the next five years, Clark established three new offices, two in neighboring suburbs and another in the city's downtown business district. They operated under the original professional corporation. The two suburban offices were relatively small, but the downtown location was even larger than Clark's original office. Clark hoped the downtown office would be his real moneymaker, but he was wrong. Within three years, the two new suburban locations were operating profitably, as was Clark's original location. However, the downtown location turned out to be a nightmare.

The downtown location could not attract patients. Perhaps it was because a renewal program for the office's neighborhood never took hold or because most people left downtown after work and obtained care where they lived. Regardless of the reason, the downtown location operated deeply in the red, losing so much money that it threatened to financially cripple the entire corporation. Clark channeled cash from the other three offices to pay creditors of the downtown location. The cash crunch soon got so bad that Clark considered bankruptcy for the entire corporation.

Clark's problems could have been avoided had he established each chiropractic office under a separate corporation. While this may not have saved his downtown office from financial woes, it certainly would have isolated it. Its failure would be a bankruptcy of only that office, not Clark's entire operation. If the office had operated under its own legal entity, it is likely Clark could have negotiated favorable settlements with its chief creditors—the bank (on an operating cash loan), the landlord (on the lease), and medical suppliers (on equipment). By operating as one corporation, Clark precluded this possibility. After all, why should creditors settle when they can claim the assets of all four offices?

Learn from Clark's mistake and use multiple legal entities for multiple locations or outlets.

One Business Unit With a Single Location or Outlet: Use at Least Two Legal Entities—One for Dangerous Assets and One for Safe Assets

What do these three businesses have in common: (1) a men's clothing store, (2) a theater operator, and (3) a consulting company? Each operation has one outlet and one line of business. But, like the businesses in the previous examples, these ventures can also benefit from multiple entities. These businesses can effectively segregate safe assets from dangerous assets by using multiple entities.

Case Study: Dave's Repertory Company and Theater

Dave is an owner of a successful repertory company and theater. Concerned after a friend suffered a devastating lawsuit judgment for a personal injury claim, he asked us how he could best protect his business. We learned that in addition to owning a valuable trade name and goodwill, Dave also owned the building housing the theater—both owned personally.

First, we advised Dave to set up a corporation in which to operate the business. This may help protect personal assets from future business claims. Second, Dave formed an LLC to own the building. The LLC, owned by Dave, his wife, and his children, leased the office to the theater company (see the next section). Should any employee or customer sue the corporation, Dave's building would not be vulnerable.

Third, Dave set up a second LLC to own the trade name to be leased to his corporation. In this way, Dave effectively isolated his asset (the building) from his business and safeguarded other valuable assets (the trade name).

Even within a multiple-entity structure, each business unit or location should be as lawsuit-proof and creditor-proof as possible. This is the best structure: a multiple entity business in which each unit segregates dangerous assets from safe ones.

ASSETS YOUR BUSINESS
SHOULD NOT OWN

Your operating business or practice must never own its most valuable assets. Usually, this is real estate, whether in the form of outright ownership or a valuable below-market lease. In other businesses, the most valuable assets may be copyrights, patents, or even high-tech equipment.

You don't want your operating company to own this valuable asset because if it did, the company's creditors can claim the asset. Your strategy should be to make your operating business as poor as possible. Then, creditors and lawsuit plaintiffs have little to gain by attacking the business. Establish other legal entities to own valuable assets and then lease or license these assets to the operating business entity. The following three tactics illustrate this strategy:

1. If your *business owns real estate*, you should have a separate entity to own the real estate and lease it back to the operating company asset. Make the tenancy month to month so it has the least valuable assets as an operating company. Remember that a lower value for the operating company means less attractiveness for creditors. Also, document the sale and leaseback, and follow legal formalities (i.e., the business must pay rent to the other entity).

2. If your *business has a valuable lease*, have a separate entity own the lease and have your operating company sublet it on a month-to-month basis. This is especially crucial if your business depends on its location. Again, all formalities between the entities must be followed.

If your business hits hard times, you can always close the shop, and your creditors cannot claim the lease. They can only claim the operating entity's sublet, until the end of the month. Next month, you can set up the same business using a different legal entity in the exact same location! Your lease-controlling entity sublets the same location to your new business. You have effectively secured your valuable location, while protecting it from creditor and lawsuit threats.

3. If your *business owns other extremely valuable assets*, such as copyrights, trademarks, patents, and high-tech equipment, have another entity own these assets and then license or lease them to the operating business. By now, you understand the tactic, but always follow legal formalities in the transactions. If not, you could lose your protection.

STICK TO WHAT YOU KNOW

You may want to stop lawsuits before they arise. One growing trend is the use of professional employer organizations (PEOs—see Chapter 68). This will remove all of the employee lawsuit headaches and exposure from your life and allow you to spend more time growing your business.

CHAPTER SIXTY-EIGHT

REMOVE HEADACHES AND COSTS WITH PEOS

As a small to mid-size business owner, you are no longer able to focus on just the selling of your product or service to maximize productivity and profitability. You may spend a great deal of time trying to tackle a variety of issues, which include recruitment and retention of qualified employees, medical insurance costs, competitive benefits, regulatory compliance, worker's compensation, management, and other human resource issues. In addition to all the time you spend handling these areas of concern, you have to suffer all of the liability and lawsuit risk associated with each of these challenges.

If you can overcome all of these issues (which certainly were not your motivation for becoming a business owner), then you still have to look for ways to become more efficient in your daily routine without incurring additional expenses.

THE SOLUTION

A professional employer organization (PEO) is an organization that provides an integrated approach to many administrative concerns faced by an employer. Your PEO enters into an agreement with you under which the PEO becomes a coemployer to your employees by providing human resource and personnel services. The PEO establishes and maintains the employer relationship with the workers by handling employee payroll and employee taxes; providing benefits; and assuming the responsibility of worker's compensation, labor law compliance, and risk management. Basically, the PEO handles the daily tasks required to maintain a prospering business and gives you, the employer, the time to do what you really should be doing. Many times, a PEO costs less than it would to actually hire staff to accomplish these same objectives.

BENEFITS

A PEO saves time and money. It will give you time to manage your business without having to worry about such challenges as meeting government compliance issues, handling payroll and payroll taxes, or finding a fringe benefits package for your employees. You can have human resource experts available to you who will help reduce accounting costs yet will not be on your payroll. Some PEOs also have legal counsel on staff to help you keep up with the current labor laws. Avoiding liability should be of great interest to you because asset protection is an integral part of Wealth Protection planning.

GOVERNMENT COMPLIANCE

Keeping up with government compliance is yet another obstacle employers must face. A PEO will work with you to ensure that you are kept well informed of such issues as discrimination laws, COBRA, workplace safety, civil rights, and tax issues within your industry.

HEALTH BENEFITS

A PEO will have a health benefits package that can be offered to your employees. Because the total number of employees in the PEO dictates all discounts, you can take advantage of the PEOs and get a rate on health insurance that is generally only available to larger companies. Also, with most PEOs, you can design your own program to offer your employees the healthcare coverage they need most.

WORKER'S COMPENSATION

Your PEO will also handle your worker's compensation claims. Because many PEOs offer expertise in risk management, your worker's compensation costs may also be reduced significantly.

> *Note:* If your business is prone to certain kinds of worker's compensation issues, then the PEO can work with you to help you reduce your costs by including your employees in their worker's compensation policy (where your adverse experience may not have such a negative impact on your premiums).

PAYROLL

Payroll administration is a basic function of a PEO. Your PEO's staff will make sure that the checks your employees receive are on time and accurate and will provide answers to any payroll questions from your employees. Some of the other payroll responsibilities your PEO may handle include: filing local, state, and federal government paperwork; providing support for hourly, salary, and tipped employees; establishing a variety of different payroll methods; and tax reporting and compliance.

RETIREMENT

Many PEOs offer a 401(k) plan for the employees of the business. In addition to handling the formation and oversight of the retirement plan, many PEOs offer consulting services to the employees to assist them in their individual retirement planning. These consulting services are not limited to just retirement. Some PEOs offer consulting services for educational funding or even estate planning.

FLEXIBLE BENEFITS PROGRAM OR "CAFETERIA PLANS"

Most PEOs will offer a flexible benefit plan, also called a "cafeteria plan." This benefit plan allows the employees to have some choice in designing their own benefits package. Employees are allowed to select different types and/or levels of benefits that are funded with nontaxable employer dollars. The tax savings could be enormously beneficial to both you and your employees.

Choosing a professional employer organization

As with any contract, it pays to consider several PEOs to find the one that meets the specific needs of your business. Some factors to consider are:

- *Cost:* What services are included in the base cost? What services will cost extra?
- *Financial stability:* What are the PEO's credentials? What is the PEO's reputation?
- *Technological capability:* What technological services does the PEO have available? Are these compatible with your existing systems?

Every business owner who wants to reduce hassles, decrease liability risk, and increase the time spent on the business should seriously consider a PEO as part of a comprehensive Wealth Protection plan.

Last word

Planning for businesses is intricate because each business inevitably has unique features. There are a number of useful protection tools for businesses, but they cannot be employed in a cookie-cutter generic approach.

APPENDIX 1

THE 10 COMMANDMENTS OF OFFSHORE

Although there are pitfalls to using offshore planning (as explained in Chapter 31), you can still achieve many legitimate goals offshore. The key is to follow our "10 Commandments of Offshore." For updated information on offshore planning, including common scams, visit our web site at www.mywealthprotection.com.

1. CONSIDER OFFSHORE AS AN OPTION.

If you have more than $500,000 in liquid wealth, you should consider offshore planning. You simply cannot achieve the same level of protection or claim discouragement by using domestic structures. The stability of the offshore financial centers and the security of the large fiduciaries typically utilized should alleviate any of your skepticism.

2. DON'T EXPECT TO SAVE ON TAXES THROUGH OFFSHORE PLANNING.

Ninety-five percent of offshore planning is not designed to provide tax savings for U.S. taxpayers. If you intend to save taxes offshore, you'll need a particular plan designed to legitimately reduce, or defer, taxes. General asset protection plans aim to be tax neutral. If you intend to save taxes by not declaring income, we must advise you that this is tax evasion, punishable as a felony.

3. DO NOT "HIDE" ASSETS OR INCOME OFFSHORE.

Whether your goal is asset protection, tax reduction, privacy, or investments, you must intend to disclose everything you are doing offshore to the relevant U.S. government agencies. If not, you run the serious risk that you will need to perjure yourself to keep the existence of offshore assets (and their income) a secret. Again, this is a felony punishable by jail time.

4. USE STRUCTURES RESPECTED UNDER U.S. LAW (TRUSTS, LLCs, REAL CICs).

If your asset protection plan is ever challenged in the United States, you want judges to understand and respect what you have done. This will be a much easier task if the structure you utilize is part of estate or business planning in the United States. The best structures are LLCs, certain types of trusts (generally where there are third-party beneficiaries, such as children and grandchildren), and captive insurance companies.

5. USE TRANSACTIONS THAT HAVE AN ECONOMIC SUBSTANCE.

Again, U.S. judges are becoming increasingly skeptical of offshore transactions that do not make economic sense (i.e., funding a foreign trust with most of your net worth while claiming you no longer have control of the trust). This warrants the use of entities that allow a real exchange of economic value. The leading personal entity that experts use to gain this benefit is the foreign LLC. Strategies using captive insurance companies are also excellent if they are used only when there is an economic justification to do so.

6. IF IT'S TOO GOOD TO BE TRUE, IT IS.

This is an old adage, but nowhere is it more true than in offshore planning. You simply cannot expect to achieve mind-boggling returns without risk offshore, nor can you hope to create complex offshore arrangements on the cheap. You will simply get what you pay for— and you will not like what you get.

7. USE PFIC QEF MUTUAL FUNDS.

Making sure your offshore entity is tax compliant is only the first part of the tax battle. You must also make certain that the investments you choose are U.S. tax compliant as well. You should use a large and established mutual fund that makes the effort to comply with the complex Passive Foreign Investment Company Qualifying Elective Fund (PFIC QEF) rules or to invest in a legitimately U.S. tax-deferred variable life insurance policy or variable annuity.

8. RELY ON ESTABLISHED FIDUCIARY FIRMS.

You want to make sure that the fiduciary firms on which you rely are established, have adequate references, have insurance, and are bonded, if applicable. In most offshore centers, it will not be difficult to find some of the largest accounting, investment, and banking firms in the world. Don't skimp on these services. The security of your funds depends on it.

9. WALK BEFORE YOU RUN.

It is always wise to move wealth offshore gradually, as you become increasingly comfortable with the process. We typically recommend that you begin with less than 25 percent of the amount you eventually intend to move offshore.

10. FIND AN EXPERIENCED U.S.–BASED ATTORNEY.

Of all the commandments, this one is paramount because an attorney who is an offshore expert will make sure that the first nine commandments are followed. Also, this advisor will have the contacts and the experience to make the planning process seamless and understandable for the client. Finally, an attorney is the only advisor with an absolute client privilege respected by the courts. Certified public accountants (CPAs) and financial advisors have no such privilege and can be forced to divulge any and all information you have given them. In the sensitive area of offshore planning, it is always wise to use an attorney for this reason alone.

Appendix 2
Preventing Fraudulent Transfers

Why you must avoid running afoul of these laws

Fraudulent transfer laws give creditors the right to undo certain transfers that debtors have made—and that are deemed fraudulent—so that the transferred property can be seized by creditors (including judgment creditors). In other words, under certain circumstances, the courts invalidate sales or gifts that you have made to hinder those suing you. Whatever you sold or gave away is transferred back to you, allowing the creditor to seize the property. These laws have been enacted so that debtors cannot transfer property to defraud their creditors.

Fraudulent transfer laws are important because they may partially, or totally, destroy your asset protection plan. *Asset protection is achieved by titling your wealth beyond the reach of creditors.* Fraudulent transfer laws are obstacles to that goal because they allow a creditor to get at your assets even when they are no longer in your name. This is extremely important—fraudulent transfer laws separate valid legal asset protection from illegally disposing of assets. A fraudulent transfer challenge, then, often becomes the true test of your asset protection plan.

When a transfer is "fraudulent"

Courts find two types of fraudulent transfers:

1. Fraud in fact—or "actual fraud"
2. Fraud in law—or "constructive fraud"

ACTUAL FRAUD

For actual fraud, your creditors must prove that you actually intended to hinder, delay, or defraud your creditors. This may be very difficult to prove directly because they must prove your state of mind or get you to confess fraudulent intent. To assist creditors, the courts recognize signs of fraud or "badges of fraud" that, if proved, can allow the court to infer fraudulent intent. These badges include:

- The transfer was made to a close family member or friend.
- The transfer was made secretly.
- The transfer was for less than fair value.
- The transfer was around the same time that the debtor incurred a large debt.
- The transfer left the debtor with no property.
- The transfer left the debtor insolvent (unable to pay debts as they came due).
- The debtor continued to use or to possess the property after the transfer.
- The debtor disappeared.
- The debtor had been sued or threatened with suit before the transfer.
- The debtor concealed assets.

Even if a creditor proves these badges, it does not always mean that the judge will automatically find the transfer to be fraudulent and allow the creditor to recover the property. These badges only *infer* fraudulent intent; that is, they are evidence that can allow the judge to conclude that you had fraudulent intent.

CONSTRUCTIVE FRAUD

Because actual fraud is so difficult to prove, even when certain badges of fraud exist, creditors more often rely on constructive fraud to undo transfers by debtors. Constructive fraud occurs when there is a gift or a sale of the debtor's property:

- For less than fair value (also called "fair consideration").
- In the face of a known liability.
- That leaves the debtor insolvent.

For Less Than Fair Value

Creditors must first show if they want to prove constructive fraud that the transfer was for less than fair value. Whereas showing this is not a problem when the debtor makes a gift, showing that an actual sale was for less than fair value is more difficult for the creditor because of the way a court defines fair consideration.

Fair consideration is a price that a reasonably prudent seller would obtain using commercially reasonable means. This may not mean the fair market value; it depends on what type of item or property is involved. For stocks or bonds of publicly traded corporations or commodities, fair value does mean "fair market value." Exact value of the stock/bond/commodity can easily be determined by looking up the quotes of the day of the transfer. If the debtor transferred the stock/bond/commodity for less than its price on that day, then the sale would be for less than fair value and might be a fraudulent transfer.

For items that are more difficult to value precisely, such as real estate, stock in a privately held business, antiques, and vehicles, fair consideration may be much less than fair market value because reasonable minds differ about the exact value of a piece of real estate, or a painting, or a business. Also, as the debtor, you may not have the luxury of waiting through a series of price negotiations or for the right buyer willing to pay the full fair market value price. You may want to settle for less than optimum price for fast cash. For these reasons, courts typically conclude that real estate that is sold for over 70 percent of fair market value satisfies fair consideration. For other items, like jewelry or closely held businesses, courts will look at all the facts—especially certified appraisals—to determine whether or not the payment figure was in the ballpark.

In the Face of a Known Liability

Even if a creditor attacking a transfer shows that it was a sale for less than fair value or a gift, he or she must still show that you made the transfer "in the face of a known liability." What does this phrase mean?

Courts define it to mean that you cannot transfer assets to protect against future *probable liabilities,* but you can make a transfer to protect yourself against future *possible liabilities.* Again, it is difficult to precisely define the difference between probable liabilities and possible liabilities. The courts look at the facts of each case, focusing on the timing of when the act creating the liability occurred and when you realized that you may be liable for that act.

That Leaves the Debtor Insolvent

Even if a creditor attacking your transfer can show it was for less than fair value, and even if he or she can show you made the transfer when a probable liability existed, the court will not undo the transfer unless it left you insolvent. *Insolvent* means that the market value of all of your assets is less than the amount needed to pay your existing debts as they come due. In other words, you are left in the position where you cannot pay your debts.

HOW TO AVOID FRAUDULENT TRANSFER CLAIMS

There are six more common ways to structure asset transfers to ensure that they will not be judged to be fraudulent:

1. *Transfer before the liability arises.* Simply put, a transfer cannot be deemed fraudulent if you make the transfer *before* a probable liability arises, which underscores why it is so important to set up your asset protection plan sooner rather than later.

2. *Show that the transfer was for purposes other than asset protection.* Support your transfer with adequate correspondence and documentation that the transfer was part of an estate or an investment plan. Often we put language in the legal documents—or *preliminary recitals*—that confirms that the transfer was for purposes other than creditor protection alone.

3. *Document what you receive in the transaction—higher is better.* This is especially important if the transfer was made for past services. Be prepared to prove that the value you received satisfies the fair value requirement. If you received property, obtain favorable appraisals.

4. *Document the value of the property you transferred—lower is better.* For the same reasons, shop around to document the lowest appraisal of transferred property. Emphasize defects or damage when working with the appraiser to help ensure a low value.

5. *Utilize overlapping asset protection techniques.* Good attorneys use *overlap* techniques to protect certain assets. For example, in addition to transferring rental property to a family limited partnership, the attorney might also recommend a mortgage on the property to an uncle for the $15,000 owed an uncle. Now, a creditor must attack the transfer to the partnership and also the mortgage.

6. *Continue your regular gifts and donations.* Even if you gifted property when a liability existed, it may not be fraudulent if it was part of an established pattern of gifting. For example, if you always paid your children's college tuition, you can probably continue without incurring sanctions.

WHY AN ASSET PROTECTION EXPERT IS SO IMPORTANT

Laws against fraudulent transfers are complex. They create a tremendous gray area—most challenged transfers are neither clearly fraudulent nor clearly legitimate. An asset protection specialist will understand the complexity and the nuances of fraudulent transfer laws. The specialist understands how transfers can be justified. Further, a specialist knows how to structure a transfer so that through the very documents that create the transfer, any claim of possible fraudulent intent is eliminated.

An asset protection plan's ultimate test is often a fraudulent transfer claim by a frustrated creditor. An experienced asset protection specialist can ensure that your plan will survive such a fraudulent transfer attack.

APPENDIX 3

INTESTACY: WHAT HAPPENS IF YOU DIE WITHOUT A WILL OR LIVING TRUST

INTESTACY DEFINED

If you die without a valid document disposing of your property—either a will or a pour-over will and living trust—the state in which you live will decide exactly how your estate should be divided. Each state has a statute that controls the distribution of a decedent's property in these circumstances. Such a statute is called an "intestacy" law because "intestacy" is the legal term for dying without a valid will (or pour-over will and living trust).

Dying without a will is the worst estate planning mistake you can make. Not only do you lose estate tax benefits and lose the probate-fee savings of a living trust, but you also *lose all control* of how your property will be given away when you die. You allow the politicians to decide how your property is divided—and they usually make a mess of things, as you might have guessed.

Read this disclaimer:

> The following is a general description of how property is divided under California's intestacy laws. Use this description to give you a general understanding of what intestacy laws are, but do not rely on this description, as laws may have changed since this writing. Check with an attorney familiar with the laws in *your* state for particular legal advice. Or, better yet, set up a living trust and a pour-over will and rest easy knowing this law will not apply to you.

SAMPLE INTESTACY LAW

If you die intestate, this is how your property will be divided:

377

1. If you have a surviving spouse but no surviving issue (descendants), parent, brother, sister, or issue of a deceased brother or sister, the surviving spouse gets everything.

2. If you have a surviving spouse and any of the following are true, the surviving spouse gets one-half of the estate:
    *   You also are survived by one child (that child gets the remaining half).
    *   You also are survived by the issue of one predeceased child (that issue takes or splits the remaining half).
    *   You leave no issue but are survived by one parent (he or she gets the remaining half).
    *   You leave no issue but are survived by the issue of one parent (they either take or split the remaining half).
    *   You leave no issue but are survived by more than one parent (they split the remaining half).

3. If you have a surviving spouse and any of the following are true, the surviving spouse gets one-third of the estate:
    *   You also are survived by more than one living child.
    *   You also are survived by one living child and the issue of a predeceased child.
    *   You also are survived by the issue of two or more predeceased children.

    There are also questions regarding how much the issue (descendants) of predeceased children should take—and state laws do differ on this point.

4. If you do not leave a surviving spouse, then your entire estate will pass to your heirs in the following priority:
    (1) To your issue (descendants).
    (2) If you have no surviving issue, then to your parents.
    (3) If you have no surviving issue or parents, then to the issue of your parents.
    (4) If you have no surviving issue or parents or issue of your parents, then to your grandparents or to their issue.
    (5) If you have none of the heirs in 1 through 4, then to the surviving issue of your predeceased spouse, if any.

(6) If you still have none of the heirs in 1 through 5, then to your "next of kin" (any blood relative, in order of kinship).

(7) If you have none of the heirs in 1 through 6, then to the parents of a predeceased spouse, if any.

(8) If you have none of the heirs in 1 through 7, then your hard-earned property will escheat (be transferred) to the state.

Unfortunately, millions of dollars in property every year escheat to the state in this way—because the decedent had no relatives or none that can be found. *Do not let the state decide how your property will be given away. Do the smart thing, and establish a living trust and pour-over will as soon as you can.*

2002 INCOME TAX TABLES

Annual Income: Married Persons				
If the Taxable Income Is . . .		Computed Tax Is . . .		
Over	But Not Over	The total of this column PLUS >>	The % in this column TIMES >>	The amount over (Taxable income less the amount in this column)
$0	$6,456	No tax withheld.		
$6,456	$18,456	$0	10%	$6,456
$18,456	$51,552	$1,200	15%	$18,456
$51,552	$109,704	$6,164	27%	$51,552
$109,704	$176,796	$21,865	30%	$109,704
$176,796	$311,904	$41,993	35%	$176,796
$311,904	Over	$89,281	38.6%	$311,904

Annual Income: Single Persons				
If the Taxable Income Is . . .		Computed Tax Is . . .		
Over	But Not Over	The total of this column PLUS >>	The % in this column TIMES >>	The amount over (Taxable income less the amount in this column)
$0	$2,652	No tax withheld.		
$2,652	$8,556	$0	10%	$2,652
$8,556	$29,652	$590	15%	$8,556
$29,652	$64,824	$3,755	27%	$29,652
$64,824	$142,956	$13,251	30%	$64,824
$142,956	$308,748	$36,691	35%	$142,956
$308,748	Over	$94,718	38.6%	$308,748

APPENDIX 5

ASSET QUESTIONNAIRE

Personal Information

Name: _____ Birth date: _____

Spouse's Name: _____ Birth date: _____

Occupation: _____ Income: _____

Spouse's Occupation: _____ Income: _____

Address: _____

City/State/Zip: _____

Work phone: _____ Fax: _____

Home phone: _____ E-mail: _____

Number of children: _____ Ages: _____

Number of grandchildren: _____ Ages: _____

Years until retirement: _____

Monthly (after-tax) income required during retirement: _____

Long-term rate of return that you expect to realize
on your retirement investments: _____

Business/Practice Information

Gross Revenue: _____

Accounts receivable: _____

Number of employees: _____

Balance Sheet

Asset or Liability	Fair market value (face for annuities death benefit for life insurance)	Date purchased	Cost basis equity, or cash value	How is asset held? Own name jointly, living trust, LP, other?
Pensions and profit-sharing plans and IRAs				
Home				
Real estate holdings				
Brokerage accounts, bank accounts, CDs				
Business interests, limited partnerships, etc.				
Disability income, insurance coverage				
Life insurance: cash value/face amount				
Long-term-care insurance				

SAMPLE EMPLOYEE CENSUS FOR RETIREMENT AND OTHER BENEFITS PLANNING

Name of business: _____

Tax status: Incorporated _____   Unincorporated _____

Date business began: _____

Date of incorporation: _____

Tax year-end: _____

Approximate contribution desired
(percent of pay or dollar amount): $ _____

Any current pension plan in force: Yes ____ No ____

(If "yes," supply details on a separate sheet.)

Do the owners have ownership interests in any other firms? Yes ____ No ____

(If "yes," supply details on a separate sheet.)

Additional comments:

_____

_____

_____

_____

_____

Confidential Employee Census

Name	Date of birth	Date of hire	Salary	See note below and check if:			
				Part-time	Non-smoker	Ownership percentage	Officer

Note: "Part-time" means that the employee works less than 1,000 hours per year. Check "nonsmoker" if known. List "Ownership percentage" of all owners.

Index